THE MISMATCHED WORKER

Contemporary Societies Series

Jeffrey C. Alexander, Series Editor

Forthcoming

THE
MISMATCHED
WORKER

Arne L. Kalleberg

CONTEMPORARY SOCIETIES
Jeffrey C. Alexander
SERIES EDITOR

 W. W. NORTON & COMPANY ⊙ NEW YORK LONDON

W. W. Norton & Company has been independent since its founding in 1923, when William Warder Norton and Mary D. Herter Norton first published lectures delivered at the People's Institute, the adult education division of New York City's Cooper Union. The Nortons soon expanded their program beyond the Institute, publishing books by cele-brated academics from America and abroad. By mid-century, the two major pillars of Nor-ton's publishing program—trade books and college texts—were firmly established. In the 1950s, the Norton family transferred control of the company to its employees, and today—with a staff of four hundred and a comparable number of trade, college, and professional ti-tles published each year—W. W. Norton & Company stands as the largest and oldest publishing house owned wholly by its employees.

Copyright © 2007 by W. W. Norton & Company, Inc.

Printed in the United States of America.
First Edition.

Composition by PennSet, Inc.
Manufacturing by Victor Graphics, Inc.
Series design by Beth Tondreau Design.
Production manager: Benjamin Reynolds.

Library of Congress Cataloging-in-Publication Data
Kalleberg, Arne L.
    The mismatched worker / Arne L. Kalleberg.
       p. cm. — (Contemporary societies)
    Includes bibliographical references and index.

    ISBN 13: 978-0-393-97643-4 (pbk.)
    ISBN 10: 0-393-97643-2 (pbk.)

    1. Job satisfaction. 2. Labor market. 3. Vocational qualifications.
4. Quality of work life. I. Title.

HF5549.5.J63K34 2006
331.1—dc22

                                        2006046719

W. W. Norton & Company, Inc., 500 Fifth Avenue, New York, NY 10110-0017
www.wwnorton.com

W. W. Norton & Company Ltd., Castle House,
75/76 Wells Street, London W1T 3QT

1 2 3 4 5 6 7 8 9 0

CONTENTS

ACKNOWLEDGMENTS

THIS BOOK elaborates a theme I have been studying since I entered graduate school at the University of Wisconsin–Madison in the early 1970s—the structural conditions that affect people's ability to find jobs that match their qualifications, interests, and needs. I began by looking at how the fit between peoples' work values and job rewards affected their job satisfaction, and how the degree of fit depended on their degree of control over their employment situations. I then moved on to study inequalities in various job rewards (earnings, intrinsic rewards, hours worked, job security, careers, and mobility); organizational sources of variation in work practices, human resource policies, and employment relations; individual differences in these rewards and workplace practices by gender, race, and age; and how all these factors differed among countries such as the United States, Japan, Norway, and Hungary.

Writing this book has given me the opportunity to pull together many strands in my research and scholarly activities into a general discussion of mismatches between people and their jobs on a large number of dimensions. I hope the resulting book moves us closer to developing a multidimensional, multidisciplinary approach to explaining mismatches between people and their work as well as their place in stratified industrial societies. Disciplinary silos have for too long limited our understanding of the interplay between individuals and the social structures within which they are embedded.

Along the way, I have accumulated a number of major intellectual debts. Two people in particular have nurtured my ideas and helped me understand how people come to be mismatched to jobs and have inspired me to continue to work in this area. I am grateful to my mentor, the late Aage Sørensen, for helping me think about the way processes in labor markets shape individual and structural forces to produce differences in mobility and careers, as well as earnings inequality. I am also thankful to Ivar Berg, whose classic book, *Education and Jobs: The Great Training Robbery* (1971), inspired my first foray into studying mismatches and was the conceptual underpinning for my master's thesis on the topic. Ivar has continued to be a source of boundless inspiration and joyful collaboration over the years. He also made incisive comments on an earlier version of the manuscript; I hope I have responded to some of his comments successfully in this final version.

During the writing of this book, I also benefited enormously from the ideas and commentary of many people, including many former students and collaborators. I am especially thankful to the people who read earlier versions of the book and shared useful and thought-provoking comments. I have tried to follow their advice while still getting the book to the publisher only a few years after the promised date.

I owe special thanks to three former students and collaborators who read the manuscript closely and offered me more suggestions for revision than I was able to respond to given the time I was able to devote to this project—Mike Wallace, Kevin Leicht, and Jeremy Reynolds. I tried to follow most of their excellent recommendations, although I was unable to address all of them. To supplement the gaps in this book, I urge readers to take a close look at their fine work on related issues. I also thank a current student, Steve Vaisey, for his comments on an earlier version, allowing me to use the data presented in Tables 3.1 and 4.1, and suggesting the title of the book.

I am also grateful to a number of other persons who read and commented on earlier versions of the book, including Roberto Fernandez, Michael Handel, and Teresa Sullivan. I also thank my editors, Jeffrey Alexander and Karl Bakeman, for their support, patience, and encouragement.

Finally, I thank my father, Theodor Kalleberg, who was ailing when I was writing this book and who died shortly before it was completed. An immigrant from Norway, he was often overqualified, overworked, and subject to earnings mismatches; his life was an inspiration to me and those who knew him. I dedicate this book to his memory.

Arne L. Kalleberg
University of North Carolina at Chapel Hill

THE MISMATCHED WORKER

Chapter One
MISMATCHING PEOPLE AND JOBS

WORK IS A CENTRAL ACTIVITY in all societies. For most people, work is the major source of their income and social status. The workplace is also where people develop social relationships and are integrated into social life. Not surprisingly, studies show that work has an important impact on one's identity and psychological well-being and is related to a wide range of attitudes and behaviors, both on and off the job.

When thinking about work and its consequences, we need to consider the characteristics of both workers and their jobs. Workers differ in their skills and abilities, family situations, life stages and experiences, and cultural backgrounds. These differences produce diversity in what people want, need, and expect from their jobs. Some needs are fairly universal: Almost all people need to earn at least a minimum amount of money, since employment is the main source of economic and social position in a capitalist country such as the United States, and money is required to obtain many of the necessities and good things in life. Other needs and wants are specific to particular people: Some workers want jobs that challenge them and enable them to use their skills, while others want to acquire additional skills so they can find better-paying work. Some workers want to work many hours, while others would be happier spending fewer hours on the job.

The work that people do also differs in various ways. Some kinds of jobs are generally considered more desirable than others, in part because they pay better and confer more social esteem, while others pay very little and are usually regarded as unpleasant or associated with low status. Certain jobs are complex and require long periods of training and high levels of skill, while others are learned quickly, often from casual observation of someone doing the activity. Some jobs, such as those dealing with customers face-to-face, need to be performed at specific times and fixed locations, while others, such as tax preparation, writing reports, or developing websites can be performed almost anywhere at any time.

When workers' jobs match their needs, preferences, and abilities, they are likely to be happy and satisfied with their work and lives, and workplaces are apt to function smoothly and effectively. On the other hand, when there is a *mismatch* or lack of fit between workers and their jobs, a variety of problems and difficulties are likely to result for the workers, their families, their employers, and society in general.

The importance—and difficulty—of successfully matching people to jobs was recognized early in our nation's history by Thomas Jefferson, who noted in 1801:[1]

> Of the various executive duties, no one excites more anxious concern than that of placing the interests of our fellow citizens in the hands of honest men, with understandings sufficient for their station. No duty, at the same time, is more difficult to fulfil [sic] (Ford 1897, 68).

[1]I thank Richard Kohn for calling my attention to this quotation from Thomas Jefferson.

While mismatching people to jobs may have been problematic even in the early days of the American republic, things are much worse today. There are a number of fundamental mismatches between today's workforce and workplace and the institutions and policies that support and govern them.

Seven Mismatched Situations

The following seven situations illustrate mismatches that are common in industrial societies such as the United States. The first three cases exemplify various kinds of mismatches between the skills or qualifications of the person and those required by the job.

1. John[2] received a Ph.D. in English two years ago and now works as a cashier in a convenience store. He is *overqualified* or *overeducated* for his job because he is not able to use the skills that he has acquired from his education; the job could easily be done by persons without a college education or even a high school diploma.
2. Latoya works as a machine operator in a textile mill that recently introduced computerized automated equipment. She is *underqualified* for her job because she does not have the skills to operate this new equipment. She knows she must upgrade her skills in order to meet the new skill requirements of her job or she will be fired.
3. Lamont lives in an apartment in a run-down area of a big city; his job as a welder in a manufacturing plant is lo-

---

[2]The examples used to illustrate the various types of mismatches are fictitious persons that have the characteristics associated with the mismatch. Any resemblance to real people is purely accidental.

cated far away in the suburbs. He experiences a *spatial mismatch* since he lives in a geographic area far from his job or the pool of jobs for which he is qualified.

These three situations do not exhaust the ways in which jobs may not match workers' needs. The following four cases illustrate other situations in which jobs either do not meet workers' preferences or are inadequate in various ways to fulfill their needs.

4. Kelly is a lawyer who has worked an average of eighty to ninety hours a week during the past four years. Her employer requires that she work that many hours; she also feels that she needs to do so in order to pay off her credit card debts. Kelly is *overworked* since she works more hours than she would prefer and works harder than she would like.

5. Emily is an accounting technician for a construction company; she works twenty hours a week. She has been unable to find a full-time job since there are no vacancies for people with her skills in her area, and she doesn't want to move because of her social ties to people in her neighborhood. Emily is *underworked* because she would like to work more hours than she is able to.

6. Ramón works full-time as a nursing aide at a local hospital. He earns seven dollars an hour, not enough to lift his family above the poverty line. Edward works as a tax preparer for much less than he earned at a bank before he was laid off; his current salary is not enough to pay his family's bills. Both Ramón and Edward illustrate an

earnings mismatch and have jobs that are not adequate to fulfill their families' economic needs.

7. Kayla is a registered nurse who works in a large hospital. Her husband, Luis, is an account executive in the biggest advertising company in the state. Kayla and Luis are both very busy and have a hard time adjusting their work schedules to be able to spend the time that they need with their families. They often experience *work-family* mismatches—conflicts between the demands of their jobs and the needs of their families.

These seven situations illustrate a lack of fit between individuals and their jobs. Such mismatches have become more common in recent years in American society, since there has been growing diversity in both what people want and need from their jobs and the extent to which jobs can satisfy these preferences and needs. The consequences of these mismatches constitute problems for workers, their families, and the society in general. Therefore it has become urgent that we understand the nature of these mismatches and the reasons behind them and develop policies that might alleviate these mismatches and their consequences.

This book will examine each of these seven types of mismatches between people and jobs. It will discuss the causes of these mismatches and the kinds of people and jobs most likely to experience them. Whenever possible, we will present data on the extent of these mismatches among jobs and labor force participants in the United States. We also consider some of the significant consequences of these mismatches for people, organizations, and American society. Finally, we will outline some governmental social policies and business strategies that might be helpful in reducing these mismatches.

TYPES OF MISMATCHES

The idea of mismatches between people and jobs assumes that it makes sense to think of them as distinct from one another. This assumption is appropriate in industrial societies, since the concept of a person "going to work" emerged with industrialization and the development of the factory system. Before that, one's work life and non-work life were intimately related, and it was not easy to distinguish between them. In preindustrial societies, work was home and home was work, since most people worked on farms that were also the places where they lived, and all family members chipped in to handle farm chores whenever they needed to be done. There was little uncertainty about what kinds of work people would do when they reached working age and workers were rarely, if ever, able to go "off the clock."

The industrial revolution changed all that, as family members, usually men but sometimes (and increasingly) women, left home to go to work in factories. Working time now had a set beginning and end, and after work people defined themselves as "not working." Moreover, people now had to find jobs, and employers with jobs to fill had to find people to work for them. The need arose to match people and jobs, and so did the possibility that this matching process might not always produce a good fit.

The notion of a mismatch is a normative one, shaped by cultural understandings of what is considered normal and the conditions under which a job might reasonably be expected to match a person or be a good fit. These cultural norms differ in different time periods. In the Depression era of the 1930s, for example, people were happy to have a job at all because of high unemployment, despite oppressive employment conditions characterized by poor work environments, inadequate health and safety protections, and lack of health and retirement benefits. Workers sought to satisfy only basic needs through their jobs, such as obtaining a living wage. Those who were lucky to have jobs at all were not apt to be distraught that these jobs might not make full use of their skills or qualifications, required them to work too many hours, or left them little time to spend with their families. While we would consider people whose jobs did not fit their skills or time preferences in this period to be mismatched, workers were not as concerned about such mismatches, since they were powerless to change things and there were no alternative jobs.

In the early twenty-first century, on the other hand, the range of needs and wants that people seek to fulfill through their work has expanded. Workers increasingly expect their jobs to satisfy their preferences for challenging work and meaningful social relationships in addition to economic success. The needs and wants that people seek to satisfy through their jobs have also become more diverse. The greater availability of information about the kinds of jobs that exist in the economy has made it easier for people to compare their jobs to others and to assess the relative goodness of their jobs. As a result, more people feel that there is a mismatch between their needs and the rewards that their jobs provide. Combined with the fact that for many people the standards of living and wages have declined, there are fewer opportunities for advancement, many have no health insurance, and so on, mismatches are also more likely to cause complaints and negative feelings on the part of workers and their families.

Mismatches thus result from the interaction between a combination of people's needs, values, and expectations on the one hand, and the characteristics and rewards associated with their jobs on the other. We must evaluate a person's skills, needs, or preferences in relation to the requirements or benefits of jobs to which he or she has access in order to conclude that a person and job are mismatched. Two people in the same job may not necessarily be equally matched or mismatched, depending on their preferences and needs. For example, whether people are considered to be overworked depends on their needs and preferences as well as the demands of their job. Some people might like to work eighty to ninety hours a week, while others feel overworked if they have to work even twenty hours a week. Moreover, whether a job that pays a minimum wage is inadequate for a person's economic needs depends in part on her or his family situation and life stage—for example, a teenager who has dropped out of school, lives at home, and works full-time may feel that working in a minimum-wage job fulfills her needs for spending money and gives her the flexibility to go out with her friends on weekends. By contrast, people who have been employed for years and have families to support may experience a mismatch if they are forced to work in jobs that pay poorly.

In order to identify the different kinds of mismatches that are likely to occur in an industrial society, we must know the dimensions along which people as well as jobs differ and what kinds of correspondences between them are considered normal (or a "good fit") and which are not (a mismatch). These questions are complex, since jobs and people both differ along a large number of dimensions.

Jobs are work tasks associated with particular skills and require certain qualifications. Most jobs involve procedures and time schedules that are often constrained by a division of labor reflecting their interdependence with other jobs in a particular workplace. In some cases, the timing of jobs is governed by the requirements of product or service delivery. For example, an increasing number of jobs in the economy involve serving customers—such as those in restaurants, hotels, convenience stores, and supermarkets—and the needs of customers may require work on Sundays or on a 24/7 basis. Jobs also differ in the extent to which they provide intrinsic rewards such as opportunities for personal gratification as well as extrinsic benefits such as money, chances for advancement, and health insurance.

People also differ in a variety of ways, many of which parallel the ways in which jobs differ. Thus, individuals have different skills and aptitudes as well as educational and other qualifications. People also vary in their preferences for working a certain number of hours and when they work these hours; some people are morning people, while others prefer to work at night. Workers also differ in the importance they place on the various kinds of benefits that jobs provide; some people attach the highest value to having a challenging or secure job, while others focus more on the economic rewards of work.

Combining the characteristics of people and jobs provides the basis for developing a typology of possible mismatches. The seven mismatched situations listed earlier suggest some of the key dimensions on which to compare individuals and jobs. These seven mismatches are diverse and represent poor fits between people and jobs based on skills and qualifications, time preferences, geographic location, inadequate earnings, and conflicts with other important roles that people play such as their family lives. The diversity of these types of mismatches reflects the variation in both workers and their jobs in a complex society such as the United States. In this book we will examine in detail these seven types of mismatches.

Skills Mismatches

Skills mismatches are situations where there is a lack of fit between people's skills or qualifications and their jobs' skill requirements. There are two general kinds of skill mismatches: *overqualification*, in which people's skills (often equated with their education and other work-related qualifications) exceed the skills required to perform the job; and *underqualification*, in which people do not have the skills required to carry out job duties adequately.

These two kinds of skills mismatches may coexist at the same time in the economy. There may be some occupations in which many workers are overqualified, such as the oversupply of computer programmers in the Silicon Valley; at the same time there are skill shortages or underqualification in others, such as the lack of qualified teachers of mathematics or physics in some high school systems.

There may also be changes over time in the extent to which overqualification or underqualification becomes more serious and attracts the interest of social scientists and the media. For example, in the 1970s, sociologists and economists focused on the causes and likely consequences of overqualification, as the rapid increase in the number of college-educated persons in the 1960s and early 1970s was assumed to exceed the growth in highly skilled jobs. By contrast, concern in the 1980s and 1990s shifted to the problem of underqualification and its relationship to rapid technological change and increased competitiveness in the world economy. Therefore, to many observers, it appeared that the nature of skills mismatch had changed and that "the skills glut seemed to have turned rapidly into a skills shortage" (Handel 2003, 137).

Geographical Mismatches

Geographical mismatches occur when geographic or spatial barriers prevent workers from obtaining jobs for which they are qualified or that meet their needs.

One type of geographical mismatch occurs when jobs move from one area to another, leaving behind workers who are not able to move and do not have the skills to fill the jobs that remain in the area. An example is *deindustrialization*, the shift of manufacturing industries from one region of the United States to another (such as from the Midwest or Northeast to the South and West) that was a prominent concern in the 1980s (Bluestone and Harrison 1982). Such geographical movements of jobs also reflect the shift from a manufacturing economy to a service economy. Geographical mismatches are also represented by the movement of jobs out of the United States altogether; such *offshoring* of both high-skill and low-skill jobs reflects the increasing globalization of the economy and is a concern to many workers and policy makers in the United States in the twenty-first century.

Another type of geographical mismatch is the lack of fit between jobs and people located in cities and suburbs. Most cities in America started with an urban-industrial core; people lived within walking distance of their jobs. As cities and transportation evolved, affluent people moved away from the city core to create the suburbs. Later the jobs followed, leaving low-income, minority residents behind in the urban core. The resulting geographical mismatch is frequently studied by social scientists by means of the *spatial mismatch* hypothesis. This idea posits that discrimination and other constraints in housing markets have denied minorities the access to homes in suburban areas to which the jobs for which they are qualified have migrated. As a result of these limits on mobility, minorities have been forced to live in inner-city areas where there are insufficient jobs that make use of their qualifications. The lack of access is compounded because minorities often have difficulty in commuting to places where suitable jobs are located, and the jobs in these locations don't pay well enough to support a family and justify the commute.

Temporal Mismatches

People often prefer to work for a certain amount of time, usually defined in terms of a number of hours per week, depending on such factors as the centrality of work to their identity and the extent to which they have nonwork interests that they wish to pursue or family responsibilities to attend to. People also differ in the number of hours they need to work in order to earn a certain level of income. For workers who are paid by the hour, income is directly linked to the number of hours they work, but salaried workers are often able to vary their hours, at least in the short run, without affecting their income.

In this book we will discuss two main kinds of temporal mismatches: *overworking*, in which a person works more hours than he or she wants (or works harder than he or she prefers within a fixed number of hours); and *underworking*, in which a person works fewer hours than he or she wants. In both cases, people are not able to work the amount of time that they would prefer or the number of hours that enable them to meet their needs.

Overworking is often associated with high-paying, high-status, professional jobs and self-employment. These jobs place relatively high demands on workers, especially early in their work careers, but they also provide workers with opportunities for high earnings and advancement to higher-paying, better jobs. On the other hand, underworking is usually related to economic hardship and often does not lead to better jobs in the future. Despite their differences, both types of temporal mismatches are likely to lead to stress and may contribute to other problems, such as conflict between work and family.

In addition to the number of hours people work, they may not be able to work the hours they prefer. This *work-schedule* mismatch is a third type of temporal mismatch and is illustrated by people who work nonstandard shifts, such as weekends or evenings, as opposed to a standard work schedule such as 9 to 5, Monday through Friday, even though such schedules may conflict with their family or other responsibilities. About two-fifths of all employed Americans worked nonstandard shifts in the late 1990s. Many of these jobs requiring nonstandard schedules are likely to expand greatly in the next few years, and are likely to involve a disproportionate number of women and blacks; these occupations include registered nurses and nurses' aides, cashiers, and retail salespersons (Presser 2003).

Finally, a fourth type of temporal mismatch is the case of a person working involuntarily in a temporary job. Temporary help agencies have multiplied in recent years, as employers have sought to cut costs and establish flexible employment arrangements with their employees (see Chapter 2). As a result, more workers are now working for such agencies. While this kind of temporary work arrangement might be advantageous for some workers, since it gives them greater variety and control over their work assignments, for many others it represents a mismatch, since they would prefer to work in traditional employment arrangements. In 2005, for example, only 32 percent of temporary help agency employees in the United States said that they preferred to work in temporary jobs (US Department of Labor 2005a).

Earnings Mismatches

Some workers cannot earn enough money to meet their needs and those of their families. In principle, earnings mismatches could occur regardless of how much money a person earns; even highly paid CEOs may feel that the amount they earn does not meet their needs, which may include airplanes, yachts, and summer cottages in exotic locales. Such high earners are not who we normally think as having earnings mismatches, however, since this reflects people's runaway expectations rather than the kinds of mismatches that concern us here.

Here we focus mainly on earnings mismatches at lower salary levels, such as the working poor, defined here as those persons who work full-time at a wage rate that is not sufficient to provide for their family's needs, keeping them below the federal government's poverty threshold, an amount which depends on family size. This admittedly arbitrary definition is useful as a point of departure, because it is utilized by the government to collect statistics on the working poor and is often the basis for deciding whether one is eligible for government aid.

In addition to the working poor, many middle-class workers may experience an earnings mismatch. Such workers have seen their earnings stagnate and decline in the past several decades, and many have experienced an income squeeze, forcing both spouses to work for pay and work for more hours in order to send their children to college, live in a good neighborhood, drive a nice car, and provide other amenities of a middle-class lifestyle.

Closely related to earnings mismatches is working in jobs that do not provide fringe benefits, especially health insurance. In the United States, people generally acquire health insurance through their employers, not from the government as a benefit of citizenship, as is the case in most other industrial countries. In 2003, 45 million Americans did not have health insurance, an increase of 5.2 million people since 2000 (Lambrew 2004). Low-wage jobs generally do not provide health insurance, although many workers on the margins of the working poor will take jobs that pay poorly if they include benefits.

Work-Family Mismatches

People's jobs may sometimes conflict with their performance in other roles and vice versa. We focus here on a conflict that affects large numbers of people in American society—when People's family lives interfere with their work lives, or when work conflicts with people's family activities and responsibilities. We define work-family mismatch in terms of work-family conflict. There are three general situations that may lead to work-family conflict (Greenhaus and Beutell 1985).

First, *time-based conflict* exists when the time commitments associated with one role make it difficult for people to fulfill their obligations in another role. An example is persons who are overworked in their jobs and thus do not have enough time to take care of their family obligations.

Second, *strain-based conflict* occurs when fatigue or frustrations produced in one role affect one's performance in another role. For example, people who are worried, tired, or tense as a result of what happens on their jobs may find it difficult to achieve a positive family life, and vice versa.

Third, *behavior-based conflict* results when the expectations regarding behavior in one role conflict with one's behavior in another role. Thus, men and women may be expected to be aggressive and objective in their dealings with coworkers or customers on the job, but warm, emotional, and vulnerable with members of their family at home.

Work-family mismatches are likely to be especially problematic for women, who are generally expected by our society to play a larger role than men in parenting, care-giving, and household activities. However, an increasing number of men are facing this kind of mismatch as well.

Interrelations among Mismatches
Since the seven types of mismatches identified above have distinct causes and consequences, we will discuss them in separate chapters in this book.

Nevertheless, these mismatches do not occur independently of each other, and one mismatch may lead to others. For example, a prominent reason why some people may not be able to find jobs that fit their skills, preferences, or needs is that they are geographically constrained for one reason or another and are not able to move to areas to find jobs that fit better their needs and preferences. This is often the case for women who are trailing spouses, who may be overqualified or may not be able to work as much as they would like because they are unable to find suitable employment in the area where their husbands are working. For example, a college professor who moves from one university to another may bring a trailing spouse who has difficulty finding suitable employment in the new location, often a college town.

Moreover, immigrants who have recently arrived in the United States, like minorities who live in the inner city, often cannot compete for jobs in their area because of their lack of skills and qualifications; they may also not have the resources to travel to other areas to search for jobs for which they might be more qualified. Geographical mismatches can thus account for some of the other kinds of mismatches we discuss in this book, since geographical constraints may affect workers' ability to obtain what they need or want from their jobs.

Members of the working poor are also likely to be under-qualified for their jobs and to lack the skills required to obtain higher-paying jobs. Indeed, it may well be that underqualification is the reason why a person is a member of the working poor. Underqualified workers may also be unable to find jobs that provide them with as many hours as they would like to work, or to find jobs at all.

In addition, people who feel that they are overworked may experience conflict between their work and family lives; one common reason why workers wish to reduce the number of hours that they work is to reduce conflict with their family life. On the other hand, people working in a job with inadequate income may be forced to take a second or third job in order to make ends meet, leading to feelings of being overworked.

Furthermore, some kinds of mismatches may coexist because they result from similar processes, especially from a disharmony between labor supply and employment demand. Thus, as suggested above, there can be a labor shortage at the same time as high underemployment; some jobs may be available because of the lack of applicants with the requisite education and training (e.g., high school math and physics teachers), while some college graduates work as bartenders. Additionally, hours in the labor market are often poorly distributed in the number of hours worked so that over- and underemployment may both occur. As a result, some workers may feel overworked at the same time as others are seeking to work more hours, reflecting the polarization that exists in temporal mismatches, as some workers work a large number of hours while others work relatively few (Jacobs and Gerson 2004).

In contrast to mismatches that are positively related to each other, there are situations in which some mismatches may be mutually exclusive and negatively related to each other. Obtaining a job that avoids one type of mismatch may thus lead to another type, and it may be difficult if not impossible to achieve good fits on all dimensions.

For example, obtaining a high-skilled job that fits one's

qualifications or avoiding earnings mismatches may require a person to work more hours than he or she desires. In addition, alleviating work-family conflict or meeting family needs such as caring for children or aging parents may require people to obtain more flexible jobs that do not fully utilize their educational qualifications or do not pay as much as they would like.

The negative relationships among some mismatches suggest that people may be forced to trade some types of good matches in order to avoid other mismatches. Understanding how and why people make such trade-offs provides insights as to what they consider most important about the job, or what economists refer to as *preference structures*.

STUDYING MISMATCHES

The characteristics of the people used earlier to illustrate the seven mismatches are fleshed out in Table 1.1. We will provide more details on each of these people in Chapters 3 9. While these people are composite individuals who do not correspond to any particular individual, they do represent types likely to experience each of the seven mismatches. Moreover, the characteristics we use to describe these individuals represent important dimensions of social experience and are variables often used to understand the nature and consequences of the mismatches. In subsequent chapters, we will elaborate on how these seven mismatches are explained in terms of the characteristics listed in the first column of Table 1.1.

While mismatches result from the interplay between characteristics of people and jobs, it is important to recognize that

Table 1.1
EXAMPLES OF MISMATCHED SITUATIONS

	Over-qualified	Under-qualified	Spatial Mismatch	Overwork	Underwork	Earnings Mismatch—Working Poor	Earnings Mismatch—Middle Class	Work-Family Mismatch	
Name	John	Latoya	Lamont	Kelly	Emily	Ramón	Edward	Kayla	Luis
Sex	Male	Female	Male	Female	Female	Male	Male	Female	Male
Race/ethnicity	White	African American	African American	White	Asian American	Hispanic	White	African American	Hispanic
Age	31	50	40	35	45	32	52	35	41
Family situation	Single, aging parents	Single, 3 children	Married, 3 children	Married, 2 children	Married, 2 children	Married, 2 children	Married, 2 children	Married, 4 children	
Education	Phd, English	HS diploma	1 year of college	Law school graduate	2 years of college	HS diploma	College graduate	College graduate	MBA
Occupation	Cashier	Machine operator	Welder	Lawyer	Accounting technician	Nursing aide	Tax preparer	Registered nurse	Account executive
Employer	Convenience store	Textile manufacturer	Manufacturing plant	Large corporate law firm	Construction company	Hospital	Accounting firm	Hospital	Big advertising company
Salary and benefits (Health insurance)	$8.50/hour, no health insurance	$12.00/hour, health insurance	$10.50/hour, health insurance	$80,000+/yr, health insurance	$11.00/hour, no health insurance	$7.00/hour, no health insurance	$40,000/yr, no health insurance	$40,000/year, health insurance	$90,000/year, health insurance
Length of time in job	2 years	20 years	10 years	4 years	15 years	3 years	1 year	10 years	15 years
Career aspirations (if any)	Teach Shakespeare	Continue at company	Find job closer to home	Be promoted to partner	Full-time work	Higher paying job	Find job similar to one he lost	Continue at job	CEO of company
Region of country	Northwest	Southeast	Midwest	West	Northeast	Southwest	Southeast	East	East

these mismatches are due primarily to social factors and are not necessarily the fault of individual workers. Some kinds of mismatches occur because the composition of the labor force or the nature of jobs is changing and are out of synch with each other. For example, the increase in women workers has made it more difficult for both men and women to balance their work and family lives. Moreover, pressures on organizations to do more with less have made it necessary for some workers to work more hours—and to work more intensely during those hours—than they would like. Other mismatches occur because social institutions and structures such as changing technology create imperfections in labor markets—for example, when changes in technology lead to a skills mismatch, or when people live too far away from jobs for which they are qualified—that prevent people and employers from obtaining jobs and workers that fit with each other.

We will examine these seven mismatches primarily from the point of view of workers and their families and focus on the conflict that may result from mismatches between workers' needs, skills, or other personal characteristics and the nature of their jobs and workplaces. Our main concern is to understand better the causes and consequences of mismatches for workers and their families. These mismatches, however, will also have broader effects on employers and society in general.

Focusing on workers is not the only way to study these mismatches. We could look at these mismatches from the employer's standpoint. Studying mismatches from the worker's viewpoint as opposed to the employer's is not the same, since a mismatch that may be problematic from the point of view of the worker may not necessarily be so from the perspective of the employer or vice versa. For example, a worker might perceive herself to be overqualified for a job, whereas the employer might see the situation as a way of bringing a worker up through the ranks by giving her progressively more challenging tasks. Similarly, a worker who feels that he is overworked might be seen by the employer as simply giving back to the company a fair day's work for a fair day's pay.

Despite our focus on workers, all seven mismatches that we consider here are not limited to specific individuals; all are likely to be shared by relatively large groups of people. Over- and underqualification, for example, are not isolated incidents experienced by our hypothetical examples of John and Latoya, but rather reflect a broader disjuncture between many workers' qualifications and jobs' requirements at any time. In other words, these seven mismatches are not only personal troubles, but also public issues rooted in structural mismatches between labor market institutions and the nature and composition of the labor force (Mills 1959).

Work-family mismatches, for instance, are ultimately due to changes in the nature of the commitment of family members to the labor market that have not been accompanied by parallel changes in the organization of work to make it easier for men and women to balance better their work and family lives. Moreover, low-wage work is problematic because the United States lacks the institutional structures to provide workers with various forms of social insurance such as health care and pensions or a safety net outside of the workplace (Osterman et al. 2001). Since these mismatches are structural in nature, alleviating them requires institutional and structural solutions, and individuals' actions to improve their own situations are not likely to be sufficient to reduce mismatches on a large scale.

Significantly, all seven mismatches we consider in this book are pressing public issues. Evidence suggests that most, if not all, of these mismatches have increased, sometimes substantially, in the United States in recent years. Work-family mismatches, for example, are now widespread and are intimately related to concerns about overworking. Both types of mismatches have profound consequences for both workplaces and families. In addition, there has been a long-term decline in adequate employment in the United States, making the study of underqualification, underworking, and earnings mismatches more important now than it has ever been (see Clogg, Eliason, and Leicht 2001, 243).

These mismatches are also burning issues at this time because they result from some of the main trends that are occurring in the labor force: *globalization*, which leads to pressures on businesses to become more competitive, increasing geographic mismatches, overworking and perhaps underworking, and earnings mismatches; *growth of information technology*, which increases underqualification; and the *geographic dispersion* of people and workers, which contributes to geographic mismatches.

Multidisciplinary Perspective
The complexity of work and workers calls for a multidisciplinary approach, and thus our explanation of mismatches incorporates ideas of sociologists, economists, and psychologists, and to a lesser extent the contributions of geographers, historians, and other social scientists.

Various social science disciplines have emphasized different ways of categorizing and identifying how people and jobs are matched. These disciplines differ in the aspects of the matching process that they emphasize and in the factors they identify as being primarily responsible for the incidence, nature, and consequences of mismatches between people and jobs.

- Sociologists have generally approached the issue of mismatch from the point of view of whether jobs are inadequate. This idea is based on the Labor Utilization Framework (LUF) (Sullivan 1978; Clogg 1979), a prominent sociological perspective that defines mismatches in terms of three types of underemployment or inadequate employment: that is, inadequate hours (involuntary part-time work); inadequate income (low-income work); and underutilization of a person's skills (overqualification). Sociologists have also studied mismatches that result from conflicts among the different kinds of roles people play in society, especially those related to work and family.

- Economists emphasize the importance of labor markets for understanding how persons are matched to jobs and examine how imbalances between the supply of workers and the demand for jobs may create mismatches. For example, economists study the consequences that arise when workers' skills and qualifications do not fit those required by the jobs that are available (e.g., Tyler, Murnane, and Levy 1995), or when people are unable to find jobs that allow them to work as much or as little as they would like (e.g., Golden 2003).

- Psychologists who study industries and organizations conceptualize the notion of mismatch broadly in terms of the lack of fit between an individual's ability, interests, personality, or beliefs and the corresponding requirements of jobs (e.g., Wilk, Desmarais, and Sackett 1995; Holland 1973) or between an individual's beliefs and perceptions and the organization's culture (e.g., O'Reilly, Chatman, and Caldwell 1991). This approach recognizes that people's attitudes and preferences may diverge from the realities of the workplace in a large number of ways, not only in terms of skills.

- Geographers have emphasized the importance of location for understanding labor market processes (e.g., Peck 1996). Introducing the notion of space raises the possibility that geographical boundaries may produce mismatches; people may not have easy access to locations where the jobs for which they are qualified are located and must either settle for jobs that they would not otherwise take or go without any job at all.

The theoretical perspective we use throughout this book draws upon insights from all these disciplines about the nature and consequences of these mismatches. Our arguments thus build on ongoing efforts to integrate the social sciences such as: *behavioral economics*, the use of psychological reasoning to inform economic problems—for instance, how emotions affect preferences for earnings and other kinds of labor market outcomes; *sociological economics*, the application of the tools of economics to questions typically asked by sociologists—for example, how labor market processes affect inequalities among men and women; and *economic sociology*, the use of sociological theories to explain economic phenomena, such as the way social institutions affect the operation of labor markets.

Plan of the Book

We seek to understand several things about the seven mismatches: What are the main mechanisms that explain why these mismatches occur? Which groups in society are most likely to experience them and how have they changed over time? What are their likely consequences? What kinds of social policies and interventions are apt to be effective in alleviating these mismatches?

Chapters 3–9 address in turn the seven types of mismatches we have identified. Each chapter summarizes the main social scientific research that has sought to explain why the mismatch occurs. We organize the literature in terms of the conceptualization developed in Chapter 2, which argues that mismatches occur as a result of the interplay between characteristics of individuals and of jobs and how these are matched in labor markets. Explaining why mismatches occur will help us predict where in the labor force and job structure the various mismatches are likely to be prevalent. Accounting for why these mismatches occur between people and jobs is an essential prelude to thinking about how we might try to minimize or eliminate them.

We also discuss how we measure the salient aspects of the mismatch. In many cases, the measurement of a mismatch is ambiguous and there are alternative ways to assess it. It is valuable to obtain empirical, quantitative estimates of the incidence of the mismatch and its correlates, since these tell us who is affected by the mismatch and where policy interventions should be directed. We also present quantitative information on the extent of the mismatch whenever possible and indicate how its incidence differs by characteristics of individuals such as gender, race/ethnicity, age, and education, and by characteristics of jobs, such as the occupations and industries in which they are classified. These empirical estimates give us a sense of the extent of the mismatch and provide suggestive evidence as to who is more likely to be affected by it. We also attempt to indicate how the various types of mismatches vary over time for different groups of people and jobs.

We then discuss some of the main conclusions of social science research about the consequences of these mismatches, especially for individuals and their families. We argue that mismatches are important to study because they are likely to have widespread consequences for the individual, such as unhappiness or dissatisfaction due to unmet needs; the family, such as stress caused by conflicts or poverty; the organization, such as lower productivity and performance; and society, such as political unrest, welfare burdens, and social disintegration (Schor 1997).

Finally we suggest social policies and strategies that might alleviate the various kinds of mismatches. We argue that reducing mismatches cannot rely solely or even primarily on the actions of individuals and their families in order to be effective. Structural and social remedies are needed to bring work structures and characteristics of workers into closer alignment in order to obtain greater individual satisfaction, organizational efficiency, and social welfare.

The kinds of mismatches discussed here are likely to occur,

in greater or less degrees, in all industrial countries. Our focus in this book, however, will be primarily on the situation in the United States. The US case is complex enough for a short book, and the American context is distinctive in many ways, which makes the study of work and workers especially challenging and interesting in this country. At the same time, there is considerable variation across countries because of national differences in institutions such as unions, government policies that regulate labor markets, linkages between educational and occupational systems, cultural belief systems and expectations of what is desirable in a job, and so on. All these factors are apt to affect the incidence, nature, and consequences of mismatches. We do not attempt to conduct a systematic cross-national analysis, but we will draw on examples and lessons for the United States from other countries whenever possible.

Chapter Two
MATCHING PEOPLE TO JOBS:
CONCEPTS AND THEORIES

IT IS NECESSARY to understand three main factors in order to explain the occurrence and consequences of the seven mismatches we identified in the previous chapter.

First, we should understand how individuals differ in their work-related needs and preferences, and why some people are better able than others to find jobs that fulfill their needs. The likelihood that people will experience the various kinds of mismatches depends on characteristics such as gender, marital status, race, age, and education. For example, dual-career couples are more likely to experience mismatch between their work and family lives; college-educated people are more likely to be overqualified for their jobs; and people who dropped out of high school are more apt to be underqualified.

Second, we have to be aware of the number and kinds of jobs available at a given time and place and the characteristics of the workplaces in which they are found. Jobs differ in the levels and types of rewards they offer, such as earnings, health insurance, and challenging work, and in the constraints they impose, such as inflexible work schedules or the requirement to travel to particular geographical areas, that may prevent workers from obtaining what they want and need. The structure of jobs also affects the likelihood that certain kinds of mismatches will occur. For example: The rapid expansion of highly complex professional and technical jobs may create skill shortages, leading to an oversupply of underqualified workers; growth of retail trade and personal service jobs may increase the availability of jobs that pay low wages and hence the number of workers relegated to the ranks of the working poor; and corporate restructuring and downsizing may create pressures on workers to work more hours than they want out of fear that otherwise they will be laid off.

Third, explaining mismatches between people and jobs requires an understanding of the labor market and the institutional mechanisms that bring jobs and people together. Labor markets match job seekers with particular qualifications and tastes to jobs that fit people's skills and preferences in varying degrees. If labor markets operated perfectly and efficiently, mismatches would be less likely to occur, since people would take only jobs that fit their needs, preferences, and skills, and employers would hire only workers that had the necessary skills and wanted to conform to the jobs' demands. No markets, including labor markets, operate perfectly, however, and so we need to identify the institutional and social factors that introduce inefficiencies, imperfections, or irrationalities into otherwise competitive labor market mechanisms, leading to mismatches.

In this chapter, we first discuss some of the ways in which individuals differ with regard to their work-related needs and preferences and to their ability to obtain jobs that fulfill them. We then consider some of the important differences in jobs that affect opportunities for people to find jobs that match their abilities, needs, and preferences. Next, we examine the mechanisms by which people are matched to jobs, or how peo-

ple with certain characteristics choose (or are chosen for) particular jobs. Finally we discuss some of the issues involved in
assessing the consequences of mismatches. This chapter will set
the stage for our examination of the specific types of mismatches in the following chapters.

Individual Differences

Demographic categories such as gender, race, and age are
among the most important attributes associated with the likelihood that a person will experience one or more of the seven
mismatches. Men and women, whites and non-whites, and
younger and older workers, for example, often have different
work-related needs and preferences. Members of these groups
are likely to differ in their preferences for working a certain
number of hours, the degree to which they are committed to
work as opposed to family and other institutions, the extent to
which they rely on their earnings to support themselves and
their families, and so on.

Economists usually assume that people's preferences for particular kinds of job rewards—for example, high income, security, or interesting work—are formed outside the labor market
and influence their decisions about such things as how many
hours they would like to work. Sociologists, by contrast, generally assume that workers' preferences may also be affected by
their work experience; for example, workers who are not able to
find a full-time job may adapt by preferring to work part-time.

Workers also differ in their types and levels of skills, education, and other qualifications, all of which affect their ability to
obtain the kinds of jobs that they want. The main concept we
will use to explain people's differing ability to satisfy their

needs and preferences in the labor market is their degree of *market power*, which derives from both individual and collective sources. Workers with more market power have more control over their employment and should be better able to find jobs that match their work-related needs and preferences than workers with less market power. The concept of market power focuses on the effects and processes of power and infers the existence of power from the varying ability of workers to realize their interests through participation in labor markets (Form and Huber 1976; Parkin 1971; Kalleberg, Wallace, and Althauser 1981).

People differ in their market power or degree of control over their employment situations for several reasons (Sullivan 1978). First, members of certain demographic groups, such as women, non-whites, and young or old people, often have less choice regarding jobs than men, whites, and people in the prime working ages (25 to 54). These constraints on job choice are due in part to characteristics such as gender, race, and age, which often cause an advantage for some and discrimination and other disadvantages, such as the lack of a network of contacts, for others.

To understand why some people are constrained in their job choices, it is helpful to distinguish between horizontal and vertical segregation (Charles and Grusky 2004). Horizontal segregation—such as the crowding of women into non-manual jobs and men into manual jobs—is rooted in cultural beliefs that these jobs are associated with gender-typical traits; non-manual occupations require traits such as an orientation toward service or nurturing that are associated with women, while manual occupations require traits such as strength and physicality that are associated with men.

On the other hand, vertical segregation—such as men being paid more and having more desirable jobs—results from cultural principles such as the belief that men are more status worthy than women. These cultural beliefs are enforced by discrimination by employers and institutions—through the educational system, for example—as well as by men and women internalizing these beliefs and thereby choosing jobs that are considered appropriate by the culture.

Second, a person may have relatively high market power from having acquired skills and qualifications that are highly valued by employers in the labor market. Thus, persons with advanced degrees are generally in a better position to obtain the jobs they prefer, as are those with specialized skills acquired through vocational and on-the-job training and work experience. These skills and qualifications help workers to avoid some types of mismatches, such as underqualification, underworking, and working in low-wage jobs, but not necessarily others, such as overqualification, overworking, and work-family conflict.

Third, a person's market power is affected by characteristics that might limit his or her employment, such as disabilities or poor health. People who are disabled or for other reasons unable to participate fully in the labor force are likely to be marginal in the labor market and apt to experience some forms of mismatch, especially those related to underworking and low-wage jobs.

Finally, a person's market power or vulnerability to mismatch depends also on collective or institutional characteristics such as union membership and belonging to an occupational or industrial group for which demand may be growing or declining. Later in this chapter we will discuss further how work structures such as occupations, industries, and unions affect a worker's market power and thereby the likelihood of mismatches.

We next provide an overview of the main demographic characteristics of the labor force in the United States, how the composition of the labor force has changed over the past half-century, and what some experts view as future trends in the composition of the labor force. We also consider why people in these different demographic groups will be more or less likely to experience the various types of mismatches.

Changing Labor Force Composition
The US civilian labor force grew sharply during the twentieth century, from about 30 million people in 1900 (about 40 percent of the US population at that time) to about 140 million by the year 2000 (about half of the total population). It is expected to grow to over 190 million by the year 2050. In addition to getting bigger, the labor force in the United States has become more diverse; it has gotten older, better educated, less white, and more female.

A commonly used indicator of the extent to which a population is engaged in paid economic activity is the *labor force participation rate* (LFPR). The LFPR is defined as the percentage of persons in the *population at risk of employment* who are in the labor force. The "population at risk of employment" is usually defined as civilians over sixteen who are not in institutions such as prisons or mental hospitals. The labor force, in turn, is made up of two groups of people—employed persons (non-institutionalized civilians over sixteen years of age who are working for pay or profit) and unemployed persons (those who are trying unsuccessfully to find paid jobs).

Table 2.1 provides some basic statistics on the demographic characteristics of the labor force in the United States. It shows that about 59 percent of the population at risk was in the labor force in 1950, compared to 67 percent of the population at risk in 2000. The LFPR in the United States is projected to decline over the first half of the twenty-first century, to about 62 percent in 2050.

Gender

Perhaps the most dramatic and far-reaching change in the labor force in recent years has been the growing participation of women in the labor force. As Hochschild (1989, 239) describes it: "Women's move into the economy is the basic social revolution of our time." This increase of women in the labor force has had profound consequences for the types of jobs that are available—for example, the rapid expansion in white-collar occupations such as clerical work—as well as for the nature of interactions among people within the workplace. It has also made it more likely that certain kinds of mismatches will occur, such as those related to balancing work with family responsibilities and needs.

Women's labor force participation rates increased steadily during the last century, growing from about 20 percent in 1890 (Committee on Techniques for the Enhancement of Human Performance 1999) to about 34 percent in 1950 and 60 percent in 2000 (see Table 2.1). The LFPR of men in the United States has always been relatively higher than that of

Table 2.1

DEMOGRAPHIC CHARACTERISTICS OF THE

US LABOR FORCE, 1950–2050[a]

	1950	1980	2000	2020	2050
LF (in thousands)					
Total LFPR,	62,208	106,940	140,863	164,681	191,825
16 and older	59.2	63.8	67.2	65.1	61.5
Men					
% of LF	70.4	57.5	52.4	51.9	52.3
LFPR	86.4	77.4	74.7	70.3	66.8
Women					
% of LF	29.6	42.5	46.6	48.1	47.7
LFPR	33.9	51.5	60.2	60.3	56.6
Race					
White					
% of LF	—	87.5	83.5	79.5	74.9
LFPR	—	64.1	67.4	65.0	61.4
Black					
% of LF	—	10.2	11.8	13.3	14.1
LFPR	—	61.0	65.8	65.0	59.8
Asian and other					
% of LF	—	2.3	4.8	7.3	10.9
LFPR	—	64.6	66.5	66.4	64.9
Hispanic origin[b]					
% of LF	—	5.8	10.9	16.0	23.7
LFPR	—	64.0	68.6	67.9	63.8
Age					
16 to 34					
% of LF	42.0	51.0	38.6	38.6	39.3
LFPR	61.9	74.0	75.7	77.8	76.7
35 to 54					
% of LF	40.8	35.0	48.5	41.1	41.9
LFPR	67.0	77.6	83.8	85.3	84.9
55 and older					
% of LF	17.2	14.1	12.9	20.3	18.8
LFPR	43	32.8	32.3	36.3	30.2

[a]Source: Mitra Toossi. 2002. "A Century of Change: The US Labor Force, 1950–2050." *Monthly Labor Review* (May): 15–28 (Tables 4 and 5).

[b]Persons of Hispanic origin may be of any race. Percentages of whites, blacks, and Asians/other add up to 100 percent (deviations due to rounding).

women, but has been declining, from 86 percent in 1950 to about 75 percent in 2000, and is projected to decline to about 67 percent in 2050. In 1950, women constituted less than a third (about 30 percent) of the labor force, compared to nearly half (about 47 percent) in 2000. Women's LFPR—at least for white women—is expected to level off in the next several decades and decline to about 57 percent by 2050 (Toosi 2002). Women's representation in the labor force is also projected to remain below 50 percent by the year 2050.

Women with children are now more likely than in the past to participate in the labor force. In the 1950s, the LFPR of women showed a big decline during the childbearing ages, when they left the labor force. This decline changed each decade, especially after the women's movement of the 1970s. By the 1990s, women's labor force participation rates looked very similar to men's, with hardly any decline in the childbearing ages (Padavic and Reskin 2002, 150).

The growth of female participation in the labor force was due to a number of factors. Women's entry into the labor force was stimulated by economic pressures such as the stagnation in earnings for middle-class workers that made it difficult for families to rely on a single breadwinner. It was also facilitated by declines in the birth rate, which lessened the demand on women to take care of children, and the growth in the divorce rate, which made it more necessary for women to earn a living. Women were also encouraged to move into the labor force for several other reasons: to take advantage of their rising educational levels, to continue their positive experience with paid employment during World Wars I and II, and to fill the multiplying jobs for which they were especially matched in the service sector and the emerging caring professions. The caring professions—teaching, social work, nursing—have traditionally provided acceptable careers for unmarried women as well as married women in the years before they had children.

Women generally have less market power and are more vulnerable to the labor market than men. This is not because women are less qualified than men; indeed, women have about as much education as men. However, women are more likely to experience discrimination in hiring and promotion and have less access to the social networks and connections that facilitate job acquisition. Women's job choices are also often constrained because of their family commitments. For these reasons, women are more likely than men to work in low-wage jobs and to be segregated into a smaller range of jobs than men (Padavic and Reskin 2002). Women are also more likely to be paid less than men even when they work in comparable jobs. Since women are also expected to play the major role in the household and raising children, they are more likely than men to experience work-family mismatches.

The increase in women workers and dual-earner households has made work-family balance a more pressing issue than it was when the US labor force was predominantly male and the typical family consisted of a male breadwinner and a wife who stayed at home with the children. Workers, especially women, with small children are more likely to experience conflicts between their work and family responsibilities, as we will discuss in more detail in Chapter 9. In addition, the growing number of single mothers has helped to increase the proportion of the working poor, many of whom consist of families headed by women.

Race and Ethnicity

The vast majority of labor force participants in the United States are white, although this proportion has declined during the past several decades, decreasing from 88 percent of the labor force in 1980 to 84 percent in 2000, and is projected to decline further to 75 percent in 2050. The fastest-growing non-white racial group comprises "Asians and other" races, whose representation in the labor force more than doubled between 1980 and 2000 (from 2.3 percent to 4.8 percent) and is expected to comprise about 11 percent of the labor force in 2050. The proportion of blacks[3] in the labor force increased slightly, from about 10 percent in 1980 to about 12 percent in 2000, and is expected to increase to about 14 percent by 2050. The proportion of black men in the labor force has declined over the past 30 years, partly because of a decline in traditional manufacturing industries and higher incarceration rates; in 2004, nearly 20 percent of black men in their prime working years (25 to 54) were no longer in the labor force. By contrast, there has been an increase in black women in the labor force because of better education, which gives them more access to jobs, and an increase in households in which black women are the sole breadwinners.

Perhaps the most dramatic increase among any race/ethnic group is among those of Hispanic origin, which increased from less then 6 percent in 1980 to nearly 11 percent in 2000 and is projected to constitute nearly a quarter of the labor force by 2050.[4] The LFPR of Hispanic men is over 90 percent. The

[3]The terms "black" and "African American" are used synonymously in this book.
[4]Those classified as being of Hispanic origin can be racially classified as white or black.

growth in Hispanics is in large part attributable to the recent waves of legal and illegal immigration to the United States from various Latin American countries, coupled with the relatively high Hispanic birth rate.

One of every seven people working in the United States in 2004 was born in another country; only a decade ago, the figure was one in ten. Slightly more than one million immigrants from all countries entered the United States in 2004. More than half of these immigrants were illegal, and many worked in relatively low-paying and often dirty jobs in industries such as services, meatpacking, and construction (N. Bernstein 2005).

Minorities are more likely than whites to be vulnerable to the negative consequences of labor market processes. Discrimination and lack of social capital such as access to social networks and contacts helps to keep non-whites—especially blacks—from finding out about and entering many jobs. Minorities are also more likely to experience disadvantages in acquiring the qualifications they need to compete for good jobs and in finding desirable places to live. For these reasons, non-whites are more likely to be part of the working poor, underqualified for many of the jobs that are available, and subject to spatial mismatches.

Age

The proportion of the labor force between the ages of 16 and 34 increased from 42 percent to 51 percent between 1950 and 1980 but declined fairly dramatically, to 39 percent, between 1980 and 2000. By contrast, the proportion of people between 35 and 54 increased sharply, from 35 percent to 49 percent, between 1980 and 2000. The decline in the younger age group coupled with the rise in workers in the 35 to 54 age group is due in large part to the aging of the large cohort of baby boomers born after the end of World War II. It is projected that the age of the labor force will continue to increase, with the largest gains occurring in the proportion of workers who are 55 and above—13 percent in 2000, but projected to be 19 percent in 2050.

The aging of the labor force has made it more likely that people will be underqualified for many of the jobs that are available, as older people's skills are apt to become outdated and obsolete because of technological change and reorganization taking place within workplaces. On the other hand, the aging of the labor force makes it less likely that these workers are overqualified for their jobs, because older workers' skills may have declined as they aged and because they have had more time to find jobs that fit their skills. Older workers are probably less likely to be overworked, as they are apt to be past the peak of their careers and so have less incentive to put in longer hours at work than they want to.

Education

The educational level of the labor force in the United States increased steadily in the twentieth century, especially the proportion of college graduates. In 1910, only about 14 percent of the US population 25 or older were high school graduates or better, and only about 3 percent had at least a college degree. By 2002, 84 percent of the population in the United States 25 or older had at least a high school diploma, and 27 percent had a college degree or more (United States Bureau of the Census, *Statistical Abstract of the United States*, 2003, Table HS-22). In 2003 a slightly higher proportion of men than women had four or more years of college (29 percent vs. 25 percent), although there was no gender difference in the percent that had at least four years of high school.

The educational attainment of labor force members is slightly higher than that of the population of the United States generally. Thus, 31.4 percent of the civilian labor force in 2002 had at least a college degree, up from 26.4 percent in 1992, while only 12 percent had less than a high school diploma. Women in the labor force have about as much education as men—for example, 31 percent of women in the labor force had at least a college degree in 2002, compared to 32 percent of male workers, while only 8 percent of women and 12 percent of men had less than a high school education in 2002 (United States Bureau of the Census 2005, Table No. 573).

Workers with higher levels of education are more apt to be overqualified rather than underqualified or unemployed, and, depending on the nature of their jobs and family situations, more likely to experience overwork and work-family conflicts. Highly educated workers are also less likely to work in low-wage jobs. As we will see in Chapter 8, though, a significant proportion of the working poor have at least some college education.

DIFFERENTIATION OF JOBS

Jobs differ in the skills they require, as well as in stability, desirability, compensation, opportunities for advancement, and other benefits. Advances in technology, globalization and internationalization, and the growth of service industries have had major impacts on the kinds of jobs found in an industrial society. These macroeconomic changes, in turn, have had a great influence on the number of hours Americans spend working, what they do in their leisure time, their consumption patterns, their attitudes toward success and failure, and a host of other attributes that shape the way they live and interact with each other. Changes in the nature of jobs and how work is organized may not always coincide with workers' skills or needs, however, and the resulting mismatches between people and jobs produce difficulties for employers as well as workers.

Jobs in some occupations and industries are more likely than others to be associated with each of the seven mismatches. Occupations differ in their skill requirements, in the extent to which they are in high demand by employers, in their level of earnings and the potential for paying higher earnings over time (dead end versus career occupations), in the degree to which they need to be performed on a fixed schedule or in a fixed location, and so on.[5]

Jobs also differ in the degree to which they can be "crafted" by individuals—that is, reorganized to fit better with their personalities, skills, and preferences—and hence the extent to which they can be altered by people as they seek to reduce mismatches by changing the activities and conditions of work.

Occupations and industries also differ in the extent to which they provide workers with sources of collective labor

---

[5]How the work of an occupation is organized may also differ considerably from one company to the next, enhancing the chances that workers in the same occupation may be overqualified or underqualified (or overworked and underworked), depending on the particular employers they work for.

market power such as membership in a union or professional association. These sources of market power enhance the chances that workers will obtain jobs that match their needs and preferences.

We next provide a brief overview of American occupational and industrial structures, how these have changed over the past century, and what some experts anticipate as future trends in these structures. We then consider several reasons why workers in some occupations and industries are more or less likely to experience the various types of mismatches.

Table 2.2

OCCUPATIONAL DISTRIBUTION OF THE UNITED STATES

LABOR FORCE, 1900–2000[a]

Occupational Group	1900	1960	1980	2000
White-collar workers	17.7	43.4	52.2	59.4
Professional, technical	4.3	11.4	16.1	18.9
Managers, administrators	5.9	10.7	11.2	14.6
Clerical workers	3.0	14.8	18.6	13.8
Sales workers	4.5	6.4	6.3	12.1
Blue-collar workers	35.9	36.6	31.7	24.5
Craft and kindred	10.6	13.0	12.9	11.0
Operatives	12.8	18.2	14.2	9.5
Nonfarm laborers	12.5	5.4	4.6	4.0
Service workers	9.0	12.2	13.3	13.5
Farmers and farm workers	37.6	7.9	2.8	2.5

[a]Source for 1900, 1960, 1980: Randy Hodson and Teresa Sullivan, *The Social Organization of Work*, 2nd edition (1995). Belmont, CA: Wadsworth. Source for 2000: United States Department of Labor, Bureau of Labor Statistics, *Report on the American Workforce 2001*, Table 10, p. 131. Numbers are percentages in each occupational group.

Occupational Differences

Occupations are groups of activities that describe the different kinds of work that people do. The categories used to classify occupations are the main way sociologists and government analysts conceptualize and measure the division of work within a society. The proportion of people in these occupational categories comprise the occupational structure, which has changed in several important ways during the twentieth century.

First, there has been an increase in white-collar occupations, from less than 20 percent of the labor force in 1900 to nearly 60 percent by 2000. There have been especially large increases in certain white-collar occupations, including professional and technical workers, which increased from about 4 percent of the labor force in 1900 to about a fifth by 2000; clerical occupations, which grew from about 3 percent of the labor force to about 14 percent during the century; and managerial and administrative occupations, which more than doubled in size over the century. These changes resulted in part from the increased complexity of work and changes in the way workplaces are organized, reflected in the growth in the administrative components of organizations (clerical work, managers) during most of the twentieth century.

Second, there has been a decline in blue-collar occupations, which decreased from more than a third of the labor force in the early part of the twentieth century to less than a quarter by century's end. The big decline in this category occurred in unskilled blue-collar workers (non-farm laborers), who saw their jobs taken over by machinery and technological innovations. The proportion of operatives, the category of semi-skilled workers of the mass-production era who operated machinery, grew until the 1960s and then decreased. Only the proportion of relatively skilled craft occupations (plumbers, electricians, mechanics) has remained fairly constant during the twentieth century.

Third, the proportion of service occupations (child care workers, police and firefighters, waiters and waitresses) increased substantially during the twentieth century. This increase reflects the growth in service industries as well as the increased size of the public sector. Note that many of the occupations associated with service industries are also classified in other categories, such as "professionals."

Finally, the biggest occupational shift during the twentieth century was the decrease in farmers and farm workers, from more than a third of the workforce to less than 3 percent by the end of the century. This decline reflects in large part the technological advances in agriculture that made it possible to produce more food with fewer workers.

Changes in the occupational structure are generated in part by changes in industries and in the goods and services produced in the economy. Occupational changes have also accompanied changes in the composition of the labor force. For example, the growth of clerical occupations during the period after World War II was fueled by the entry of women into the labor force. In addition, increases in the educational attainments of the workforce helped to stimulate the growth in skill requirements, or at least the educational credentials that managers required for entry into both white- and blue-collar occupations.

Occupational changes—whether produced by technological changes or by organizing work differently (such as by the greater use of teamwork)—may lead to mismatches, because the new occupational tasks are likely to require skills that workers do not necessarily have. The new skills are not necessarily higher or lower than previous skills; they are just different. Still, an increase or decrease in the skill levels associated with occupations is an important question for predicting whether overqualification or underqualification is likely to be the dominant form of mismatch. The issue of changes in occupational skills and their relationship to work organization has been the subject of considerable debate among social scientists for more than three decades.

Harry Braverman (1974), for example, stimulated sociological research and theory on the question of work organization and its relationship to changes in occupational skills. He maintained that the way work was divided into various kinds of jobs within an organization resulted from the conflict between capitalists (employers and their agents, managers) and workers over the way in which work was organized, rather than being determined by the requirements of the technology used. According to Braverman, capitalists sought to eliminate workers' skills by creating jobs that were as simple as possible so that labor costs (both the wages paid to workers and the costs needed to train them), and therefore workers' market power, were minimized.

Writers who felt that technology and other drivers of the labor process resulted in increases in skills challenged Braverman's view. The debate over whether skills have been upgraded or downgraded as a result of changes in the organization of work and technological change has been reviewed by Spenner (1983) and Form (1987), both of whom found that the answer to the question depended on whether you looked at the entire economy, which yielded evidence for the upgrading of skills, or at specific occupations such as printers, which provided evidence for the downgrading of skills. The main conclusion from this research is that the skill requirements have increased for some occupations and decreased for others, while at the same time technological change has displaced some workers from their jobs altogether.

Occupations are likely to differ in the extent to which their members experience the various kinds of mismatches. Thus, white-collar occupations that are relatively low skilled but have relatively high status, such as clerical work, are likely to have high proportions of overqualified workers, since employers may require educational credentials for entry into the occupation, even though the jobs may not be very complex or well paid. Members of professional and technical occupations are likely to experience overwork and work-family conflicts, since these occupations are generally in high demand and there is always more work to do. Service and sales occupations, along with less skilled blue-collar occupations, are likely to pay relatively low wages, and those who work in these occupations are apt to be part of the working poor or members of the declining middle class.

Industry Differences
Industries are groups of organizations that produce similar goods or services and operate in similar product markets. The industrial structure is used as an indicator of the extent to which a society is agricultural, industrial (characterized by the predominance of manufacturing) or post-industrial (dominated by service and knowledge-intensive industries). The main

trends in the twentieth century in the United States, as in most developed countries, have been (1) a shift from agriculture to manufacturing in the first half of the twentieth century; and (2) a dramatic shift from manufacturing to service industries in the second half of the century.

Industry differences are intimately related to changes in occupations, and in many cases, industry shifts can be said to cause occupational changes. For example, the creation of new products such as the automobile and personal computer, and new services such as big box stores such as Wal-Mart or Target, typically leads to the creation of occupations needed to produce the goods or services (auto workers, software and hardware engineers, sales clerks). The shift toward service industries and a post-industrial economy, in particular, has created strong demand for professional, technical, and other knowledge workers.

Some kinds of industrial characteristics are particularly apt to be associated with certain kinds of mismatches. For example, industries such as services and retail sales are highly labor-intensive; people rather than machines do most of the work, and businesses have relatively low profit margins. So, work in these kinds of industries may be more likely to pay relatively low wages, keeping these workers in poverty. Jobs may also be marginal because these industries are highly competitive and characterized by many small organizations; these conditions contribute to high instability among employers, making it more likely that the workers in these industries may not be able to work as many hours as they would like and may also lose their jobs. Since service and sales industries cater to customers, they often must be staffed on a 24/7 basis, leading to perceptions of overwork among the people who work in them.

Unions

Unions represent workers in their relations with employers. Historically, unions have been the main source of workers' collective power and have helped to raise their wages and persuade employers to provide them with benefits such as health insurance and pensions. Workers who are not union members have often been helped by the presence of unions, as employers of nonunionized companies feel pressured to create good jobs so as to discourage their workers from unionizing (the so-called "union threat effect").

The heyday of unions in the United States was the middle of the twentieth century, from the 1940s through the early 1970s. This was the period of the capital-labor accord, during which businesses in many of the basic manufacturing industries such as automobiles and steel shared their profits with labor unions in return for labor peace. The interests of employers and workers were aligned during this period. The capital-labor accord began to break down in the early 1970s, as growing economic pressures on employers to become more competitive and flexible led them to mount an offensive against the rigidities imposed by unions. Companies moved to states that had good business climates, which often means a low unionization rate, or moved jobs out of the country entirely (see Chapter 5).

As a result of this onslaught on unions by employers, there was a massive decline in union membership in the United States during the latter part of the twentieth century. The percentage of workers who belong to unions has steadily fallen from nearly 35 percent a half century ago to about 12.5 percent in 2004. This decline was especially marked in the private sector, where union membership fell from 25 percent in 1975 (it was 39 percent in 1954) to 8.2 percent in 2004. This reduction in union membership was accompanied by the decrease in blue-collar workers, traditionally the occupational groups in the US most likely to belong to unions.

By contrast, the union membership rate in the public sector (local, state, and national government) rose from 25 percent in 1975 to 35 percent in 2004 (Farber 2005). This divergence in union membership in the public and private sectors reflects the lack of market competition for the products of the public sector and the lack of fiscal discipline in this sector, both of which make it likely that unionized collective bargaining will be more effective in the public sector.

LABOR MARKETS: MATCHING PEOPLE AND JOBS

Labor markets are the main tool used by economists and other social scientists to conceptualize the interplay between the characteristics of people and jobs in producing matches and mismatches. Labor markets are the arenas in which people are matched to jobs and where employment relations are created between workers and employers. Labor markets are generally associated with the economies of capitalist societies, although all industrial societies, including planned societies such as communist or socialist nations, have systems like labor markets whereby people and jobs are matched to each other.

Labor markets have been studied most systematically by economists, since markets are a central concept in that discipline (Granovetter 1981). Sociologists have also turned their attention to labor markets, especially in the past thirty years or so, as they have come to recognize their importance for understanding structural sources of inequality, particularly differences in earnings and career advancement. Both economists and sociologists have offered useful insights for understanding how labor markets operate and how they may create mismatches between people and jobs.

Efficient Labor Markets?
Economists generally assume that people are matched to jobs in competitive, efficient labor markets. In competitive markets, there are many buyers (employers) and many sellers of labor (workers), and each party has a great deal of information about the other and is able to make good decisions. Labor markets are also bounded geographically, sometimes to a city or region, but for many occupations (computer programmers, engineers, or sociologists) the labor market may be national or international in scope.

Individuals are assumed to compete with each other for jobs in labor markets (Sørensen and Kalleberg 1981). Job-seekers and job vacancies may be conceptualized as two queues that are matched in the labor market (Thurow 1975). Job-seekers who are ranked higher in the labor queues (because of a person's market power, characteristics such as education and other qualifications, or demographic characteristics that may be preferred by employers, such as being a male or white) have the greatest choice in where and how they work and are thus more likely to have jobs that match their needs and preferences.

In well-functioning, efficient labor markets, employers should be able to hire workers who meet the requirements of the jobs they are seeking to fill. Workers, on the other hand, should be able to find jobs that match their needs and values to the extent that their skills and other attributes make them attractive to employers—that is, to the extent that they have greater market power or rank higher in labor queues. Economists assume that in efficient labor markets, there should not be mismatches such as labor shortages or overqualified workers, or, in any event, any mismatches that occur are temporary and are not likely to last long. Models of labor markets based on the assumption that these markets operate according to competitive principles have proved useful in explaining many aspects of the behavior of employers and workers as they seek to create and maintain successful matches between persons and jobs.

In reality, however, labor markets don't always operate efficiently, and various types of inefficiencies may cause them to depart from the competitive model. For example, contrary to economists' expectations, workers and employers may have limited information about the choices available to them, and so may not be able to make rational and realistic comparisons among the possibilities. In addition, workers may not be able to move to the location where jobs are available because of geographical constraints imposed by family responsibilities, long commuting times, or the lack of suitable housing. Moreover, workers may be prevented from competing for certain jobs because they are not union members, do not have the appropriate certifications or licenses, or other reasons.

When labor markets operate inefficiently, the matching of persons to jobs may result in matches that are unsatisfactory from the point of view of either workers, employers, or both. For example, people may be forced to take jobs that do not utilize their skills and qualifications, require too few or too many hours, pay wages that do not enable them to support their families, or conflict with their family responsibilities. Moreover, sometimes employers cannot find workers that have the skills needed to perform jobs, and must hire underqualified workers who are not as skilled as they would like.

Economists thus generally assume that mismatches reflect market disequilibria that are temporary phenomena. They assume labor markets will correct themselves and that equilibrium will be restored in the long run. Economists also argue that various kinds of mismatches, such as skills or temporal mismatches, reflect the unwillingness or inability of workers or employers to adjust to each other (Holzer 1996). Employers may say there is a labor shortage when in reality they are not willing to raise wages to a level that will attract more skilled workers, for example, and workers may be considered to be underqualified because they are not willing or able to acquire the skills needed to qualify for the jobs that are available.

The ability of workers to find jobs that match their needs, preferences, and qualifications depends in part on the balance between labor supply and employment demand in a particular labor market. If labor markets are tight—that is, demand for labor exceeds the supply of qualified workers—then workers can be pickier about which jobs to take. On the other hand, when labor markets loosen and there are more workers looking for jobs than there are job vacancies, employers have more choice about which workers to hire, and the incidence of mismatches (from the workers' point of view) is likely to be greater.

Institutions and Work Structures

Sociologists also study labor markets. By contrast to economists, sociologists focus on the institutions in the society and economy that affect the operation of labor markets and shape the nature of the relations between employers and workers. Sociologists have developed theories of how jobs come to acquire certain characteristics, such as whether a job is high- as opposed to low-paying, or why some jobs are more likely to depend on other jobs. These theories of job structures help to explain the range of job opportunities that exist at any time for workers to be able to satisfy their needs and interests. Sociologists also highlight the importance of considering workforce diversity in gender, race/ethnicity, age, and education. These characteristics are associated with differences in the needs and preferences that people seek to fulfill through work, as well as the abilities of individuals to acquire the market power needed to find jobs that meet those needs and preferences.

Some sociologists, like economists, tend to see mismatches as relatively temporary dislocations. For example, Emile Durkheim (1933, 374–88) identified several abnormal forms of the division of labor, especially the "forced" division of labor, which is a structural condition that results in people doing social functions that do not fit well with their natural talents. He regarded such mismatches as a temporary and transitional condition that characterized the evolution from a preindustrial to an industrial society. As the mechanical solidarity that integrated preindustrial societies broke down, he argued, disequilibria were created between the kinds of jobs available in the society and the needs of individuals. While they existed, such disequilibria resulted in problematic mismatches, as Durkheim (1933, 375) noted in his criticism of the forced division of labor:

For the division of labor to produce solidarity, it is not sufficient, then, that each have his task; it is still necessary that this
task be fitting to him.

Durkheim believed that as organic solidarity developed further, the various institutions of society would become better
coordinated, and the abnormalities represented by mismatches
between the division of labor and individuals' needs and preferences would be eliminated (Sullivan 1978, 6).

Mismatches also result from what some sociologists call
structural lags, in which old customs and ways of behaving persist despite changes in institutions and other realities (Riley,
Kahn, and Foner 1994). An example of structural lag is the
persistence of the "career mystique" (the belief that workers
will invest their time and energy during their prime working
years in return for future advancement) despite the changes in
workplaces that have made it more difficult to stay and advance
with a single employer (Moen and Roehling 2005). Such structural lags are generally assumed to diminish over time, as
cultural expectations catch up to institutional realties.

Other sociologists have regarded mismatches not as transi-
tory, but as rooted in structural conditions associated with
industrial societies. Karl Marx, for example, argued that the
development of capitalism would increase the "reserve army of
the unemployed" that would give employers more leverage
in dealing with workers. This situation would lead to mismatches such as low wages for some workers, unemployment
for others, and underemployment for still more. Nevertheless,
Marx (1961) tended to view the labor market in ways that were
similar to orthodox economists, since he treated labor as a com-

modity bought and sold freely on competitive labor markets. While Marx did not provide a systematic analysis of labor markets other than the competitive ideal, Max Weber (1947) developed numerous concepts relevant for the analysis of labor market structures. Weber's discussion of *open and closed employment relationships*, in particular, offers a useful conceptual tool for examining ways in which workers may reduce competition in labor markets by exercising their collective power in these markets. Thus, he argued that in closed employment relationships, participation is limited to those who have met the criteria established by the incumbents, such as licenses or educational credentials. For example, doctors in the United States have restricted the participation in the labor market for physicians to those who have graduated from medical schools.

Sociologists often utilize the concept of the *employment relationship* to analyze outcomes of matching processes. The employment relationship involves an exchange between an individual and employer and has social, economic, legal, and psychological aspects. The exchanges that underlie the employment relationship are shaped by the relative power of employers and workers to satisfy their wants and needs in labor market transactions. The concept of market power, introduced earlier in this chapter, helps to identify the conditions that enable some workers to obtain better fits than others in employment relationships.

By focusing on the sources of power in employment relationships, sociologists go beyond the labor market to take into account the interplay between nonmarket and market behavior. They point to the institutions, structures, and processes that occur outside the labor market and affect what happens in the markets themselves (Farkas and England 1985). Work structures or institutions are the patterns by which societies deal with the problems of production and distribution (Kalleberg and Berg 1987). Institutions such as unions, professional associations (e.g., the American Medical Association), or business firms are relatively permanent features of societies that influence the operation of labor markets and help to flesh out what might otherwise be considered labor market imperfections. By emphasizing the impact of nonmarket structures on labor market mechanisms, sociologists have developed explanations of how market processes are embedded in social institutions.

Societies are made up of a complex set of institutional arrangements that may not always be closely aligned with each other, thereby leading to disjunctions and the creation of mismatches. Organizational theorists have described linkages among institutions in terms of the concept of *loose coupling*. In the United States, for example, there is a relatively loose coupling between the educational system and the occupational structure, two of the major institutions in an industrial society. Because there is not a close connection or articulation between school systems and employers in the US workers trained in particular skills have no assurance that their skills will be useful in a job but must seek such jobs on labor markets that may be more or less friendly to them. By contrast, Japan, France, and Germany are societies in which there is tight coupling between educational and occupational institutions. College graduates in Japan or France or high school students in Germany can be more confident than their counterparts in the United States that they will find jobs that make use of their educational experiences.

The loose coupling that characterizes institutions in the United States suggests that mismatches are likely to be the rule rather than the exception. A variety of actors in the economy and society—managers, unions, the Congress, the courts, the White House, Wall Street, educational institutions—are continually engaged in creating diverse initiatives, rules, and policies, and these are motivated by principles that often diverge from one another. For example, Wall Street's interest in the financial bottom line is likely to be opposed to unions' desires for job security for their members. Once begun, these initiatives are likely to take on a life of their own. The divergence of these initiatives, and the complexity of the phenomena associated with them, makes the alleviation of mismatches a major challenge for policy makers, not to mention workers themselves.

Finally, social networks affect chances that people will experience mismatches with their jobs. Network institutions are important for acquiring information about jobs and for being hired in these jobs. Yet people differ in the extent to which they are excluded from social networks and in the degree that they are able to use networks to provide useful information and resources. Nonwhites and women, for example, may be left out of the old white men's clubs that facilitate hiring their own. Effective network relations constitute a form of social capital that workers can use to find and obtain jobs that fulfill their preferences and thus help them to avoid mismatches.

CONSEQUENCES OF MISMATCHES

Mismatches are important to study because they are likely to have negative consequences for individuals and their families, as well as for their employers and the society in general. Psychologists have taken the lead in studying the attributes of individuals that make them more or less suitable for different kinds of jobs and in identifying the factors that influence their decisions about which kinds of jobs to take. They have also helped to conceptualize the kinds of mismatches that have important consequences for individuals and families, as well as for their relations within organizations.

Psychologists have been particularly helpful in explaining workers' reactions to situations where they have jobs that do not match their needs or skills. Lack of fit is a stressor and has been shown to make people dissatisfied with their jobs (Kalleberg 1977). A mismatch is an unstable situation psychologically; workers (and perhaps employers) will seek to change some dimension of the employment relationship to improve the fit between the person and the job. Workers might change their skills (upgrading them, for example), lower their expectations or preferences or, in the extreme case, leave the job completely. This last strategy accounts for the positive correlation between lack of fit and job turnover (Chatman 1989; O'Reilly, Chatman, and Caldwell 1991).

Workers may also seek to improve the fit between their goals and their jobs by gravitating to jobs commensurate with their ability. The gravitational hypothesis posits that individuals eventually sort themselves into jobs that provide a good fit to their interests, values, and abilities. Gravitation is a market-correcting mechanism and individuals should, over time, move into jobs that provide a better match with their abilities. For example, individuals with higher cognitive ability should gravitate toward jobs that require that ability, while those with lower cognitive ability are more likely to move into jobs demanding less cognitive ability. Finding a job that better fits one's abilities may involve moving from one firm to another (Wilk, Desmarais, and Sackett 1995), suggesting that there may be psychological (as well as economic and social) reasons behind job turnover and labor market mobility.

Moreover, workers might try to alleviate mismatches by attempting to change the structure of their jobs or the organization by means of *job crafting* (e.g., Wilk, Desmarais, and Sackett 1995; Wrzesniewski and Dutton 2001). This idea assumes that formal job requirements do not fully determine what happens on the job, but that individuals have the latitude to design their jobs by making physical and cognitive changes in the task (i.e., the form or number of activities one engages in) or relational changes (i.e., whom one interacts with while doing the job) (Wrzesniewski and Dutton 2001). Job crafting can reduce mismatch—for example, an overworked person may reduce the scope or scale of her work activities, while an overqualified worker might take on additional responsibilities. However, the structure of the organization may limit job crafting possibilities; narrowly defined job descriptions in companies with strong command and control cultures and structures may not give workers much latitude to change the way the work is done.

Sociologists have also discussed the consequences of mismatches between people and jobs. In the 1950s and 1960s, for example, the concept of *status inconsistency* was in vogue, and sociologists sought to assess the consequences of status inconsistency for a variety of workers' attitudes and behaviors. Examples of status inconsistency include an occupational status that exceeds one's level of educational attainment (similar to our definition of overqualification) or the opposite (underqualification), or an income level inconsistent with one's educational status. Individuals in this situation were generally assumed to experience negative consequences such as stress (although often these anticipated consequences were not found) and to be drawn to political movements (radical as well as fascist) that they hoped would help them remedy the situation.

People may also turn to deviant behavior in order to satisfy their needs and preferences if they are unable to fulfill them through legitimate jobs (Merton 1968). For example, people denied access to legitimate occupations because of discrimination or lack of education may turn to illegitimate occupations such as dealing drugs, gambling, or working in a strip club to support themselves and their families.

The Time Dimension: Age and Career Stage

The extent to which a job matches one's needs and preferences is likely to differ over time at various stages of one's career. What was once thought to be a good match might later turn into a mismatch—for example, as workers' skills, abilities, and motivations change and evolve over the course of their careers. Similarly, mismatches might arise as skill requirements and demands change because of technological innovation or reorganization of the workplace.

The degree to which a mismatch exists also depends on one's position in his or her life and career. For example, work-family conflicts are more common in the middle stages of life when people are raising children, rather than at the beginning or end. Some jobs require that workers work long hours in early career stages when they are working their way up a career ladder; this pressure may not mesh well with family time, but workers agree in the hope that they will be able to work fewer hours when their career is well established. In other words, workers may not be willing to sacrifice family time for longer hours on the job forever, but hope that they would eventually have more time with their families when they became more established. An example is young academics seeking tenure at a university; many female professors put off having children until their tenure is assured.

The consequences of mismatches also depend on a person's position in life. A particular status assumes different meanings at different ages. Some mismatches may be acceptable in the early years of one's working life, as the career has not yet begun to unfold. During the middle years, as careers approach their lifetime peaks, earnings and status are as high as they are ever likely to be, and the psychosocial and other consequences of a mismatch are apt to be more severe (Elder and Rockwell 1979, 8–9). Perception of a mismatch and the extent to which it is seen as problematic vary by life stage; overqualification may be viewed by some as a normal part of the career at the early stages. The expressions "early achievers" and "late bloomers" reflect our assumptions about levels of achievement assumed to correspond to (or match) particular life stages.

The importance of considering the timing of life events may help to explain why studies of status inconsistency in the 1960s and 1970s sometimes failed to find the expected negative effects. Elder, George, and Shanahan (1996, 263) argue that it is not surprising that studies found effects of stress associated with status inconsistency between education and occupational status only when age and life stage were taken into account. Being overqualified is more normative for the early career, for example, and may serve as a sort of apprenticeship; it becomes more stressful among older, middle-aged men who have begun to feel that advancement is not likely in the future.

CROSS-NATIONAL DIFFERENCES

This book focuses primarily on the United States and the kinds of mismatches that are fairly common in this country. As we saw in the last chapter, the US case is complicated enough. Nevertheless, there are important lessons that employers and policy makers can learn from considering mismatches in other countries.

Cross-national differences in mismatches result from variations in institutions such as unions and worker organizations, labor and employment laws, education and training systems, and welfare benefits. Moreover, there are differences in nations' cultural values that affect the extent to which workers regard work as a central life activity and what they are likely to need, value, and expect from their jobs. Some examples will illustrate the kinds of cross-national differences that are likely to produce differences in mismatches.

Countries differ in the linkages between their educational and work systems. For example, skills mismatches are found less often in countries such as Japan, Germany, or France in which the educational system is more closely coupled with the work system. In these countries there is a greater integration between education and work than in the United States, which makes it likely that the transition from one to the other will be smooth, lowering the chances that workers will be overqualified or underqualified for their jobs. Well-developed educational systems and institutions that promote vocational training, such as the German dual vocational system, supported by an institutional framework of chambers of industry and commerce and artisan chambers, have helped avoid the skill shortages that have characterized sectors of the American economy (Marsden 1999; Rosenbaum 2001).

Countries also differ in their policies regarding work time, which often result from union bargaining at the government level. In France, unions negotiated a 35-hour workweek that took effect in 2000. Moreover, in contrast to the United States, the number of work hours per week and per year has declined in most Western European countries in recent decades. In some cases (e.g., the Netherlands), reducing the number of hours worked and creating part-time jobs were enacted as a policy to reduce unemployment. These policies suggest that mismatches related to overworking would be less likely to occur in these European countries than in the United States.

Countries also differ in their welfare systems, which include income transfers and the provision of benefits such as health insurance. Most countries provide state-sponsored health insurance as a right of citizenship, and health insurance is not a factor in the mismatch equation in those countries. By contrast, health insurance is a big factor in the United States, where most citizens get their health benefits through their jobs. Hence, a job that matches a worker's preferences on many other levels may be a very bad match in the United States if it doesn't include health benefits.

The existence of other elements of a social safety net is also related to low-wage employment and a group of working poor in a country. In such a comparison, the United States fares very poorly. For example, the proportion of people living in poverty (defined as 50 percent of the median income of a country) is 17 percent in the United States, a figure higher than in any other country in the OECD (Organization for Economic Cooperation and Development), nearly double the percentages in Germany and France, and almost three times as many as in Norway and Sweden (Mishel, J. Bernstein, and Allegretto 2005, Table 7.14).

Countries also differ in the extent to which they provide mechanisms to help workers balance their work and family lives. In the Scandinavian countries, and to a lesser extent in continental Europe, government regulation of the employment relationship, as well as the availability of publicly subsidized child care and preschool have supported employees in their dual roles as workers and parents. Policies range from mandated maternity and parental leaves (with earnings replaced by social insurance) to sick leave policies, shorter full-time workweeks, and laws limiting work hours. In the United States, government policies intended to reduce mismatches between work and family are much more limited, although some employers have family-friendly policies to ease the conflict between work and family (see Chapter 9).

These examples of cross-national differences in institutional structures and cultural values illustrate ways to alleviate the kinds of mismatches that we discuss in this book. They thus serve as sources of ideas for social policy interventions designed to reduce these mismatches, an issue we will return to in the final chapter.

Chapter Three
SKILLS MISMATCHES:
OVERQUALIFICATION

JOHN IS A THIRTY-ONE-YEAR-OLD, unmarried white male who received a Ph.D. in English literature two years ago from a prestigious university in the northwest part of the United States. He wrote his dissertation on Shakespeare and would like to teach this subject at a university. There were jobs open in English departments at various universities in the eastern US, but he did not look for jobs outside his area because he felt that he had to stay in the Northwest to care for his aging parents, who did not want to leave the home and neighborhood they had lived in all their lives. Since there were no jobs open for English teachers who were experts in Shakespeare, John took a job as a cashier in a convenience store, stocking the shelves when needed. He has worked at the convenience store for two years. He started at minimum wage, but six months ago he was promoted to head cashier with a salary of $8.50 an hour. He does not receive health insurance from his employer, but he is relatively healthy and so this has not been a problem for him so far. John feels bored in his job most of the time, although he hasn't yet been able to find a better job in the area. He worries that he might have wasted the six years he spent in graduate school.

People like John are *overqualified* for their jobs; they have jobs that do not enable them to use the skills and abilities that they have acquired as a result of their formal education as well as their work experience. There are many other anecdotal examples of people overqualified for their jobs—college graduates working as low-level clerical workers, highly skilled software programmers and other dot.com workers who were laid off and had to take low-skill jobs to make ends meet, Spanish majors who graduated from college but are now working in supermarkets, engineers working as bartenders, psychologists with master's degrees working as teaching aides, and so on.

All these workers have a discrepancy between their educational qualifications and skills and (1) opportunities to use their abilities and knowledge on their jobs and/or (2) jobs that provide them with a level of earnings commensurate with the investments they have made in their education. Most research on overqualification has focused on the market for college graduates (Freeman 1976), though a person at any level or type of educational attainment could be overqualified for a job.

While we use the term "overqualification" to refer to mismatches in which jobs are not commensurate with people's educational attainments, others have used alternative labels to describe such mismatches. These include *overeducation* (Rumberger 1981), *overtraining* (Kalleberg and Sørensen 1973), *occupational mismatch* (Smith 1986), *skill underemployment, underutilization*, and an *education-jobs gap* (Livingstone 1998).

We prefer the term "overqualification" rather than "overeducation" since the latter suggests that the primary and perhaps only purpose of education is to enable one to obtain a job. Education, of course, does more than simply prepare people for work; it also enriches people's lives, makes them more intelligent and aware of things, and so on. For these reasons, "it is impossible to be overeducated for life, while it is possible to be overqualified for a job" (Brynin 2002, 650).

The terms "education-jobs gap" or "occupational mismatch" are also problematic, since they are too general and have also been used to refer to the opposite kind of mismatch, in which one's educational qualifications and preparation are not adequate for the skill requirements of the job (see Chapter 4).

WHY EDUCATION IS RELATED TO OCCUPATIONAL ATTAINMENT

In American society, one's educational attainment is generally assumed to be a good predictor of the quality of the person's job, since education is the main mechanism that sorts people into various kinds of occupations. People with higher levels of formal education generally expect to work in occupations that pay better and have more status than average jobs. Indeed, this is a major reason why young people choose to go to college at all; they anticipate that their investments in education will pay off in obtaining a higher-quality job after they complete their education.

The assumed positive correlation between education and occupations has been attributed to several alternative mechanisms. First, people with more education are thought to have higher levels of skills and abilities than those with less education, and thereby to be more productive in the workplace. The association of level of education with skills results from the fact that people learn various technical and social skills in colleges and universities, as well as the fact that colleges select skilled and able people in the admissions process.

To the extent that education represents an accurate measure of a person's skill level, a close correspondence between education and occupation suggests that labor markets are efficiently matching jobs to the people likely to be capable of performing them. This scenario is consistent with the economic theory of human capital, which holds that people invest in education in order to become more productive and that employers hire people for jobs and reward them based on their beliefs about their levels of productivity.

The assumption that education accurately reflects skill levels was challenged by the sociologist Ivar Berg (1970; reissued in 2003) in his landmark study titled *Education and Jobs: the Great Training Robbery*. Using data from the *Dictionary of Occupational Titles*, he argued that, despite the claims of human capital theory, a person's educational attainment does not always correspond to his or her levels of skills. On the contrary, Berg found evidence that employers frequently hire people with required levels of education to work in jobs that do not make use of their education, and that employees with more education are not necessarily more productive and in some cases were actually less productive than workers with less education if, for example, they quickly become bored with the job, as John appears to be. Moreover, Berg's results showed that the rise in educational requirements for jobs in the United States reflected primarily the increase in educational attainments of workers, not the actual technical requisites of jobs.

An alternative explanation to the human capital theory consistent with Berg's results is that completion of a certain number of years of formal schooling acts as a signal to potential employers that a person is likely to possess particular skills and abilities, regardless of whether or not this is actually true. Employers have imperfect information about the skills and abilities of job seekers in the labor market. Since better information is costly and time-consuming to collect, employers tend to depend on signals such as educational attainment.

The acquisition of a college degree is a sign to employers that the person has some technical skills and the ability to write and think. A college degree also signifies that the person is apt to possess so-called "soft skills" such as the ability to interact and deal with people, teamwork skills, a positive work attitude, sense of responsibility, motivation to succeed, and other cultural traits required to perform a variety of occupational tasks.[6] Soft skills are especially vital in today's service economy, since many service jobs involve dealing extensively with customers (Smith 2001). Colleges help to train students to show up to work on time, work hard, follow supervisors' instructions, get along with fellow students, work as a team, and other tasks useful in the world of work.

This strategy of relying on educational credentials to provide information on job-seekers has been called *credentialism* (Collins 1979). Here, the focus is on educational qualifications (i.e., the credential) rather than on skills and ". . . whether overqualified means overskilled is a moot point" (Brynin, 2002, 650). Credentialism suggests that there will not necessarily be a close correspondence between the skills people have acquired through formal education and the skill requirements of their jobs, since what matters is the credential, not the skills.

From the credentialing perspective, the importance of education derives not so much from the technical or social skills

[6]Here's a website to test your soft skills: content.monstertrak.monster.com/resources/archive/jobhunt/softskills.

derived from schooling but rather the fact that people have been able to attain a diploma or credential proving that the person has satisfied the requirements imposed by the educational system (Bowles and Gintis 1976). Indeed, the focus on the credential may actually hinder students from acquiring the skills that they might learn at school.

The use of educational credentials is particularly important in the United States, which appears to rely on them more than any other country in the world (Collins 1979, 19). Managers and employers in the United States often appear to place more emphasis on the attainment of particular levels of education and degrees than on the content of the educational experience; the credential is often more important in cultural terms than the skill content of what is learned in educational institutions. A person possessing educational credentials is a member of a status group (such as college-educated managers) that controls access to certain kinds of jobs and rations economic privilege (Collins 1979). Educational credentials provide people with a relative advantage over those with less education, as opposed to giving them an absolute level of technical skills and productivity.

How we interpret the nature of the mismatch between education and occupation depends on whether the skills or credential theory best explains what happens to people as a result of their educational experience. If education teaches people greater technical or social skills, then overqualification represents a condition whereby people are unable to use their work-related skills on their job. On the other hand, if education acts primarily as a credential, then overqualification reflects a situation in which people who have attained a certain level of education are unable to obtain the kinds of occupations and earnings returns that they expected to receive based on their assumptions.

EXPLAINING OVERQUALIFICATION

Overqualification reflects the gap between the educational attainments of persons and the number of occupations that make use of those attainments. The evidence suggests that there has been a growth in overqualified workers during the past thirty years. Understanding this increase requires us to explain why the supply of educated persons has exceeded the supply of jobs appropriate for them. We need to understand two related issues.

First, we need to explain why there has been such a large and sustained increase in the educational attainment of the labor force in all industrial countries, but especially in the United States, which has a higher percentage of college graduates than other countries and thus a higher capacity for overqualification. Second, we need to explain why skills requirements of occupations have not increased along with the rise in educational attainments. We consider each of these issues.

The Expansion of Higher Education

There has been a major expansion of educational attainment in the United States and other industrial countries, as we discussed above. The growth in educational attainments reflects the growth of the *knowledge society* or *postindustrial society* (Bell 1976), labels that highlight the accelerated pace of technological advancement and the growing prevalence of complex work with data and people as opposed to producing goods and material things.

Economists have underscored the view that more is better with regard to education, which is widely regarded as an investment in work skills and thus in enhanced productivity (Freeman 1976). We discussed earlier the controversy raised by this perspective and indicated that it is not necessarily the case that education enhances skills. In any event, in addition to assumed greater skills and productivity, there are numerous social reasons why societies turn out so many educated persons, including the general benefits of education, its status-enhancing characteristics, and its role in producing more enlightened citizens. These social factors have contributed to credential inflation, as progressively higher levels of educational attainment are needed in the competition for higher-level jobs.

Since education is a signal that one has acquired membership in an elite group and is viewed as an avenue to upward mobility and success in life, there is tremendous demand for education on the part of ambitious young people and their parents as they seek to enhance their social status. This demand may well exceed any rational calculation about its economic value (Collins 1979), or even any realistic calculation of the child's academic abilities. Colleges and universities, many of which have gone online and are offering degree programs via the Internet, have a vested interest in producing greater numbers of college graduates, since numbers create and maintain jobs in the education industry. Moreover, governments see the expansion of educational opportunities for all its citizens as an indicator of the nation's success in providing opportunities for material success and promoting equality (Brynin 2002, 637–38).

Do Jobs Require Less Skills?

Whether jobs require more or less skills now than in the past is a very complex question, and, as we discussed in the last chapter, the overall evidence is ambiguous; it is likely that skill requirements for some occupations have increased while they have decreased for others, suggesting that some workers may be overqualified for their jobs at the same time that others are underqualified (see Chapter 4).

In any event, the expansion of educational attainment has not necessarily been accompanied by an increase in the kinds of occupations that require people to make use of their high levels of education. Most white-collar jobs now require a college degree, but not because a college degree is required to perform these jobs. The requirement could also result from the surplus of college-educated workers.

Many writers have argued that market economies such as the United States have not been able to generate enough skilled and rewarding jobs to utilize the increased educational levels of workers (Batenburg and de Witte 2001). While there was an increase in education-intensive industries and occupations after World War II, this growth slowed considerably in the period after 1970 and has lagged behind the expansion of higher education ever since.

A number of studies have suggested that upgrading the skills of jobs and occupations has not been prevalent since the 1970s (Halaby 1994). There are various explanations of the slowdown in growth of high-skilled occupations as well as the downgrading of the skills connected with some occupations. The use of computers, for example, has made it possible for employers to automate formerly highly skilled jobs, resulting in new jobs that require fewer skills (Levy and Murnane 2004).

Employers may also have created more low-skilled jobs as an overreaction to fears of a coming shortage of workers qualified to perform skilled and autonomous work (see Chapter 4; Rosenbaum and Binder 1997, 73).

Moreover, the pressures on organizations in the 1980s and 1990s that led organizations to downsize their workforces and outsource production (see Chapters 6 and 8) forced many workers to take jobs that were less desirable and lower-skilled than their previous jobs. In addition, many people had to start their careers at lower levels than before and hence were more likely to be overqualified. Evidence indicates, for example, that increasing numbers of workers were placed in first jobs that did not utilize their educational investments (Brynin 2002). Since opportunities to advance to more highly skilled jobs declined, people remained overqualified for longer periods of time.

HOW MANY WORKERS ARE OVERQUALIFIED?

Determining how many people are overqualified for their jobs requires us to have measures of both people's skills and qualifications and the requirements of jobs. Both these concepts— what kinds of skills one has learned in school and the extent to which occupations require these skills—have proved difficult to measure validly and reliably.[7] As a consequence, social scientists have been able to estimate only crudely whether or not people's skills and credentials exceed the skill requirements of their jobs.

[7]See Halaby (1994) for a critique of various ways that people have tried to measure overqualification.

Measuring Educational Qualifications

Studies of overqualification generally use the number of years of formal schooling as the indicator of a person's level of educational qualifications and skills. Information on years of schooling is fairly easy to obtain and permits social scientists to analyze differences in skills and qualifications for different groups of people and different time periods.

We should recognize at the outset that there is no indicator of qualifications that can unambiguously measure this concept in all work situations. In particular, equating years of education with skills is obviously limited in many ways. Skills are multidimensional and cannot be equated simply with formal education. Education probably best reflects what economists call general skills, such as the ability to write or reason, that can be used in a wide variety of work settings. Educational attainment is less valid as an indicator of job-related skills specific to particular companies and not easily transferable from one workplace to another. Such firm-specific skills are often acquired through work experience, not by going to school. Moreover, some skills have little to do with formal education, such as the people skills that are increasingly important in a service economy.

Using years of education as an indicator of qualifications also neglects to consider differences in the quality of schools and one's level of achievement in school, the type of curriculum, and one's major field. All of these characteristics affect the level and types of skill and thus the kinds of jobs that a person is qualified for. Not all college graduates are in equal demand—for example, there may be a shortage of science and technology majors and a glut of English majors such as experts on Shakespeare; there may also be greater or lesser demand for college graduates in various geographical areas within the United States as well as at different times.

In the United States, the number of years of formal education attained by labor force members has increased steadily over the past few decades, as we discussed in the previous chapter. In 2003 nearly a third of the labor force had at least a college degree, up from slightly more than a quarter in 1992 (US Census Bureau 2005). This increase continues the long-term growth in the proportion of the labor force with college degrees.

Measuring Job Skill Requirements

The skill requirements of jobs are perhaps even harder to measure. Several approaches have been used; each has its limitations and is subject to various degrees of measurement error.

Sociologists have for a long time conceptualized jobs as empty places or slots in the societal or organizational division of labor; jobs are assumed to have an existence independent of the people who work in them. According to this view, employers create jobs based on the exigencies of the division of labor within organizations and then hire workers who fit into this existing structure.

Following this perspective, skill requirements are measured by assessing directly the complexity of the skills associated with jobs and occupations. This approach relies on assessments of the General Educational Development (GED) required to perform jobs adequately that have been made by analysts at the United States Department of Labor and published in the *Dictionary of Occupational Titles* (e.g., 1991). Researchers have converted these assessments into equivalent years of education. We use this approach below in assessing the extent to which workers in the United States are overqualified.

Other social scientists have argued that job requirements depend on the characteristics of workers in those jobs; they have questioned whether it is even possible to measure a job's skill requirements independently of the skills, abilities, and other characteristics of the individuals working in the job (Halaby 1994, 50). Proponents of this view point out that employers may tailor the job to fit the characteristics of particular employees, or workers may be able to craft the job—for example, highly skilled workers may be able to stretch their jobs' skill requirements. An approach consistent with this reasoning measures the level of skills required by an occupation by means of the average level of education of those who work in that occupation; persons are then considered overqualified if their level of education exceeds the average for their occupational group by a certain amount (e.g., Clogg and Shockey 1984).

Estimating How Many People Are Overqualified
Berg (1970) estimated the educational requirements of jobs using GED-equivalent scores (the first approach discussed earlier) and compared these to the educational attainments of the labor force. He found that the proportion of overqualified workers in the United States increased between 1950 and 1960.

Table 3.1 extends Berg's analysis and presents information from the General Social Surveys on the percentage of full-time workers in various social groups in the United States who were overqualified for their jobs in three different time periods from 1972 to 2002. Given the lack of precision with which individual skills and job requirements are measured, these estimates are fairly conservative; overqualification is defined here as educational attainment at least *three years greater* than the estimated educational requirements for the job[8] (Vaisey 2006).

The estimates in Table 3.1 indicate that about one in five full-time workers in the United States was overqualified in the years from 1993 to 2002. This percentage represented an increase from previous years and was about twice as large as in the years from 1972 to 1982.

Women were slightly less likely than men to be overqualified, although the gender gap in overqualification has appeared to narrow slightly during the thirty-year period from 1972 to 2002. Nonwhites were more apt to be overqualified than whites in each of the three periods. Younger workers were more likely to be overqualified than older workers in the years from 1972 to 1992, although this age gap disappeared in the most recent period.

College-educated workers were more likely to be overqualified than workers with less education, as we would expect. Over half of the workers with more than a college education were overqualified in the period 1993 to 2002, a marked increase from earlier years.

Researchers are usually unable to distinguish whether overqualification is due to skills learned in school or the credential earned through completion of a particular level of schooling. An exception is Livingstone's study (1998, 53),

---

[8]Vaisey's measures of the educational skill requirements of jobs were obtained from the GED scores found in the *Dictionary of Occupational Titles* (Autor, Levy, and Murnane 2003).

Table 3.1

Estimates of Overqualification[a] among US Workers, by

Selected Demographic Characteristics, 1972–2002[b]

	% Overqualified		
	1972–1982	1983–1992	1993–2002
Gender			
Males	11.6	16.1	20.3
Females	9.4	14.5	19.8
Race			
White	10.4	15.0	19.4
Nonwhite	14.0	17.8	22.6
Education			
Less than H.S. (0–11 years)	0.4	0.6	1.3
High school graduate	5.5	4.7	6.0
Some college (13–15 yrs)	12.5	15.0	17.1
College graduate	17.7	25.7	29.8
College plus (17–20 years)	39.7	45.3	51.0
Age			
25–34	13.9	16.1	20.8
35–44	11.0	17.8	19.0
45–54	9.2	13.3	20.1
55–65	6.6	10.1	18.9

[a]Overqualification is defined as educational attainment that is three or more years greater than the educational requirements of the job.
[b]Source: General Social Survey data (Vaisey 2006).

which developed ways to measure the two types of overqualification—as a *performance gap* between workers' educational attainments and the actual task requirements of their jobs and as a *credential gap* between educational attainments and established job entry requirements. He found that these two types of overqualification are correlated, but moderately (.47)[9], suggesting that although there is some overlap between the skills gap and the credential gap, each also represents a distinct dimension of overqualification.

CHANGES IN OVERQUALIFICATION: TRENDS AND CYCLES

The percentage of Americans overqualified for their jobs increased steadily from the 1970s to the present (see Table 3.1). The proportion of workers in almost all demographic groups defined by gender, race, age, and education who were highly overqualified (i.e., whose years of education exceeded the educational requirements of their jobs by at least three years) also appeared to increase steadily during the period from 1972 to 2002 (see Vaisey 2006). For example, the proportion of highly qualified men and women increased by nearly ten percentage points from 1972 to 2002. Livingstone (1998, 84) also used data from the General Social Survey and found that especially the performance gap between educational attainment and job requirements increased during the past twenty-five years.

Overqualification is also projected to continue to grow in the future. The Bureau of Labor Statistics projects that by 2010, only 20.7 percent of all jobs will require a college degree or more. A quarter of the US population already has this level

---

[9]A correlation coefficient is a statistical measure of how much two variables (such as an event or quantity) are related to each other. It is a number between -1 and 1; a correlation of -1 indicates that a high (or low) value on one variable is always associated with the opposite value on the other variable, while a correlation of 1 means that if one variable has a high (or low) value, so will the other. A correlation coefficient of zero means that there is no linear relationship between the variables.

of education (Tufekci 2004), and this percentage will undoubt-
edly also continue to increase.

While it appears that overqualification has increased steadily for at least the past thirty years in the United States and is
expected to continue to grow, there are at least two alternative
ways that we might consider overqualification a temporary,
rather than permanent, feature of the labor market.

Overqualification and Business Cycles

Overqualification might be considered temporary if it was a result of a business cycle, reflecting supply and demand in labor
markets. In tight labor markets, when the supply of vacant jobs
exceeds the number of job seekers, we expect less overqualification, since job seekers have more jobs from which to choose and
hence are likely to be unwilling to take jobs that are not commensurate with their educational qualifications.

By contrast, we would expect overqualification to be more
common in loose or slack labor markets, when the supply of
job seekers exceeds the number of vacant jobs, since then job
seekers have fewer jobs to choose from and thus are more likely
to be forced to take jobs that do not match their educational
qualifications. In loose labor markets, employers have a greater
pool of applicants from which to select potential employees,
and thus may tend to raise the level of education required for
the job (an example of credential inflation), even though the actual skill requirements of those jobs may not be any greater.
See Bills (1992) for a discussion of the way job requirements
for the same occupations vary depending on the supply and demand for labor.

This reasoning suggests that workers were especially likely

to be overqualified during bad economic times such as the Great Depression in the 1930s. Unemployment was very high during this period, and there were not enough jobs for everyone who wanted one, much less a sufficient supply of good jobs. Hence, many people with relatively high levels of education were unable to find jobs that made use of their skills and qualifications.

Overqualification emerged as a notable phenomenon again in the 1970s, when, for the first time since the Depression, college graduates had difficulty obtaining college-level jobs. Schoolteachers, for example, especially women, had a hard time finding jobs in elementary and secondary schools. The market for college-educated manpower was generally depressed in the 1970s, as the number of workers with at least four years of college education grew by 7 percent per year between 1970 and 1980. During this period, the large baby boom cohort went to college, lowering the economic value of the college degree. From 1980 to 1989, by contrast, the number of workers with at least four years of education grew by only 4.5 percent a year, an amount that the economy was better able to absorb (Tyler, Murnane, and Levy 1995).

If overqualification is a result of the business cycle, we might also expect to see a greater number of overqualified persons in regions of the country that are particularly hard-hit by economic recession. For example, it used to be the case in the Pacific Northwest before the advent of Microsoft and other high-tech businesses that when a dominant manufacturer such as Boeing laid off workers because of decreased demand for airplanes, many people with doctoral degrees who were unable or unwilling to move from the area were forced to take relatively low-skilled jobs in order to make ends meet.

The idea that overqualification is related to the business cycle is consistent with the arguments made by economists such as Richard Freeman (1976) who maintain that a surplus of educated people relative to jobs that require their level of education is due to a temporary market disequilibrium, in which individuals' demand for education outstrips the ability of the economy to make use of these educated persons. This surplus of educated people results in overqualification, which in turn leads to a reduction in the earnings advantage associated with education, which in turn leads to a decline in the supply of educated people until the earnings advantage for attending school is raised.

The *cobweb* model illustrates this reasoning (Freeman 1976). It suggests that overeducation (which economists define as a decline in the economic returns for education, or the amount of earnings associated with different levels of education) results when the supply of educated persons exceeds the number of jobs that require college degrees. Overeducation is assumed to be a self-correcting mechanism, however, as low returns to education act as a disincentive to going to school. Hence, people will obtain less education, which in turn increases the value of education, and so on.

Freeman's prediction that the demand for college education should decrease as a result of the overqualification experienced by workers in the 1970s, however, did not happen. Employers' demand for education continued to be strong, and individuals sought to maintain their position in the labor queue by obtaining college degrees. They believed that attending college was important, if only as a defensive necessity in order to remain competitive in the labor market.

As we noted above, business cycles have some effect on the extent of overqualification. For example, unemployment rates are positively related to the proportion of workers in the United States who were overqualified for their jobs (Vaisey 2006). On the other hand, the increase in overqualification in the United States is not completely accounted for by unemployment rates, suggesting that overqualification is not just a temporary market disequilibrium or business cycle phenomenon.

Is Overqualification a Career Stage?
Overqualification might also be considered a temporary situation if it represented only a phase in one's career, especially at the beginning of one's working life. In this situation, overqualification is temporary for an individual; in the previous case, it was temporary for the labor market. Young people tend to try out various kinds of jobs to see if they like them, and they may well be overqualified for some of these jobs. If this is the case, then being overqualified might be part of paying one's dues in anticipation of obtaining better jobs later. Overqualification would be a normal part of life and not regarded as problematic in terms of consequences for the individual.

There are good reasons for employers to hire overqualified workers for entry-level jobs. Employers may hire highly educated workers based on their potential and promise and assign them to low-skilled, entry-level jobs to expose them to all aspects of the organization, and then bring them up through the ranks, promoting them to increasingly highly skilled jobs. There is some evidence that employers use unskilled entry-level jobs to screen people for higher level jobs (on-the-job screening), and so what might appear to be overqualification may actually reflect the use of these jobs as screens for higher level jobs (Rosenbaum and Binder 1997).

There is also evidence that overqualification may be a life-cycle phenomenon. Tyler, Murnane, and Levy (1995, 24), for example, concluded that

> . . . newly minted college graduates working in latté bars (or in other jobs that do not require a college degree) is nothing new, and that being underemployed at age 22 does not mean being underemployed at age 30.

Tyler et al. (1995) showed that the earnings of 22- and 23-year-old college graduates were quite low in both 1979 and 1989, yet both groups made substantial progress by age 30.

Some of the results in Table 3.1 also suggest that overqualification is a life-cycle phenomenon, although the extent of age differences in overqualification appears to differ over time. In the period 1972 to 1982, the highest proportion of highly overqualified workers was among those aged twenty-five to thirty-four; the percentage declined steadily among progressively older groups. In the period from 1983 to 1992, the thirty-five to forty-four age group was more likely to be overqualified than the youngest age group.

By contrast, the extent of overqualification in the last period (1993 to 2002) is fairly consistent among the four age groups; about a fifth of workers in each age group are highly overqualified. Contrary to the life-cycle explanation of over-qualification, the latter result suggests that workers are highly overqualified at all ages, rather than only in the early part of their careers.

CROSS-NATIONAL DIFFERENCES

Overqualification is especially likely to occur in the United States, since in this country the relationship between educational and occupational systems is loosely coupled and not highly coordinated; control of the educational system is decentralized, and one's occupational destination is put off until the very end of the educational experience.

This situation is different in Japan and many European countries, where a student's career is decided fairly early by the educational decisions he or she makes, and students are tracked to prepare them for particular kinds of careers. In these countries there is a lot of pressure to get into the right schools, but once admitted, one's future career prospects are relatively predictable. In this case, the relationship between education and occupation is fairly close, making overqualification less likely but still possible. The relationship between educational and occupational institutions is also fairly tight in apprenticeship systems, such as the German dual vocational system, where an apprentice gains experience in a particular company while going to school (Marsden 1999).

Nevertheless, overqualification characterizes other countries as well (Borghans and de Grip 2000), and most of the recent research on this topic has focused on European societies (Burris 2005). Overqualification is also found in the Dutch labor market, for example, since people have limited opportunities to enter the occupation for which they are trained. About one-third of the Dutch labor force was underemployed during the period from 1977 to 1995 (Batenburg and de Witte 2001). Overqualification is also common and increasing in Portugal and Britain, where over 40 percent of the labor force was overqualified in the early 1990s (Brynin 2002). Overqualification is also endemic in rapidly developing and less developed countries, where opportunities for skilled jobs are likely to lag behind educational attainments.

CONSEQUENCES OF OVERQUALIFICATION

It is generally assumed that overqualification has negative consequences for workers. The United States is widely viewed as a meritocracy, in which occupational attainment depends largely on people's achieved characteristics, especially their educational achievements. Americans accept these cultural norms of meritocracy and believe that education is an avenue to higher job rewards and that it is only fair that people with more education should receive higher rewards in the labor market. If a person invests in education and does not receive the expected rewards, dissatisfaction with work and disaffection and feelings of alienation from society are likely to result.

Overqualified workers are assumed to be dissatisfied mainly because they are unhappy with the intrinsic qualities of a job, or the degree to which jobs are interesting, challenging, and meaningful. Workers who are overqualified are assumed to be bored with their jobs and to feel that they have been unfairly treated by their employers and perhaps by society. There is evidence that workers who are overqualified for their jobs are more dissatisfied with them (Kalleberg and Sørensen 1973; Burris 1983).

Workers who are overqualified for their jobs are also expected to be disaffected and hence politically alienated and more likely to vote for leftist political parties. The Carnegie Commission on Higher Education issued dire warnings of a political crisis because of the growth in overqualified or unemployed college graduates (cited in Burris 1983, 455); however, Burris (1983) found no evidence to support these political consequences of overqualification. Moreover, while Vaisey (2006) found that overqualification was somewhat related to political leftism and negatively related to the view that hard work leads to success, these results were observed only for men.

There are a number of reasons why the effects of overqualification on political and job attitudes may not be stronger. One is the difficulty of measuring overqualification, as we discussed earlier. Different results are sometimes found, depending on the various ways overqualification is measured. Moreover, it may be that studies have not examined the consequences of overqualification over the course of one's career; if overqualification is temporary, either in a person's life course or a business cycle, then it is not likely to be problematic. Further, it might be the case that American workers adapt to overqualification by lowering their aspirations or redefining success in terms of family and personal happiness, and other nonwork goals (Burris 1983).

It might also be the case that workers defined as overqualified on the basis of objective criteria (a comparison between their level of education and the years of schooling required by the job) might not perceive that they are overqualified. Suggestive evidence of this was provided by Livingstone (1998, 91), who found that the correlation between a measure of subjective underemployment (the person's perception that the job does not make significant use of his or her qualifications) and more objective measures was fairly small; one's perception that he or she is overqualified correlated only .19 with a measured credential gap and .26 with a performance gap.

Overqualification is also assumed to have economic consequences (Sicherman 1991; Cohn and Kahn 1995). Indeed, people's negative reactions to being overqualified may result as much from unfulfilled aspirations and expectations for a certain level of income as from being unable to utilize their technical skills (Burris 1983). Richard Freeman in his influential book, *The Overeducated American* (1976, 4–5) defined overqualification in terms of the declining earnings of college graduates relative to nongraduates:

> I use the term [overeducated] to denote a society in which the economic rewards to college education are markedly lower than has historically been the case and/or in which additional investment in college training will drive down those rewards.

Since education is a comparative marker, not an absolute one, it may be the case that college graduates can be occupationally mismatched (overqualified) but still not lose their relative income advantage (Smith 1986). From the late 1970s to 2000, there was a rising gap in wages between college graduates and high school graduates; however, the college wage differential has shrunk slightly since 2000 (Mandel 2005), mainly because high school wages have stagnated less than those of college grads.

From a macro-level, societal point of view, overqualification may lead to wasted talent, as people who lack the credential cannot get access to jobs for which they are really qualified. College graduates may tend to squeeze high school graduates out of their jobs, and so on:

> . . . a college education was once sufficient for the attainment of a good job. It is clearly no longer sufficient, but at the same time, it is all the more necessary (Smith 1986, 95).

To the extent that education serves as a credential unrelated to one's actual skill levels, people who lack the credentials for whatever reason, including lack of funds or opportunities to attend college, are at a major disadvantage in the competition for jobs with college graduates. This situation hurts them and their families, since they are deemed ineligible for jobs that they are really capable of doing.

The reliance on credentials may also be detrimental to employers, since it can deprive them of potential employees who might be quite capable. This reliance is also economically inefficient from a societal point of view since it affects allocation of resources to various types of educational institutions. As the experience of the United States during World War II showed, many people assumed to be incapable of doing jobs for which they did not have the educational requirements actually performed very well at these jobs once they were given the opportunity (see Chapter 4).

The irrationality of requiring that applicants have levels of education higher than the education required for their jobs was illustrated clearly by Berg's study cited earlier. One conclusion of his analysis is that it is often inappropriate to use education as an indicator of one's skill level. This idea has implications for race differences in employment, as revealed in the US Supreme Court case of Griggs vs. Duke Power Company. In this case,

> Willy Griggs, a young African American employed by the Duke Power Company, and other minority persons . . . sued for relief from their employer's requirement that only high school graduates could earn promotions to better paying jobs to which white workmates had been promoted without such diplomas. . . .

The United States Supreme Court, in a unanimous decision (with one recusal) argued that it was

> illegal to use educational achievements that were in place regarding personnel actions that were discriminatory without demonstrably valid reasons of "business necessity" (Berg 2003 xxxix).

REDUCING OVERQUALIFICATION

Overqualification is a structural mismatch that is fairly permanent in industrial societies (Brynin 2002). David Livingstone (1998, 53) describes the pervasiveness of overqualification:

> The idea that some people are denied the opportunity to use their full capability at work has been around as long as there have been class societies in which rewarded work has been hierarchically organized and gifted children have been born into the lower ranks . . . Of course, in any market-driven economy, paid workplaces are continually changing and there are always mismatches between employers' aggregate demand and re-

quirements for employees on the one hand, and the aggregate supply and qualifications of job seekers on the other.

We have argued that overqualification is a mismatch that results from the supply of people with particular educational attainments being greater than the number of jobs that make use of these attainments. Alleviating this mismatch requires action on both the supply side (the production of educated persons by educational institutions) and the demand side (the creation of skilled jobs by employers) of the labor market. There are several ways in which the incidence of overqualification can be reduced; each faces considerable obstacles.

First, educational institutions need to be more responsive to the changing skill requirements of employers. Preparing students for the jobs that actually exist via vocational schools or community colleges, for example, rather than simply generating more university and college graduates, might help to improve the match between persons and jobs (Rosenbaum 2001). This strategy would have to overcome the strong cultural values associated with higher education in the United States (e.g., that more education is always better), as well as the tendency in our culture to give higher status to white-collar occupations than to blue-collar work.

Second, employers might be encouraged to reduce their reliance on educational credentials as a signal of a person's skill level. This change would provide greater opportunities to people who do not have the needed credentials and enable companies to maximize their use of the human capital available to them. De-emphasizing credentials would also facilitate the development of alternative educational institutions, and apprenticeship and training programs, to prepare people for jobs.

Adopting this approach to alleviating overqualification means that employers must find another way to obtain information about people's skills and abilities other than simply looking at their formal educational credentials. In response to the concern that workers do not have sufficient soft skills, for example, some states such as New York, have developed innovations such as a nationally recognized work readiness credential that would certify that a potential worker understands the importance of work habits such as punctuality, willingness to accept supervision, and ability to work in a group. This credential should be available by 2006 and would be administered by the United States Chamber of Commerce in conjunction with various state agencies (Lazaroff 2005).

Third, overqualification would decline if more high-level, high-skilled jobs were created. Employers can choose to compete by implementing competitive strategies that utilize work systems in which jobs are broadly defined and require workers to be cross-trained and multiskilled. A number of companies who adopted such high performance work practices have experienced increased productivity and profits. We will discuss these strategies in more detail in Chapter 10.

Finally, mechanisms that promote more efficient matching of persons to jobs would help alleviate the incidence of overqualification. Workers need better information on actual job requirements, and employers would benefit from knowing more about potential job candidates than simply their level of education and the credentials that they have obtained. More efficient matching of job requirements to job seekers is likely to become more feasible in the future because of advances in technology such as the Internet, which will facilitate the development of more effective, computerized systems to match persons with jobs. Such informational systems might also provide ways in which employers can look beyond educational credentials in hiring workers who are suited to the job.

Chapter Four
SKILLS MISMATCHES: UNDERQUALIFICATION

LATOYA IS A FIFTY-YEAR-OLD African American woman who has a high school diploma. She is a single mother and has three teenage boys. She lives in the Southeast and has worked for a textile manufacturing company for the past twenty years. Her job was to operate machines that spin the yarn into cloth and then cut the cloth into various shapes. She earns twelve dollars an hour, which she feels is adequate given her level of education and the cost of living in her area. She also has opportunities for some overtime and receives health insurance benefits from her employer that enable her and her three boys to receive the medical attention they need.

Last year, Latoya's company acquired computerized equipment that spins the yarn and cuts the cloth automatically. Therefore the company no longer needs workers such as Latoya to operate the old machines. Her managers liked Latoya and wanted to keep her at the company, so they gave her the opportunity to take a course to learn to operate the computers that run the automated equipment. While she would like very much to continue working at the company, Latoya has not yet taken them up on this offer, since she does not feel confident about her ability to operate computers; she has a phobia about computers and gets very nervous around them. Her managers have told her that she either has to learn how to operate the computers, or she will have to leave the company, because there are no longer any jobs available there that make use of her skills.

It is easy to find anecdotal examples of people who work in jobs for which they lack the necessary skills—an engineer promoted to manager of her division who does not have the leadership skills to get the people she supervises to work together effectively, and a newly arrived immigrant unable to read the instruction manuals containing the procedures for dealing with customers who have various kinds of complaints.

We use the term *underqualification* to refer to situations in which the skill requirements of jobs exceed the skills and abilities of workers. This mismatch is in many ways the flip side of overqualification. By contrast to those who are overqualified, workers who are underqualified are less likely to be college graduates or to have relatively high levels of education. The issue of underqualification is likely to focus on a mismatch of skills, not on credentialism, since credentials matter most at entry, and workers who do not have the necessary credentials are not likely to get the job in the first place.

There are several situations in which employers may be willing to hire and retain workers who do not have sufficient skills. For example, employers may hire underqualified workers because they think that with appropriate on-the-job training, they can be trained to perform the job adequately. Moreover, when labor markets are tight (labor demand exceeds labor supply), as they were in the United States in the late 1990s, employers may be so desperate to hire anyone that they are willing to hire and offer relatively high wages to low-skilled workers. People may also be in jobs for which they are underqualified if their job security is guaranteed through mechanisms such as tenure (college professors), seniority rules (union members), and civil service protection (government employees).

In still other cases, managers may promote people within the organization to jobs they are not capable of performing. This tendency is called the "Peter Principle," which holds that people are promoted up to their level of incompetence. Thus, people are promoted from jobs they are good at as a reward for good performance, until they are finally matched to jobs that they are not able to do well. Once they reach such jobs, they are no longer able to excel and so may remain in them for long periods (Peters and Hull 1969).

Workers who are underqualified may be able to stretch their skills and qualifications so as to meet their job's requirements. In other situations, if a person is extremely underqualified, it is likely that he or she will lose the job or not be hired in the first place. Underqualification is thus intimately related to structural unemployment, a situation in which job seekers are not able to obtain jobs that are vacant (or lose the jobs that they currently have) because they lack the necessary skills and qualifications.

Explaining Underqualification

From time to time, the media, government, social scientists, employers and other interested parties have expressed their concern that there is a shortage of skilled workers to meet the demands of the American economy.

An early warning about the "coming skills mismatch" was voiced by the Hudson Institute's *Workforce 2000* report published in the late 1980s (Johnson and Packer 1987), which raised dire predictions that American workers were unprepared for the jobs that would be needed in the United States by the year 2000. While many of the findings of this report were not supported by subsequent research and were criticized by many analysts (e.g., Mishel and Teixeira 1991), the report helped fuel the widespread belief that a labor shortage was coming as large numbers of baby boomers retired and there were fewer skilled workers to replace them.

More recently, various observers have expressed alarm that many people in the US labor force are unprepared for today's high-tech jobs because of declines in the quality of education and in the performance of students (Handel 2003). For example, *Business Week's* Aaron Bernstein recently noted (2002, 129):

> Corporate America's biggest difficulties . . . will come at the high end of the labor market. The number of workers with a college degree has more than doubled since 1980 . . . Even so, the rapid expansion of supply barely kept pace with demand.

The concern that the number of college graduates will be insufficient to meet employers' demand in the 2000s—like the worry about a skills shortage that was prominent in the United States in the 1980s and 1990s—contrasts sharply with the emphasis of most social scientists in the 1970s. As we saw in the last chapter, the focus in that period was on the mismatch produced by overqualification and the belief that educational attainments exceeded the skill requirements of many jobs.

Explaining the incidence of underqualification requires us first to understand why workers may not have the necessary skills for their jobs. Then, we will need to understand why the skill requirements of jobs may have exceeded people's skills, at least for some types of skills and in some kinds of occupations.

Have Workers' Skill Levels Declined?

A Nation at Risk, the 1983 report prepared by the United States National Commission on Excellence in Education, raised concern that the skill levels of workers in the United States have declined in recent years, despite the well-documented increases in years of schooling completed (see Chapters 2 and 3). The authors expressed alarm at declining test scores (high school and college entrance test scores and poor international rankings) and the low quality of public schools, which they felt were associated with a decrease in young people's academic skills. In addition to the decrease in the quality of American schools, declines in skills were also attributed to poor home environments and other underclass conditions. The authors of the report were especially worried that this decline in skills would hamper the international competitiveness of American companies.

Addressing the question of whether some workers' skills have declined must consider the variety of skills enumerated in Chapter 3. Thus, there could have been decreases in individuals' cognitive ability as well as other job-relevant knowledge and skills, including soft skills. Moreover, some of these skills could have declined while others increased.

Regrettably, there has been relatively little research on trends in workers' skills other than cognitive ones. Studies of underqualification rarely identify the kinds of skills assumed to be in short supply, and there is often disagreement about whether these are technical or social skills. For example, it is generally believed that there is a scarcity of workers with the higher-level cognitive skills associated with college graduates. However, some studies suggest that employers are less concerned about these kinds of cognitive skills as opposed to soft skills such as work habits, motivation, demeanor, and attitudes (Handel 2003, 150, 157). As we discussed in Chapter 3, the college degree is often taken as an indication of persistence, diligence, and other soft skills.

Underqualification is likely to be concentrated within certain groups in American society. We might expect that some groups are especially likely to be underqualified, such as young workers, who have not yet obtained the skills needed for a range of jobs, and older workers, whose skills have been made obsolete by technological change. Much of the recent concern about shortages of skills has focused on young workers, but similar complaints have been made about young workers for at least the past several decades, suggesting that underqualification may be an age or life cycle effect, not a cohort effect[10] (Handel 2003, 140).

Have Jobs' Skill Requirements Increased?
There are various reasons to suspect that the levels and types of skills required by certain kinds of jobs may have increased. Most writers place considerable importance on the role of technological change in raising skill requirements and creating skills shortages and underqualification. Technological change

---

[10]A cohort effect is something that happens to a group of people who share a common characteristic, such as being born in the same year. People in the same cohort experience a similar slice of history, such as similar educational experiences or technological innovations.

and sectoral shifts from blue-collar manufacturing jobs to knowledge- and information-intensive jobs that are characteristic of a postindustrial economy have raised the cognitive skill requirements of jobs, as sociologist Daniel Bell (1976) anticipated in his book *The Coming of Post-Industrial Society.*

Technological change is probably most likely to create mismatches between people's cognitive and technical skills and jobs' skill requirements (Barley 1996). As organizations adopt new technologies, persons who worked under the old systems may not have the skills needed to operate the new technology and thus do not have the skills to do the new jobs. A strong back and willingness to work hard were about all that were needed at one time to work in a manufacturing plant; now one needs at least a high school diploma and often some college education, at least an associate's degree.

The consequences of technological change for underqualification are illustrated by the case of older workers in Davidson County, North Carolina. Here in 2004 a Belgium-based floor manufacturer, Unilin Flooring, committed to an $80 million plant and 330 jobs over five years. Over a year later, the opening of the plant has been delayed because the plant is still trying to hire the first 100 workers, despite offering competitive pay averaging $16 an hour and the promise of job security. There is no shortage of workers; the unemployment rate for the area is over 5 percent. The problem is that many potential workers who were displaced by the county's 3,200 lost furniture manufacturing jobs in the past four years lack the skills required to operate the new automated machinery. The local community college is providing job training for the plant, but some of these programs are not yet in place, and it will take as much as two years to produce workers able to operate Unilin's machinery.

The textile industry in North Carolina provides another example of the impact of technological change on skill levels. Textile plants in this region began to send low-skilled jobs offshore to countries where wages are much lower than in North Carolina. The textile companies then built new plants to replace the old ones that closed, but, unhappily for many North Carolina workers, these new plants demanded different skills than the older ones. The textile workers who stayed in North Carolina are not likely to find jobs that enable them to use their former skills.

These examples illustrate how a company may adopt advanced technology in an effort to enhance efficiency and how this may lead to an upgrading in required skill levels. However, it is not always the case that technological changes lead to jobs that require more skills; sometimes, more sophisticated equipment is easier to operate, as illustrated by the automated cash registers in grocery stores that scan bar codes and do not require that checkers know the prices of the various items. Thus, the introduction of computer technology does not always constitute an impediment to the ability of people to do their jobs (Berg and Shack-Marquez 1985).

Besides technological change, other factors may cause upgrading of skills. Restructuring of work organizations, such as the adoption of team-based work systems, is one example. These systems place great emphasis on communication among workers, and may require workers to have complex interpersonal skills. Moreover, there has been an increase in the horizontal division of labor—that is, a growth in the number of

occupational specialties, reflected in the expansion of professional and technical work—that relies on workers having au-
tonomy and control over their tasks, as opposed to occupations
in the vertical division of labor—that is, positions in the hier-
archy of organizations, such as managers versus clerical occupations—which are more often supervised by a chain of command
and control. The growth of the horizontal division of labor has
reduced opportunities for employment in semiskilled and unskilled jobs.

The textile and furniture manufacturing industries in North
Carolina also illustrate how skill levels required by jobs may
increase due to business decisions—in this case the decision to
move production offshore in order to cut labor costs. The shift
of jobs to plants overseas has resulted in a loss of highly paid
but relatively unskilled jobs (such as Latoya's) in North Carolina. The jobs left behind in North Carolina were highly
skilled, and the displaced workers were unable to perform
many of them. Moreover, new jobs that are being created are
often high-skilled jobs in various service industries. As a consequence, many textile and furniture workers are underqualified
for the jobs that were now available and can no longer find jobs
that suit their skills.

It may be the case, however, that not all skill requirements
are increasing. There may be a polarization of skills taking
place in the economy, resulting in simultaneous increases and
decreases in the skill requirements of jobs. Some occupations
and industries may have experienced substantial upgrading of
skills, while other job skills are being downgraded (see Chapters 2 and 3). These opposing changes may even happen in the
same industry; the introduction of automated equipment may

make some jobs simpler, while at the same time creating new, highly skilled jobs that require extensive computer programming and the ability to repair computer hardware.

Moreover, the different kinds of skills required by jobs may not all be changing in the same way. The measuring of job skill requirements by years of education, discussed in the last chapter, for example, emphasizes cognitive and technical skills. A study by Howell and Wolff (1991) found that there was an increase in cognitive and interactive skill requirements between 1960 and 1985. However, they also found that there was no growth in motor skill requirements, which increased in the 1960s but decreased in the 1970s and 1980s, as demand for machinists and operatives declined, in part because of outsourcing and offshoring of jobs.

Unfortunately, few studies have examined changes in the diverse skill requirements of jobs, which range from basic skills such as reading and writing to higher-level cognitive skills and soft skills. A study of employers (Holzer 1996, 60) found that they emphasized soft skills, such as work attitudes and communication skills, that signaled general employability and readiness for work as opposed to the kinds of technical skills typically measured by schooling, grades, and test scores. Soft skills are likely to grow in importance as the economy continues to emphasize services and dealing with customers rather than manufacturing, and as work organizations require more teamwork and employee involvement in the workplace.

STUDYING UNDERQUALIFICATION

Providing evidence on the extent of underqualification raises many of the same challenges for measurement and data collection as assessing overqualification, and many of the issues we discussed in the previous chapter are equally salient here. We need to obtain measures of both the skills and other qualifications of workers and compare these to the skill requirements of jobs. As with overqualification, our information on the extent and distribution of underqualification is not as good as we would like.

Measuring People's Skills

As we indicated in the last chapter, the most common measure of a person's skills is the number of years of schooling that he or she has completed. As we discussed in the previous two chapters, the amount of education that Americans have attained has generally risen over the past half century. However, the trend in educational attainment was relatively flat among young workers in the years 1975 to 1990, a period when concerns about skill shortages were particularly great (Handel 2003, 142).

As we also saw in Chapter 3, years of education is in many ways a limited indicator of a person's level and types of skills. It reflects the quantity of education, not its quality. In addition, the number of years a person has attended school is a broad and heterogeneous measure and may not accurately reflect the wide variety of skills assumed to be in short supply. These skills include basic or intermediate reading, writing, and math skills; problem-solving skills; technological competencies; interpersonal abilities; and soft skills including attitudes such as responsibility, effort, and commitment.

Test scores are another commonly used indicator of skills, although these reflect primarily a person's cognitive skills. The evidence suggests that test scores for young people in the United States are as high or higher today than they were thirty years ago (Handel 2003, 149). But it is often difficult to draw conclusions about the connection between test scores and job-related skills. People can often perform tasks at higher levels than their test scores indicate, in part because people pick up tacit skills or know-how in real-life situations on the job (Handel 2003, 147). Such tacit skills are difficult to measure, since they are often specific to particular work situations, but they are no less important than more commonly measured skills. Examples of tacit skills include postal workers learning how to deliver the mail most efficiently without getting bitten by dogs on the routes; office workers knowing who to butter up in order to get things fixed or to obtain needed supplies; and college professors learning what meetings are important to attend and which can be missed without penalty.

Measuring Skill Requirements of Jobs

Jobs require many kinds of skills, and ideally all should be taken into account when assessing the skill requirements of jobs. The diverse skills required by jobs include motor skills such as manual dexterity and coordination; interpersonal skills; organizational and managerial skills such as leadership, the ability to work autonomously and make decisions, and teamwork; verbal and language skills; analytical skills such as math and logical reasoning; and diagnostic skills such as synthetic reasoning.

Some of these skill requirements may not be highly related to each other. For example, the motor and cognitive skills required by jobs are not correlated with each other, and neither is closely associated with jobs' interactive skill requirements, as a study by Howell and Wolff (1991, 489) found. These authors also reported that motor skills were negatively correlated with educational attainment. These findings suggest that a single measure of skills is not apt to draw realistic conclusions about the skill requirements of jobs.

Extent of Underqualification in the United States

Statements about a skills shortage or underqualification are often based on anecdotal observations of specific cases and are usually not well grounded empirically in data representative of the labor force in general. As with overqualification, assessing whether a person is underqualified by comparing his or her skills to the skill requirements of the job is not straightforward, and there may often be considerable ambiguity about whether there is indeed a mismatch.

One reason for this haziness in measuring underqualification is that skill requirements for jobs may be elastic; they can stretch in both directions, depending on the skill levels of the workers. As we suggested earlier, some workers may be able to craft their jobs to fit better their skills and abilities. Moreover, workers' qualifications may be elastic, and workers may sometimes do jobs for which they were assumed to be underqualified. Thus,

> . . . the skills workers can develop and for which they are rewarded are partly a function of the jobs employers offer, rather than the intrinsic capacities of individuals acting as a kind of hard constraint (Handel 2003, 147).

Workers assumed to be underqualified for their jobs may indeed be able to perform these jobs well if given the motivation and opportunity to do so, as illustrated by two dramatic examples.

First, during World War II, workers in the United States were able to perform hundreds of thousands of jobs for which they had little or no training, education, or experience. The war effort required a huge mobilization of people to do jobs for which they had little experience, and their heroic efforts in performing them suggested that people could do these jobs well if they were challenged and motivated to do so. A vivid example was the case of women in blue-collar manufacturing jobs in World War II, when wartime mobilization enabled women to enter men's jobs on a large scale (Milkman 1987). "Rosie the Riveter" and her female colleagues performed ably in blue-collar occupations such as welding during the war, when they were given the chance to work in these jobs after men left to fight overseas. After performing capably in these jobs during the war, however, manufacturing industries were defeminized after World War II; women were forced to give up these jobs to make room for men returning from the war, and once again took their place in traditionally female occupations or left the labor force altogether.

A second example of underqualified workers rising to the challenge of skilled jobs if given the chance is the generally favorable evaluations by employers of the performance of the large number of former welfare recipients who have left welfare since the mid-1990s. About three-quarters of those formerly on welfare worked for pay at some point in the year after leaving the welfare rolls and usually worked full-time. About a third of current recipients are employed, despite their low levels of education (Moffitt 2002). Far from being underqualified and unemployable, these persons have been able to stretch their skills to perform well in the jobs made available to them.

In light of this ambiguity in the fit between jobs and persons' skills, measuring the extent of underqualification is more difficult and fraught with error than assessing changes in either job skills or workers' skills. Furthermore, the way we measure workers' skills may differ from the way we assess the skill requirements of jobs, and few studies have developed comparable indicators of both (Handel 2003, 155). This parallels the situation for overqualification discussed in the previous chapter.

There have been several attempts to measure the extent of underqualification for large, representative groups of workers. A survey of a cross section of employers in the mid-1990s (the National Employers Survey), for example, found that employers felt that between a fifth and a quarter of their current production or front-line workers were underqualified for their jobs (National Center on the Educational Quality of the Workforce 1994). Unfortunately, these estimates did not take into account these workers' ages or their length of time on the job, and previous estimates that might be used to assess whether these figures were comparatively high or low were not available (Handel 2003, 156).

Another study that linked information from employers to data from their employees (Moss and Tilly 2001) found that about a quarter of recently hired high school dropouts were underqualified, since they held jobs that their employers felt required a high school diploma (Handel 2003, 150).

An alternative way of measuring underqualification is by the wage differentials among people with different amounts of education. The growth in the college wage premium—that is, the gap in wages between college versus high school graduates—from record lows in the 1970s to highs in the 1980s was interpreted by some economists as reflecting a rise in skill requirements for jobs; this argument is often referred to as "skill-biased technological change." This increased wage differential also signaled to some that there was a growing skill shortage, since employers needed to pay higher wages to attract skilled workers (Katz and Murphy 1992).

However, there is considerable evidence that the growth in wage inequality was not due to skill-biased technological change. Galbraith (1998, 19–20), for example, argues convincingly that economic inequality results not from growing skill differentials evaluated in a free and efficient labor market. Rather, economic inequality results from "political battles . . . driven by the interaction of economic policy, economic performance, and the existing structures of monopoly power."

A related way of measuring underqualification is by whether there are vacancies in particular occupations. Some occupations, for example, are in chronically short supply, such as nurses and computer programmers. However, this shortage does not necessarily mean that there is a shortage of qualified workers for these occupations. We need to consider the wages that employers are offering to attract workers in various occupations before we conclude that there is really a shortage of people with these skills in the labor market. For example, when New York City increased the wages for teachers, their shortage of teachers was quickly eliminated.

New York's experience suggests there never was a shortage, only an unwillingness of qualified teachers to work at previous pay levels. This will come as no surprise to economists, who say that real shortages are rare in a market economy. At the right price, supply grows to meet demand (Rothstein 2002, A16).

Since underqualification and overqualification are in some sense two sides of the same coin, the strategy for measuring overqualification that we used in the previous chapter (comparing a person's years of educational attainment to the years of education required by the job) might also be used to assess the extent of underqualification.

In Table 4.1, we present estimates from the General Social Survey on the extent to which people in the United States are underqualified for their jobs. The measures of educational requirements of jobs are the same as those used in Table 3.1 and were obtained from the *Dictionary of Occupational Titles* (see Autor, Levy, and Murnane 2003). The criterion used to define underqualification (people's years of schooling are at least three years less than the educational requirements of their jobs) leads to fairly conservative estimates of the extent to which the educational requirements of jobs exceed individuals' educational attainments and is the mirror image of the criterion used in Table 3.1 to measure overqualification.

Taken as a whole, the results in Table 4.1 do not support the argument that underqualification is increasing in the United States. The percentages of persons in every demographic group have declined over time, suggesting that concerns about a coming skills shortage have been exaggerated.

These estimates indicate that about 20 percent of men and 12 percent of women in the United States were underqualified for their jobs in the period from 1972 to 1982. The gender gap in

Table 4.1

ESTIMATES OF UNDERQUALIFICATION[a] AMONG US WORKERS, BY

SELECTED DEMOGRAPHIC CHARACTERISTICS, 1972–2002[b]

	% Underqualified		
	1972–1982	1983–1992	1993–2002
Gender			
Males	19.9	11.8	7.2
Females	11.9	9.5	6.7
Race			
White	16.9	10.4	6.9
Non-white	18.4	13.1	7.4
Education			
Less than H.S. (0–11 years)	51.0	47.1	41.2
High school graduate	8.4	7.8	7.0
Some college (13–15 yrs)	4.4	2.8	2.5
College graduate	5.5	3.3	2.2
College plus (17–20 years)	1.5	1.2	0.6
Age			
25–34	9.0	7.8	5.5
35–44	14.6	7.8	6.4
45–54	23.8	14.0	7.4
55–65	27.5	22.1	11.4

[a]Underqualification is defined as educational attainment that is three or more years less than the educational requirements of the job.
[b]Source: General Social Survey data (Vaisey 2006).

underqualification has narrowed since then, and the percentage of both men and women who have at least three fewer years of education than that required by their jobs has decreased over time; in the years from 1993 to 2002, only about 7 percent of men and slightly fewer women were underqualified by this measure.

We might also expect underqualification to be more common among groups that are educationally disadvantaged, such as nonwhites. Table 4.1 suggests that nonwhites are more likely to be underqualified than whites, but the gap is relatively small and has narrowed in the most recent decade.

Underqualification is also more apt to characterize workers with a high school degree or less, as shown in Table 4.1. The percentage of workers with a high school diploma who are underqualified has declined over time, from nearly six out of ten in the years from 1972 to 1982 to slightly less than 50 percent in the decade from 1993 to 2002. These estimates suggest that the problem of skill shortages is concentrated among those with less than a high school degree, just as overqualification is greatest among college graduates (see Table 3.1). By contrast, relatively small percentages of workers who have attained a college degree or more are underqualified by these measures.[11]

Underqualification also appears to be most prevalent among older workers. Nearly a quarter of workers aged 45 to 54 and over a quarter of workers aged 55 to 65 were underqualified in the years from 1972 to 1982. These numbers underscore the problem of using years of education as the sole measure of skills; most of these older workers have accrued job-specific skills and work experience that make them more valuable to their employers. They may not have achieved a college education because in their generation, college degrees were not as widespread.

The corresponding percentages for workers aged 45 to 54

---

[11]This is a ceiling effect—the more education people have, the less likely it is that their jobs will require more education than they have.

and aged 55 to 65 for the most recent decade (1993 to 2002) are about 7 percent and 11 percent. By contrast, relatively small proportions of the youngest workers were underqualified (less than 10 percent in the years from 1972 to 1982 and less than 6 percent in the period from 1993 to 2002). It appears, then, that the proportion of workers in the United States who are underqualified has declined over time in all age groups.

CONSEQUENCES OF UNDERQUALIFICATION

Underqualification may have consequences for individuals, organizations, and the society in general. For individuals, not having the skills to perform the job may put them at greater risk of unemployment. It may also negatively affect a person's self-esteem, as one is more likely to experience failure at work if he or she lacks the skills to perform the job well.

From the point of view of the organization, employing underqualified workers is apt to create inefficiencies in the workplace that may hinder the development of innovation and forestall the implementation of new technologies. These consequences may endanger the organization's profits and performance. In turn, such skill shortages may encourage organizations to outsource these activities to countries such as India that have the trained workforce to do the work, often at much lower wages.

Skills shortages may also lead employers to alter job descriptions and to change the mechanisms and institutional linkages that affect hiring and promotion. For example, there is evidence that some employers modified their human resource policies and work organization in response to their need for skilled workers by strategies such as reducing their dependence on workers' skills, by increasing the amount of supervision and decreasing the complexity of jobs; developing special accommodations to retain good workers, such as creating part-time positions and more flexible hours; and developing networks with schools to provide a pipeline of new, skilled workers (Rosenbaum and Binder 1997, 69). These closer linkages with schools facilitated the flow of skilled workers to the organization but made it more difficult for people outside these networks to get access to jobs.

These actions have consequences for society as a whole. Outsourcing production to skilled workers abroad who are willing to work at lower wages represents a cost to the citizens of the country that loses these jobs, who are often displaced as a result of the movement of jobs offshore. This trend may eventually affect a country's competitive advantage and perhaps its trade balance.

These potential negative consequences for society were a major reason for the concern about skill shortages in the United States in the 1980s, when it was assumed that the existence of a large group of underqualified workers would lead to an underutilization of capital and a decline in productivity and economic performance. It was assumed that workers with insufficient skills would be unable to take advantage of the potential productivity inherent in the technology and other types of capital in which employers have invested.

It would be incorrect to attribute the poor economic performance of US companies in the 1980s to individuals' low skills, however. This assumption unfairly puts the blame on the victim as opposed to structural reasons such as inadequate investments in training, inefficient work organization, incentives imposed on businesses by financial markets that discouraged new job creation, and misguided trade policies.

Underqualification as a Form of Structural Unemployment

People who are underqualified for their jobs are at considerable risk of losing their jobs altogether, becoming unemployed. The term *structural unemployment* refers to joblessness produced by a lack of fit between workers' skills and those that employers demand. This mismatch may increase because of changes in business conditions, rapid technological change, restructuring of work methods and production techniques, or changes in the local industry mix. Structural unemployment may be viewed as an extreme form of underqualification, since it represents a persistent mismatch between the jobs that are available in the labor market and the people seeking jobs. In the case of structural unemployment, the jobs that are vacant do not match the skills of job seekers, so that no match is possible.

To return to the example of textile workers in North Carolina, the fact that these workers were highly skilled at manufacturing textiles does not help them get jobs when there are no textile jobs left in the area. At the same time, high-technology computer jobs can be filled only if there are sufficient workers with those skills willing to work in them at prevailing wage rates.

One form of structural unemployment is technological unemployment, in which jobs are eliminated because of the introduction of new technologies such as computers and other electronic devices, as was the case with Latoya's job. New technology and product market competition (both domestic and international) encourage employers to reevaluate their production methods and staffing needs.

Structural unemployment, like underqualification, results from the interplay between individuals' skills and the requirements of jobs, and is not due exclusively to either one or the other. Economists' theories of structural unemployment tend to put the blame on the supply side of the labor market, arguing that unemployment is created because people do not have the required characteristics, such as adequate training, formal education, labor market experience, and work attitudes; because there are too many workers; because workers are not willing to work at the wages offered by employers, and so on. An apt example is the lack of workers willing to rebuild New Orleans after the devastation brought by Hurricane Katrina unless wages for such work were increased; labor was so scarce that Burger King offered a $6,000 signing bonus to anyone who agreed to work for one year at one of its New Orleans outlets (Rivlin 2005).

These theories assume that employers are rational and do not hire people who do not possess sufficient skills. By contrast, Berg and Shack-Marquez (1985) argue that we should not confuse the problem of structural unemployment with the traits of unemployed persons, especially their demographic and human capital attributes. Rather, they maintain that the availability of jobs is most strongly related to unemployment, as well as job seekers' access to information about jobs.

Like underqualification, structural unemployment also creates negative consequences at several levels. For individuals, structural unemployment means that the person no longer has a job because of a lack of requisite skills. People have to change careers, move from one area to another, or obtain additional training and education in the hope of finding work.

For organizations and society, structural unemployment means that needed jobs are not filled and products or services are not produced. There is underutilization of productive capacity, both with regard to human capital and physical capital, and lost opportunities as organizations and societies are not able to take advantage of the potential for innovation and the productive capacity that exists when seemingly underqualified workers are given the opportunity to demonstrate their abilities.

REDUCING UNDERQUALIFICATION

There are two main ways to reduce underqualification: lower the skills required to perform jobs or provide workers with the skills needed to do the jobs.

The first approach—reducing the skills required by jobs—is likely to be limited in its effectiveness. Employers' abilities to reduce job skills in order to control the work process and reduce labor costs are inhibited in some industries by the available job tasks or technologies. For example, some high-end jobs, especially in service industries, are hard to computerize or to routinize to make them easier for workers with fewer skills. Moreover, all jobs require some skills; workers may well be underqualified even for low-skill jobs if they lack the requisite abilities and know-how to do them. Many low-skill jobs actually involve considerable skills, even if they generally pay low wages; they often require non-cognitive skills that are acquired through experience, such as taxi drivers knowing the best routes to get to various destinations at different times of the day. Finally, reducing the skills required to perform jobs is likely to create other kinds of mismatches, such as overqualification and low wages.

The much more preferable alternative is to provide workers with job training or continuing education of some kind, whether through educational institutions or on-the-job experience. The key questions are who provides this training and who pays for it—the government or employers. Too often the burden of retraining falls exclusively on the individual. As we argue throughout this book, mismatches such as underqualification need to be addressed by a combination of government and business policies and cannot be left up to the individual to solve.

Public schools can provide some skills training, but such training is likely to be inadequate. The kinds of job-related skills obtained through formal schooling are apt to be general and not directly applicable to what people actually need to do their jobs. Formal schooling may be more useful in providing people with soft skills such as appropriate work attitudes, work ethics, and so on. Community colleges and other vocationally oriented schools are better able to provide workers with technical skills that may qualify them for specific jobs. Businesses are encouraging community colleges to develop job-training programs as illustrated earlier in this chapter by the textile industry in Davidson County, North Carolina (see also Wirtz 2002 and Chapter 10).

In any event, effective mechanisms to facilitate the transition from schools (community colleges, universities, vocational schools, or other educational institutions) to workplaces are especially needed. Social policies should seek to create systematic pathways from school to work, or to produce a tighter coupling between these two institutions (Rosenbaum and Binder 1997). This connection would help ensure that the training programs are useful in preparing people for jobs that actually exist.

In order to combat the shortage of skilled manufacturing workers, businesses need to supplement these government efforts by enhancing their training programs and the resources they devote to training. Companies in the United States have tended to underinvest in training. A study conducted in the early 1990s, for example, found that the median training budget for US establishments was only $56 per employee over a two-year period (Knoke and Kalleberg 1994).

In addition to increasing spending on training and education, employers can alleviate skills shortages by developing better strategies to recruit and retain workers, such as increasing their diversity efforts to bring in more minority workers; offering more flexibility and child care to working mothers; and recruiting and training hard-to-place workers such as welfare moms, people with disabilities, and ex-prisoners. These groups are said to be deficient in their soft skills as well as technical skills. By encouraging and providing these potential workers, often regarded as underqualified, with the necessary resources to work, employers can reduce possible skill shortages and provide these workers with the opportunity to demonstrate their ability to work productively.

Businesses in the United States may be reluctant to train workers because they are afraid that their newly skilled employees will leave and they will lose the investment they made in training them. This concern is heightened by the greater insecurity of employment relations reflected in the growth of nonstandard work such as temporary and contract work that has made it less likely that workers will remain with the company long enough for it to recoup its investment in training. This fear is known as the "free-rider" problem; firms do not wish to provide public goods (in this case, training) that workers may take with them to another employer.

There may be lessons for the United States in the ways other countries have dealt with the free-rider problem. In Germany, for example, there is a fairly close relationship between public and private sectors in the training of workers. The clearest example is the dual vocational system, whereby students work at a particular company while going to school, facilitating their transition to a job when education is completed. This system is supported by an institutional framework based on local employer-led chambers of industry and commerce and artisan chambers, which together play a central role in managing apprenticeship training. Membership in these chambers is compulsory, and about 90 percent of employers are members. These chambers help to prevent "free riding" and reinforce the quality of training (see Marsden 1999, 224–5).

The German situation also illustrates the importance of unions for enhancing the quantity and quality of worker training. Unions have historically played this role in the United States, and the decline in union representation has contributed to the relatively low investments employers have devoted to training programs. Where unions are still active, employer-based training is more likely to occur. For example, the United Steelworkers of America is currently cross-training 3,000 experienced workers at US Steel Corporation in a secondary discipline, such as teaching a pipe fitter to run a press. Ten years ago, such cross-training was not provided; it has been introduced recently in response to competitive pressures and to avoid expensive downtime (Maher 2005).

Social policies and business investments need to reinforce each other. Employers cannot be expected to solve mismatches due to underqualification on their own and need to be supported by governmental social policies. For example, if the needed workers truly cannot be found within the United States, the federal government might need to expand the H1(b) visa program again to allow more workers with needed skills to immigrate to the US. Government support is also needed to enhance the educational attainments of workers though increased national investment in schools and by providing college aid to middle-class as well as poor and minority students.

Chapter Five
GEOGRAPHICAL MISMATCHES

LAMONT IS A FORTY-YEAR-OLD African American man who has worked as a welder in a manufacturing plant for the past ten years. He dropped out of college after one year in order to take a job when his first child was born. He earns $10.50 an hour, barely enough to pay the rent and provide food for his wife and three children, especially if he is able to work some overtime, but he has nothing left over at the end of the week after paying the bills. He does, however, receive health insurance from his employer, which is very important to Lamont since his oldest child has a severe disability.

Lamont and his family live in a three-room walk-up apartment in the middle of a big city in the Midwest. His company recently decided to relocate the manufacturing plant at which he works to the suburbs, to a larger and more modern facility on a bigger piece of land next to a major highway. This new location will reduce the company's transportation costs, there is plenty of parking space for employees' cars, and the property taxes are lower. Unfortunately, Lamont can't afford to live in the suburbs near the plant, since there are few apartments for rent in that area and he has not been able to save enough money to make a down payment on a house. He now has to commute to the plant from his apartment. The commute is difficult; the trip takes nearly three hours each way and requires him to take three buses, but he cannot afford to buy a car. He has been late to work six times in the past two weeks, since the bus service is not reliable, even if he gets up very early in the morning. He doesn't know how long he can continue this long commute before he gets fired, but he hasn't been able to find any jobs for which he is qualified in the area where he lives. Unfortunately, he may not have his job much longer; his company has decided to relocate its manufacturing operation to Mexico, where costs are even lower and there is less hassle with labor laws and unions. Lamont's goal is to find a job closer to where he lives.

Lamont's situation underscores the importance of space or location for understanding labor market processes and the creation of mismatches. Lamont is *geographically mismatched* because he lives far from the area in which his job is located. His company's decision to move his job to another country will make the mismatch even worse and ultimately cause him to be unemployed.

Geographical immobility is a form of mismatch between people and jobs and may lead to some of the other kinds of mismatches we discuss in this book. In order to obtain good matches in the labor market, people must be able to find jobs that fit their needs and preferences, which may require them to move from one area to another. Inability to move to where the jobs are may lead to mismatches such as overqualification and underqualification, overworking as well as underworking, working in low-paying jobs or jobs that do not enable workers to take care of their familial needs and responsibilities.

We will discuss several types of geographical mismatches in this chapter. First we consider the offshoring of jobs to other parts of the world, which has become increasingly common as the economy has become more global and internationalized, as well as mobility of jobs within the United States, such as the shift of textile industries from the Northeast to the South. Second, we discuss the problem of spatial mismatches between workers who live in central cities and jobs that are located in the suburbs.

INTERNATIONAL AND REGIONAL MISMATCHES

Jobs move from one location to another, both within the United States and from one country to another. Employers generally move jobs to take advantage of cheaper labor in another location or to otherwise reduce costs of production. Mobility of jobs is usually expected to be accompanied by the movement of workers, who are encouraged to move to areas where the demand for jobs is growing and away from areas of job decline. Coordinated movement of jobs and workers is considered desirable and normal, since it facilitates the job creation process and economic development and innovation.

While some people follow their jobs to other areas, others are unable to do so because of barriers that limit their mobility, leading to geographical mismatches. Constraints on mobility arise from various sources. Some workers cannot afford to move because they have insufficient savings to transport themselves and their families and possessions or to make a down payment on housing in the new location. Others feel that they are unable to move because of ties to a particular location, which may be produced by family relations (for example, John, in Chapter 3) or deep-rooted loyalties to a particular area.

Globalizing Production and the Offshoring of Jobs
American companies, like companies throughout the world, are increasingly offshoring jobs; they are shifting their production to foreign companies as well as to subsidiary organizations they own in another country. The jobs that are offshored include low-wage jobs, such as textile and furniture manufacturing and corporate call centers, as well as high-technology jobs such as microchip research and development. At present, China is probably the fastest-growing destination for companies looking to outsource manufacturing, engineering, and product development, while India is a favorite location for information technology and back-office activities such as finance, accounting, and purchasing (Friedman 2005). Moreover, treaties such as NAFTA (North American Free Trade Agreement) have lowered the barriers to the mobility of capital and labor among countries in North America and have encouraged US textile manufacturers, for example, to move their production to lower-cost areas in Mexico.

Companies shift their production to offshore locations for several reasons. One strong motivation is to cut costs, especially labor costs, thereby improving profits. The countries to which American jobs are exported typically pay much lower wages than those in the United States and do not require employers to meet our high standards for occupational safety and health. Employers thus have greater latitude in designing jobs. Another reason for offshoring is to find workers with skills that might not be available in the United States. The seven major institutions that constitute the Indian Institutes of Technology, for example, provide a huge pool of highly skilled workers in India. The combination of these two reasons—high-skilled workers and low wages—characterizes the labor force in India and China and constitutes a powerful inducement to businesses to move jobs to these locations.

For example, Conexant Systems, a Newport Beach, California, maker of microchips, currently does 50 percent of its semiconductor design and other high-tech engineering work in Hyderabad, India, employing about 700 engineers. This percentage is up from 10 percent last year, and the company plans to increase this figure to 65 percent by the end of 2006. The reason is that it can hire Indian engineers for $25,000 a year in salary and benefits compared to $100,000 in the United States (Flanigan 2005). Similarly, Intel plans to spend about $1 billion over the next five years to expand its research and development in Bangalore, India, while Cisco Systems will invest $1.1 billion and triple its staff in India over the next three years.

Offshoring is not a new phenomenon. Multinational corporations based in the United States, for example, have exported jobs to their overseas operations for some time, and offshoring has been a major source of their profits. In 1979, for example, 94 percent of the profits of Ford Motor Company, 63 percent of the profits of Coca-Cola, and 83 percent of the banking profits of Citicorp came from their overseas operations (Bluestone and Harrison 1982, 42).

Offshoring has accelerated in recent years, however, mostly because of technological advances such as computers and communications. These advances enable work, workers, and capital to be moved quickly across national borders. In addition, the time difference between Asia and the United States now makes it possible for work to go on around the clock. For example, documents sent to India at the close of the business day in New York can be edited and returned by the next morning. Jobs that are particularly likely to be offshored include those in information technology, finance, accounting, and human resources.

Regional Mobility of Jobs

The demand for particular kinds of jobs also varies among areas within the United States. Heavy industrial manufacturing jobs—"smokestack industries"—were once concentrated in the Midwest, while the computer industry was born in the Silicon Valley of California. The location of jobs in these industries has changed over time, and there are many examples of industries and companies moving from one community or region to another. Thus, textiles were once manufactured mainly in New England, then moved to the South, and then more recently moved to low-wage countries in Asia and Latin America.

The movement of jobs from one region to another (especially from the Northeast and Midwest to the South and West) caused considerable concern in the United States in the early 1980s; many labor leaders and social scientists were worried about the "deindustrialization of America," or the " . . . widespread, systematic disinvestment in the nation's productive capacity" (Bluestone and Harrison 1982, 6). This movement resulted largely from the slowdown in the economy that began in the 1970s, which led to an increase in plant shutdowns and jobs disappearing from communities as employers sought to increase profits by cutting jobs and moving to areas of the country such as the South, which had better business climates, often equated with the absence of unions.

Such movement of businesses (often called "capital flight" or "capital mobility") involved shutting plants down and relocating them, a process that

> . . . earned the epithet "runaway shop" in the 1930s, and again in the 1950s, when industries such as shoes, textiles and apparel left New England for the lower-wage, nonunionized South (Bluestone and Harrison 1982, 8).

As a result of this mobility, there was a net gain of nearly 3.7 million people in the South and West during the 1970s.

The problem with this mobility strategy, from Bluestone and Harrison's (1982) point of view, is that it diverted capital from productive investment in basic manufacturing industries to investments in mergers and acquisitions and foreign investment, activities in which profits may be greater. The trend to deindustrialization was thus driven by characteristics of capital markets, which rewarded managers for short-term, bottom-line profits attained through downsizing and reducing labor costs, rather than for strategies that might be better for the community and company in the long run, such as investing in training and community development.

Consequences of International and Regional Mismatches
Mobility of jobs is often associated with dislocations of people, families, and communities. People whose mobility is constrained are more likely to be unemployed or be forced to take jobs that do not fit them well and illustrate one of the types of mismatches we discuss in this book. As we have noted earlier, this is a common situation for trailing spouses, usually women, who find themselves restricted in their labor market options

because they are living in a particular area due to the husband's job situation. For family reasons, these trailing spouses are often not in a position to move to areas where there are better job opportunities for them.

Another factor that limits people's abilities to follow the jobs to other regions is what happens to a community when companies pull out. Large-scale job losses in a particular area create wholesale community decline; even if workers want to move, they cannot sell their houses because all their neighbors want to sell too, and nobody wants to move into a declining neighborhood. Housing values plummet, making the option of selling one's house and moving much less likely.

The consequences of mobility of jobs are often severe for communities as well as individual families. As companies pull out of towns, they take with them the tax base, leaving relatively little support for schools and other social services, further depressing housing values as well as making these communities less attractive places to live.

Reducing International and Regional Mismatches

Despite the cost advantages, there are also disadvantages to offshoring jobs. For example, it is often difficult to achieve teamwork and to enforce quality standards across oceans and time zones. In addition, call centers in India are struggling with high employee turnover (Rives 2005), which may increase as the standard of living of workers in India and other countries rises and workers are less likely to be willing to work for low wages.

Nevertheless, there is reason to believe that the offshoring of jobs and the movement of jobs from one region to another will continue in the future. The mobility of jobs is likely to accelerate as the pace of social change continues to increase. We cannot turn back the clock and try to stop the flow of capital and labor across geographical areas. Protectionist policies will not be effective when so much work is carried out through the Internet, for example. The big question that needs to be addressed regarding the mobility of jobs is how to help workers who are victims of job loss to adapt to the new jobs that are being created.

In the case of the international migration of jobs, it is not reasonable to expect that people will leave the United States to follow the jobs. We need to provide these displaced workers with alternative job opportunities in the United States. Training programs are needed for the workers left behind; the implementation of such training programs raises the same kinds of questions we discussed at the end of Chapter 4.

It is also necessary to temper the consequences of the movement of jobs from one area to another. Communities, for example, would benefit from as much advance notice as possible that plants are planning to leave. This would give them the opportunity to discuss this decision with employers and prepare for this displacement.

SPATIAL MISMATCHES

The role of space in the labor market has also been discussed and researched by social scientists in terms of *spatial mismatch*; we will elaborate on this type of mismatch in the remainder of this chapter. The spatial mismatch hypothesis has been used to explain why certain groups of workers, especially racial minorities, have relatively high unemployment rates and low incomes.[12] This hypothesis, first articulated by John F. Kain (1968), suggests that space constitutes a barrier especially for minorities in the labor market. It thus addresses "the issue of job accessibility and the relationship between race, the housing market, and the labor market" (Fernandez and Su 2004, 546).

The spatial mismatch hypothesis states that inequalities in the housing market because of racial segregation spill over and cause inequalities in people's job opportunities. It refers to a spatially specific matching problem—the inability of inner-city residents, usually racial minorities, especially blacks, to compete successfully for jobs for which they are qualified. These jobs often require relatively low skills and are likely to have moved to the suburbs.

This hypothesis asks whether the movement of businesses and jobs from central cities to the suburbs in the United States during the 1970s and 1980s helped to create problems of unemployment and low-wage employment for workers (especially blacks) who were unable to move from the inner cities (e.g., Holzer 1991, 105). Much of the work related to the spatial mismatch hypothesis deals with the plight of the urban poor left behind by the decline of traditional manufacturing work and the rise of a suburban-based service sector job market (Kasarda 1990; Wilson 1996). This problem is compounded if public transportation is inadequate for moving people to jobs, which it often is.

---

[12]Women's jobs may be less affected by spatial mismatch than men's. Because of high levels of sex segregation in the labor market, women are still largely confined to relatively few female-dominated jobs that are generally available in most geographic areas.

Spatial mismatch is also illustrated by the situation that often occurs in many expensive and desirable places to live, resort towns such as Aspen, Colorado and college towns such as Chapel Hill, North Carolina. People who work in service occupations (e.g., janitors and food service workers) and other relatively low-paying jobs created by the resorts and colleges in these places usually cannot afford to live in these areas but must commute—often long distances, utilizing less-than-ideal transportation systems—from areas in which housing is less expensive. In 2000, more than 18,000 household workers (nannies, cleaners, and others) in the New York City area, for example, spent at least 90 minutes daily commuting to jobs paying less than $25,000 (Berger 2004). And in South Carolina, about 800 workers commute two hours each way to Myrtle Beach, where they flip burgers or clean hotel rooms for $6 or $7 an hour (Halbinger 2002).

Explaining Spatial Mismatch

Spatial mismatches result from two trends in the movement of jobs and people. First, job growth, especially in manufacturing industries, has occurred more rapidly in the suburbs and has declined in many cities. This reflects a long-term, functional transformation of cities from manufacturing centers to loci of information processing, which involves loss of blue-collar jobs and an increase of knowledge-intensive jobs in administration, finance, the professions, and other white-collar service occupations.

In the late nineteenth and early twentieth centuries, cities in the United States had employment bases that featured low-skilled manufacturing jobs that provided unskilled immigrants with opportunities for jobs and advancement. In the latter part of the twentieth century, employers moved many of these manufacturing jobs to the suburbs, since these geographic areas offered them cheaper and more abundant land to build factories and greater accessibility to highway transportation to bring in raw materials and export finished products. This transformation of the cities is intimately related to the broader processes of globalization and economic restructuring, as well as to the kinds of regional and international mobility of jobs discussed earlier. Thus, while there was an increase in entry-level jobs in the US during the years from 1975 to 1985, this job growth occurred in the suburbs, not the inner cities (Kasarda and Friedrichs 1985).

A second trend is that minorities, especially blacks, live mainly in the inner cities and are unable to move closer to the jobs for which they are qualified (see Massey and Denton 1993). Middle-class people originally left the inner cities in search of a better education for their children. High degrees of racial segregation in the suburbs of many metropolitan areas have constrained the ability of blacks to choose where they want to live. Minorities also generally lack the education and other skills to qualify and compete successfully for the information-processing and high-skilled service sector jobs which are more likely to be found in the inner cities, although they can still compete for low-skilled service jobs, such as those in hotels or fast-food restaurants.

Thus, minorities do not have easy access to the suburban jobs for which they are qualified and are likely to be underqualified for the jobs in the inner cities close to where they live.

They are also less likely to have access to social networks and other sources of information about job opportunities in the suburbs and cannot afford the high transportation costs associated with the long commutes it often takes to get to them. Moreover, members of these groups may also be discriminated against by employers as they seek to obtain these jobs. The consequences of these trends is that inner-city minorities are more likely to be unemployed or working in jobs that pay less than those for which they are qualified.

Whites who live in the suburbs, on the other hand, are more likely to be able to obtain jobs in the inner cities. While they too have relatively long commutes from the suburbs to their jobs in the inner cities, these jobs are relatively well-paying, and so they are better compensated for their long commutes. Suburban dwellers are also more likely to have the cars and other means to ease this commute. By contrast, inner-city black residents are not able to obtain jobs in the suburbs that pay enough to compensate them for their long commutes (see Mouw 2002), as was illustrated by the example of Lamont at the beginning of this chapter.

The spatial mismatch hypothesis attributes the occurrence of geographical mismatches to frictions or constraints in housing and labor markets, not primarily to discriminatory behaviors on the part of employers in denying jobs to blacks (Kain 1968). Since blacks are discouraged and constrained from applying for suburban jobs because of the long commutes involved or their lack of information about these jobs, employers are not faced with the choice of hiring them. This puts suburban employers below the radar of Equal Employment Opportunity (EEO) enforcement, since they can avoid hiring minorities simply by moving to locations where blacks are not able to find housing in which to live or to easily commute to these jobs from their homes.

The growth of high-skill jobs in the areas in which minority workers live and for which they are not qualified has thus helped to create a growing mismatch between skills of minority workers and job requirements. This, in turn, has fueled the creation of concentrated poverty in an urban underclass, whose members are not able to find jobs for which they are qualified. For them, work has disappeared, and these workers may be underqualified for or underemployed in the only jobs to which they are likely to have access (Wilson 1996).

Evidence for the Spatial Mismatch Hypothesis

The spatial mismatch hypothesis has been controversial and has generated a considerable number of studies seeking to test its central predictions. Holzer (1991) reviewed the empirical evidence gathered during the previous two decades and noted that there was considerable support for a number of its key propositions. For example: There has been population growth in the suburbs; manufacturing jobs have moved from the central cities to the suburbs (Fernandez 1994); there has been an increase in the central cities of jobs in the financial, trade, and service sectors; there continues to be racial segregation in the suburbs, especially for blacks (Massey and Denton 1993); there has been a greater increase in unemployment in cities than in the nation as a whole (Kasarda and Friedrichs 1985) or the suburbs; job requirements tend to be higher in the inner cities than in the suburbs (Holzer 1996); and the wages of blacks (especially black males) have deteriorated compared to their white counterparts.

Not all of these trends are due to spatial mismatch, however. For example, the higher unemployment rates and lower wages of blacks may be explained by reasons other than spatial mismatch. The higher black unemployment rates in the cities as compared to the suburbs may also reflect patterns of selective migration, as blacks with greater employment opportunities have moved to the suburbs (Holzer 1991). In order to provide a convincing test of the spatial mismatch hypothesis, studies need to take into account alternative explanations, including metropolitan area characteristics such as size, industrial structure, and modes of transportation, as well as characteristics of individuals in these areas such as their educational attainment, age, and family background.

Social scientists differ in how they have specified the central independent variable, spatial mismatch or geographic job accessibility, which has been defined as residential segregation, living in central cities versus the suburbs, the suburbanization of employment, and measures of access to jobs such as commuting distance or travel time. Studies using different measures of spatial mismatch have often reached different conclusions regarding its consequences for unemployment (Ihlanfeldt and Sjoquist 1998). For example, studies utilizing measures of job access such as commuting time tend to support the spatial mismatch hypothesis, while some studies of the outcomes of programs designed to help families relocate to suburban areas did not (see Fernandez and Su 2004, 548–53). Studies using data from the 1950s to 1970 did not provide convincing evidence that blacks experienced substantial unemployment due to spatial mismatch, whereas data from the 1980s tended to show that spatial mismatch did have significant consequences for the employment of blacks (Holzer 1991, 118).

A more recent review of the literature on spatial mismatch by Fernandez and Su (2004, 553) reached a similar conclusion (see also Ihlanfeldt and Sjoquist 1998):

> In sum, much research has appeared that tests key predictions of the spatial mismatch hypothesis as it has been laid out by Kain. Although it is unlikely to be a complete explanation, this research is generally persuasive in showing that job accessibility—generally measured in spatial terms—is an important contributing factor to minorities' labor market difficulties.

Spatial mismatch thus appears to be an important explanation, although not necessarily a complete one, of the racial gap in unemployment and other labor market outcomes. The explanation of racial differences may involve factors associated with race, in addition to those related to space. Other factors—employer discrimination, human capital factors such as education, and social capital indicators such as access to social networks and contacts—may also be important in explaining racial differentials in employment (Ellwood 1986).

The role of race in addition to space has also been underscored by studies of racial patterns in hiring. Some studies have noted that employers may use location as a space signaling device, helping them to act on their preferences against hiring minorities by not hiring people who live in the inner city. In this case, employers are acting in a discriminatory way (not a racially neutral way, as in Kain's original notion), and are using location or space as a means of racial preference.

Consequences of Spatial Mismatch

A major consequence of spatial mismatch is relatively high levels of unemployment of minorities—especially black males—in urban areas. There has been a dramatic deterioration of employment rates of less educated minorities, especially young African Americans, in inner cities during the past two decades (Holzer 1996). Moreover, unemployment rates are likely to understate the actual problem of joblessness, as people often become discouraged, drop out of the labor force, and thus are no longer counted as unemployed (see Chapter 7). Thus, nonparticipation in the labor force as well as unemployment may be a direct result of spatial mismatch. Such joblessness leads to the greater need for government expenditures for unemployment insurance and welfare assistance for those who do not have jobs.

In addition, spatial mismatch has contributed to a growing polarization of economic opportunities in cities where affluent white residents work at privileged jobs with high incomes and are spatially segregated from a growing group of unemployed, urban poor blacks who have incomes far below the poverty line. Low-income residents are at a considerable economic and cultural disadvantage in the new service economy because of the local nature of services and the reliance on interpersonal skills.

The racial inequality associated with spatial mismatch may help to explain why the race gap in earnings in the United States has not narrowed since the 1980s. Spatial mismatch may also indirectly contribute to racial tension in inner cities and prevent people from having good relationships with people in their neighborhoods.

Spatial segregation can also be seen as the root of a whole series of other ills that affect whites in addition to blacks. For example, spatial segregation drives up white housing values in the suburbs and increases housing inequality, in some places to the point that white families can't afford suburban housing and good schools either (see Warren and Taig 2003).

Reducing Spatial Mismatch

Spatial mismatch is " . . . one dimension of the changing geography of metropolitan opportunity" (Ihlanfeldt and Sjoquist 1998, 851). In recent years, the simple dichotomy between cities and suburbs has become less useful, as many inner suburbs now share the problems faced by inner cities (Ihlanfeldt and Sjoquist 1998, 851). Changes in the location of jobs away from cities and inner suburbs toward more distant suburban areas have created new spatial mismatches and problems of unemployment and underemployment. As one newspaper reporter described the challenges raised by this shift:

> You have a metro economy that used to offer a living wage to high school dropouts. It's a huge challenge to figure out how to employ the undereducated (Hummel, *News & Record*, 9/26/04).

Reducing spatial mismatch requires several related policy interventions targeted at the various aspects of the problem and involves reducing the constraints in both the housing and labor markets.

First, it is necessary to create ways to enable minorities to live in the suburbs and thereby to gain access to jobs located there (Holzer 1996). We need to reduce or remove the frictions in the housing market, perhaps through the provision of affordable loans to minority families or otherwise removing the barriers to home ownership in the areas where jobs are located. Steps might also be taken to facilitate the travel of minorities to jobs in the suburbs, a policy intervention that would not require them to live in the suburbs. Good public transportation, for example, is a vital element in any public policy, since it would increase the ability of minorities to move from areas of job decline to areas where jobs for which they are qualified are more plentiful.

Second, more jobs for which blacks and other minority group members are qualified need to be created in the inner city. Various kinds of urban development programs might be effective in bringing more jobs to the inner cities. Strategies to create lower-skilled jobs directly through mechanisms such as urban empowerment zones, for example, and providing tax incentives to employers to create jobs offer promising alternatives. Cities should develop strategies to increase economic growth and job opportunities, perhaps by lowering taxes to attract more business and reducing the zoning regulations that raise housing costs. In addition, ways of promoting entrepreneurial activities among inner-city blacks and minority residents, such as providing venture capital to new businesses, need to be implemented.

Third, we must recognize that part of the spatial mismatch problem is that some minorities are underqualified and do not have the skills required for jobs in the new economy. Providing more efficient matching opportunities or creating jobs in the inner city will not solve the problem. Here, policies to deal with spatial mismatch overlap with the strategies to combat skills shortages or underqualification discussed in the previous chapter. It is necessary to increase the job-related skills and credentials of minorities to make them more competitive for the jobs located in the inner cities. Also, better ways need to be found to help blacks and other minorities ease the transition from school to work. Better linkages need to be established, for example, between schools and employers (Holzer 1996).

Finally, removing barriers to transportation or providing more training opportunities might help blacks and other minorities have better access to suburban jobs, but these strategies are not likely to be effective if employers are using location to discriminate against minorities (Fernandez and Su 2004, 563). It is necessary to supplement these policy interventions with careful monitoring of hiring patterns to ensure that equal opportunity laws are being enforced.

These diverse policy recommendations underscore the need for a complex, multidimensional strategy to alleviate problems of spatial mismatch. This strategy needs to focus on the underlying reasons for spatial mismatches—racial housing segregation, poor mass transit, lack of good jobs in the inner cities, poor training opportunities for inner-city minority residents, and employment discrimination. It is easier to identify remedies than to make them a reality, however, and there are considerable obstacles that need to be overcome. Given the complexity of the necessary policy interventions, a strategy to ease spatial mismatch must encompass various kinds of initiatives—tax policies to encourage businesses to create more and better jobs in inner cities, housing policies to provide support to low-income families and to remedy spatial segregation, income subsidies to supplement low-wage jobs, and workforce development and training policies to improve the qualifications of workers.

While these challenges are daunting, they are well worth considering, since reducing spatial mismatches will help alleviate a number of the other mismatches we discuss in this book, especially underqualification, underemployment, and earnings mismatches.

Chapter Six
TEMPORAL MISMATCHES: OVERWORKING

KELLY HAS BEEN A LAWYER with a large corporate law firm in a Western city for the past four years. She is thirty-five-years old, white, and graduated from a prestigious law school about five years ago. Kelly is currently an associate in this firm and hopes very much that she will be promoted to a partner in a few more years, with a much higher salary and greater job security. She is ambitious and hard-working and has worked an average of 80 to 90 hours a week during the past two years. During many weeks, she rarely sees her two young children, leaving home before they are awake and returning home after they are asleep. Luckily, Kelly's husband, Mike, is a stay-at-home husband who has chosen to put his own career as a management consultant on hold for a few years to help Kelly to get her career started at the law firm.

Kelly would like to work fewer hours, but the number of hours she bills to clients is what the firm uses to measure a lawyer's productivity. She feels that she cannot cut back on her work schedule, because she fears that it would hurt her chances of being promoted to partner. Kelly also feels she cannot afford to work fewer hours because the bonus she receives at the end of the year is tied to the number of hours she bills to clients; she and her husband depend on her bonus to supplement her regular salary (more than $80,000 a year) and to pay for occasional child care for their two young children. Her job also provides her family with health insurance.

People make choices about how they use their time. Unlike many other choices, these are zero-sum choices—since there are only so many hours in a day and weeks in a year, choosing to spend time in one activity necessarily limits the opportunity to do other things. Many workers are called upon to decide how much time they will spend at work; they could choose, for instance, to work an extra five hours at their job or to devote more time to family, hobbies, leisure, or to religious or community pursuits.

Choices about time commitments, however, are not always voluntary, because they depend in part on the demands of one's job and workplace (Epstein and Kalleberg 2004). Some people work more hours than they really want because they need the money or are pressured by their boss into doing so. In addition, some people work harder and more intensely at work than they would like.

There are two different ways to classify the *overworked*; we discuss both in this chapter. First, overwork refers to the situation where people work *more hours* than they want—for example, full-time workers who want to work part-time, or people who desire to work fewer hours than they actually do.

Second, people might be overworked if they must work *more intensely* or harder than they want, regardless of how many hours they work. Work intensity refers to the pace of work—how hard or fast a person works or how stressed people feel at work. Some jobs are especially likely to involve too much to do and not enough time to do it, a mismatch that produces what some authors have called a "time famine" (Perlow 1999). People often respond to such time famine by time deepening, or trying to do more within a given time period. Thus, they may engage in activities such as multitasking (reading the newspaper while watching television), speeding up the activity (visiting six countries in six days), or substituting quicker activities for more time-consuming ones (eating fast food instead of cooking a gourmet meal) (Robinson and Godbey 1997, 38–42).

These two kinds of overwork are often related and may occur together. For example, it has often been said that burnout was the disease of the dot-com era, and workers in high-tech industries such as computer software programming worked a large number of hours per week or year and worked very intensely during these hours. Reporters on deadline to file their stories or students who pull all-nighters during exam week to study for finals or finish papers are examples of situations in which the two kinds of overwork occur simultaneously for brief periods of time.

In other situations, one might be overworked in one way but not the other. Some people work many hours but do not work very hard—for example, night watchmen, who may not see anyone for long stretches of time as they wait for something to happen. On the other hand, some workers may work very intensely but only for a few hours or even minutes, as in the case of jockeys riding in races.

Hours Worked

There are two general perspectives on why people work more hours than they prefer. On the one hand, some writers argue that pressures to work more hours than desired may result from people's needs and preferences. Needs generated by families or preferences as consumers lead people to work more hours in order to earn more money or to advance their careers, hoping for higher earnings in the future. An alternative view is that overworking results primarily from pressures that employers impose on workers, requiring them to work longer hours through mechanisms such as forced overtime. Employers may do this to increase productivity or to pick up the slack caused by downsizing or layoffs. We consider each of these mechanisms in turn.

First, workers may choose to work more hours than they prefer in order to obtain greater job rewards, especially earnings, which for some people are tied directly to the number of hours worked. Bell and Freeman (1995), for example, argue that the great inequality in wages and economic rewards in the American economy creates incentives for workers to work harder in order to earn more money. They compare the situation in the United States to Germany, where there is greater equality in wages and more job security. As a result, German workers tend to work fewer hours on average than Americans.

The choice to work more hours may not be completely voluntary. Workers' families may create needs for them to work more hours to earn more money; they might want to own a house in a neighborhood with good schools. Moreover, the growing sophistication of marketing and advertising has stimulated needs for more consumer goods and produced greater consumer debt, leading to so-called "unpreferred preferences" to work more hours (George 1997, 33).

The nature of the time-money exchange is an important part of the temporal aspect of employment. When people receive a fixed annual salary, for example, the hours-money exchange is less explicit than it is in systems based on hourly pay. In the latter, the employer has more direct control over the worker's time, and workers who wish to earn more money must work more hours.

Dual-earner couples are particularly likely to work more hours than they prefer and are more apt to face a time squeeze. They may wish to be seen as committed, productive workers who have the potential for advancement. Clarkberg and Moen (2001) speculate that the rising sense of a time squeeze in American society may stem from all-or-nothing assumptions about how work is organized and scheduled. That is, employer demands and institutionalized features of work cause work hours to come in prepackaged bundles; workers are faced with the choice between either no hours or 40 hours for each partner since realistic part-time options are scarce.

A second perspective on why people work more hours than they prefer looks to the requirements imposed by the employer (or by the job) to work more hours. There are a number of pressures and incentives for employers to overwork existing employees rather than hiring new ones. One source is technological change such as the development of computers and mobile communication devices that have made possible a 24/7 economy and have awakened demand for services that need to be performed day and night. For example, people are more likely now than in the past to feel that they should be able to buy groceries or speak to a customer service representative at any time.

There are also greater competitive pressures on businesses to cut costs, which may lead employers to mandate that workers work more hours, including overtime, rather than hire additional regular or temporary workers. There may also be a scarcity of workers for some jobs, caused in part by employers' lack of investment in training. Employers also demand that workers spend more hours at work to take up the slack created by downsizing and the move toward leaner organizations. Sometimes this involves working off the clock, as recent criticisms of certain employers such as Wal-Mart have pointed out (Greenhouse 2004). The survivors who have been fortunate to keep their jobs are often asked to take on additional responsibilities and may feel that they must comply with their employers' wishes, and work more hours (and more intensely during those hours) to protect their jobs from future layoffs.

Employers' efforts to increase the number of hours that their employees work are made possible by the absence of countervailing forces that offer protections to workers. The continued decline of unions and lack of enforcement by government agencies of labor and employment laws and practices that have historically protected workers have encouraged employers to mandate that their employees work longer.

Recent attempts[13] to change labor laws governing overtime are a vivid example of this decline in institutional protections. Altering these laws may cause large groups of workers to be considered exempt from the Fair Labor Standards Act, for example, thereby encouraging employers to ask these workers to work overtime without compensation (Weintraub 2003).[14] The

---

[13]These changes have been approved as the Department of Labor's "FairPay Overtime Initiative"; see www.dol.gov/esa/regs/compliance/whd/fairpay/main.htm
[14]See also www.epinet.org/content.cfm/overtime_2003.

pressure to have members of professional occupations work more hours without additional compensation is consistent with the finding that the most highly educated and professional workers are also most likely to be overworked (Jacobs and Gerson 2004).

It is likely that both of these explanations of overwork are partly true; overwork results from an interaction between employee preferences, employer demands, and the institutional context. Employers may be largely responsible for the increased number of hours that people work, although workers comply with employers' demands in order to satisfy their increasing tastes for consumer goods and other needs or desires (Schor 1991).

Empirical Evidence on Hours of Overwork

The concern that Americans are overworked was brought to national prominence by Juliet Schor in *The Overworked American* (1991) and grew during the 1990s. Schor reported, based on data obtained from questions in the Current Population Surveys, that Americans are working a greater number of hours each year than in the past. She also argued that working time has increased at the expense of leisure time and that Americans are working more hours than people in other industrial nations, especially in Europe. While some of these national differences are due to the fact that Americans work more hours per week, most of them result from the lower number of weeks worked per year in Europe than in the United States. The average American works 46.2 weeks per year, compared to the average French worker (40.5) and the average Swede (35.4). Workers in the US have much less vacation time than their counterparts in Europe (Alesina, Glaeser, and Sacerdote 2005).

Schor's argument stirred considerable controversy, and some writers disagreed with her conclusions. In particular, John Robinson and Geoffrey Godbey (1997) used data based on diaries in which people record their daily activities and concluded that leisure time in an average workweek has actually expanded. The time diaries showed that people often multitasked, so that the time they spent at work was also used for nonwork activities such as running errands and personal chores. Conclusions based on time diaries are also controversial, however, and have been criticized on several grounds—for example, the busiest people may not have time to fill out such diaries, so that the time pressures faced by the busiest workers are ignored (Jacobs and Gerson 2004, 15–18). In any event, the apparent increase in leisure seems to be due mainly to decreases in housework, not in paid work (Jacobs and Gerson 2004, 26–31).

The average number of hours per week worked by men and women in the United States has not changed much from 1970 to 2000; the percentages have remained constant at about 43 hours per week for men and 37 for women. The weekly figure contrasts with the number of hours worked per year on which Schor based her results; the latter computation makes often unrealistic assumptions about how much vacation time people take and how many weeks people work per year.

While there has not been much change in the number of hours worked, there has been a change in the inequality among workers in the time they spend on the job. There has been an increased polarization of working hours; some people are working very long weeks, while others work shorter weeks. Between

1970 and 2000, the proportion of men who work more than fifty hours a week has increased from 21 percent to about 27 percent, and the proportion of women has increased from about 5 percent to 11 percent. By contrast, the proportion of men who work fewer than thirty hours a week has increased from about 5 percent in 1970 to nearly 9 percent in 2000, and the proportion of women working fewer than thirty hours a week has grown from nearly 16 percent to about 20 percent (Jacobs and Gerson 2004).

This growing polarization in the number of hours worked represents a "time divide" (Jacobs and Gerson 2004) between people who work many hours and those who work few hours. Thus, there has not been a uniform trend in the United States in the growth of leisure or in the rising time demands of work. Instead, changes in family life have affected different groups of workers and those in different family situations in disparate ways.

Differences in the amount of time spent at work are linked to sharp and growing disparities in education; well-educated workers are more likely to put in long work weeks. So too are professionals and managers, and those who work in large firms (Jacobs and Gerson 2004). Moreover, the shift from single- to dual-income households (see Chapter 9) has created a marked increase in the working time of couples who face significantly longer work weeks. The growth of dual-earner couples has made the issue of overwork more often a household or couple phenomenon as opposed to an individual one. In the past, one spouse worked long hours in the labor force and the other took care of things at home. Now, dual-earner couples are faced with the challenge of jointly managing their domestic responsibilities while also meeting their obligations at the workplace.

The number of hours one works does not by itself necessarily mean that a person is overworked. As we have argued throughout this book, whether someone is mismatched for the job also depends on the person's needs and preferences. We all know or have heard of workaholics who enjoy putting in long hours at the office or traveling on business. These people thrive on working long hours and have no desire to reduce the number of hours they spend on their jobs. Since their job requirements are in line with their preferences, we do not consider these workers overworked (O'Connor 2004). On the other hand, some people feel that working even a few hours a day or week is too much and would like to cut down on their hours if they were able to do so. In order to know whether or not someone is overworked, then, we need information on whether a worker spends more hours at work than he or she needs or prefers.

There are several ways to obtain information on whether one works more hours than he or she wants. One way is to ask the worker to indicate the actual number of hours he or she works at his or her job during an average week and then ask: "Ideally, how many hours, in total, would you like to work each week?" Workers whose actual number of hours exceed their ideal number are considered overworked. Table 6.1 presents information obtained in this way from the 1997 National Study of the Changing Workforce (for a description of this study, see Bond, Galinsky, and Swanberg 1998).

In the late 1990s, about six out of ten men and women in the United States wanted to work fewer hours per week than

Table 6.1

ESTIMATES OF PERCEIVED OVERWORKING

IN THE UNITED STATES[a]

	Men	Women
Actual hours worked>Ideal hours[b]		
Total hours usually worked (all jobs)	47.3	41.4
Ideal hours	37.5	32.1
Difference (actual vs. ideal)	9.8	9.3
Actual hours>ideal hours	60.2	60.1
Actual hours at least 5 hours>ideal hours	58.4	58.6
Actual hours at least 10 hours>ideal hours	47.4	48.8
Actual hours at least 20 hours>ideal hours	28.3	27.9
Want to spend less time on paid work[c]		
Full-time wants fewer hours	22	15
Full-time wants part-time	9	21
Part-time wants fewer hours	2	3
Want to work fewer hours and earn less money[d]		
1989	5.6	5.3
1998	7.6	12.2

[a]First three rows (total hours, ideal hours, difference) refer to actual hours; all other figures are percentages.
[b]Source: National Study of the Changing Workforce, 1997. Reported in Jacobs and Gerson (2004), Table 3.1.
[c]Source: General Social Survey, 1998. Reported in Reynolds (2003), Table 2.
[d]Source: General Social Surveys, 1989, 1998, author's calculations.

they actually did. For men, the average difference between actual hours worked (47.3 hours a week) and ideal number of hours (37.5) was 9.8 hours. For women, the difference was 9.3 hours (41.4 minus 32.1).

There appears to be a gender difference in preferences for the number of hours worked; men typically want to work full-time and women typically prefer somewhat less than full-time hours. The vast majority of those who wanted to work fewer hours wanted to work at least five hours less than they actually worked. And about half of the 60 percent of workers who wanted to work fewer hours (three in ten in the overall labor force) want to work at least twenty hours less than they actually worked.

The gaps between actual and ideal hours were greatest for highly educated workers, those in managerial and professional occupations, workers in the middle aged range (36 to 55 years old), and married workers. For women, the biggest gap is for married women with an employed spouse (Jacobs and Gerson 2004, Table 3.2), consistent with the conclusion that dual-earner couples are most likely to experience a time squeeze or leisure pinch.

An alternative way to assess how many people are over-worked is to ask respondents if they want to spend more, less, or the same amount of time at work, if it was up to them. The General Social Survey in 1998 asked workers the following question:

> Suppose you could change the way you spend your time, spending more time on some things and less time on others. Which of the things on the following list would you like to spend more time on, which would you like to spend less time on, and which would you like to spend the same amount of time on as now? The possible responses for each activity, including paid work, were much less time, a bit less time, the same amount of time, a bit more time, and much more time.

Workers were also asked whether they preferred to have a full-time or part-time job. The second panel of Table 6.1

presents the percentages of full-time and part-time men and women workers who were classified as overworked on the basis of these questions (Reynolds 2003). These results suggest that 22 percent of men and 15 percent of women who work full-time would like to work fewer hours. An additional 9 percent of men and 21 percent of women work full-time but would like to work part-time; these workers would like to change their work status in addition to simply working fewer hours.

In addition, 2 percent of men and 3 percent of women work part-time and would like to work fewer hours. When we add these percentages together, we see that 33 percent of men and 39 percent of women are classified as overworked. These figures from the General Social Survey reveal smaller proportions of overworked workers than those suggested by the first measure, derived from the National Study of the Changing Workforce, and indicate that women are more likely to report being overworked than men.

Information from the General Social Survey (not shown in Table 6.1) also indicates that workers with higher levels of education (especially a college degree or more) were more apt to report that they were overworked; whites were more likely to say they were overworked than blacks; and workers aged 40 to 59 were more apt to prefer to work fewer hours than younger or older workers.

Both of these measures of overwork may encourage wishful thinking, since they do not take into account that—at least for many workers who are not salaried but paid by the hour— working fewer hours means they will earn less money and perhaps lose health benefits. For salaried workers, this trade-off may not be relevant, since the number of hours worked is not tied directly to one's earnings (Reynolds 2003, 1182–83). Economists, for example, often think in terms of a trade-off between labor and leisure and define overworking or overemployment as the situation

> when there are workers employed who are willing but unable to reduce their hours of paid work at their current (or comparable) job even if they are prepared to accept (proportionately) lower current or future income" (Golden 2003, 1).

The General Social Survey takes into account this trade-off between time and money by also asking workers this question:

> Think of the number of hours you work and the money you earn in your main job, including any regular overtime. If you had only one of these three choices, which of the following would you prefer: work longer hours and earn more money; work the same number of hours and earn the same money; work fewer hours and earn less money?

The third panel of Table 6.1 reports the percentage of men and women in 1989 and 1998 who said that they preferred to work fewer hours, even if it meant earning less. These percentages indicate that much lower proportions of workers are willing to work fewer hours if it means earning less money, underscoring the negative financial consequences of working less. While some workers want to work fewer hours, they feel that they cannot do so because they can't afford (or don't wish) to earn less money. Comparing the percentages in the first and second panels in Table 6.1 to those in the third panel highlights the fact that financial concerns are a major reason why people work more hours than they otherwise prefer, presenting an obstacle to people working less.

The percentages of workers who prefer to work fewer hours even though it means earning less have also increased over time, from 6 percent to 8 percent among men and from 5 percent to 12 percent among women. The higher rates among women may reflect a hidden cost of women seeking employment in full-time careers and the conflicts this has for the family (Chapter 9). The figures in the third panel of Table 6.1 are fairly conservative estimates; other studies that ask about trading off hours for money have found higher percentages of workers classified as overworked (Jacobs and Gerson 2004).

The percentage of persons who are overworked as judged by the trade-off criterion is substantially higher among women; whites; parents of young children; those who work many hours per week; and managerial, professional, and technical workers (Golden 2003).

WORK INTENSITY

Workers may also be overworked if they have to work harder or faster or do more things than they are comfortable doing, regardless of the number of hours that they spend at work. We refer to this form of overwork as working more intensely than one wants.

Workers may be required to work harder or more intensely than they prefer because of organizational changes such as downsizing and restructuring that have occurred more frequently during the 1980s and 1990s. These restructurings have led to layoffs for many workers and forced the remaining workers to work harder for fear that they too will lose their jobs.

An indication that some of the increase in hours and intensity of work stems from the downsizing culture of the 1990s is provided by the results of a poll taken December 3–6, 1995, in connection with a special report published by the *New York Times* (1996) called the *Downsizing of America*. This report chronicled the experiences of millions of middle-class Americans who suddenly lost their jobs. The survey found that 82 percent of workers said that they would work more hours—and 71 percent said that they would take fewer vacation days—if it increased their chances of keeping their jobs.

A faster required work pace may also result from pressures to increase productivity generated by greater competition from both foreign and domestic companies. Thus, workers may be asked to work faster and harder because of increased speed of machinery or more ambitious production targets (Cleeland 2002). In addition, the growth of service industries has increased pressures to work more intensely in order to accommodate customers' demands. The fact that more workers now deal directly with customers (as opposed to working in a factory or office) may have led to workers having to work harder to please these customers and, indirectly, their employers.

A study of the work practices of a software engineering team in a high-tech corporation provided insight into the social contexts that created a time famine among workers (Perlow 1999). These workers were under great time pressure to get things done, and they developed work patterns that interfered with their ability to complete their tasks and were detrimental to their nonwork lives. These work patterns were perpetuated by several features of the social context of the workplace: a crisis mentality that required workers to focus their attention on work in order to deal with the crisis, a reward system that encouraged workers to be heroes for working long hours, and constant interruptions that made it difficult to complete one's own work in order to deal with unscheduled and unforeseen work. If work had been structured differently, workers would have been able to get their work done more efficiently and avoided the creation of a time famine.

Work Intensity: Empirical Evidence

One indicator of work intensity is the amount of time pressure that workers experience on the job. Empirical evidence indicates that the proportion of Americans who feel time pressure has increased in recent decades. For example, the percentage of adults (aged 18–64) who say that they always feel rushed on their jobs has increased from 24 percent in 1965 to 38 percent in 1992, although this percentage declined slightly, to 33 percent, in 1995 (Robinson and Godbey 1997, 232).

Another indicator of work intensity is the extent to which people say they feel overworked. This perception is directly related to the number of hours people work. In 1997, for example, 37 percent of full-time workers and 19 percent of part-timers felt that they were overworked (Galinsky, Kim, and Bond 2001). Among those working fifty or more hours a week, 45 percent said that they were overworked, compared to 6 percent of those who worked between one and nineteen hours a week. About a quarter of those who worked the same or fewer hours than they prefer said that they felt overworked, compared to 44 percent of those who worked more hours than they preferred. These results suggest that the two dimensions of overwork are positively related to each other; people who work a large number of hours are more likely to feel overworked.

However, even workers who work relatively few hours in a week—and even fewer hours than they prefer—may still feel that they are overworked, consistent with the idea that people may be overworked and underworked at the same time (see Bluestone and Rose 1997).

CONSEQUENCES OF OVERWORKING

People who feel that they are overworked are likely to experience negative consequences with regard to their health and well-being. They are also apt to feel resentment toward their employers and coworkers. Moreover, they are likely to experience work-family conflict (Chapter 9); in particular, single mothers and dual-earner parents are likely to have difficulties coordinating their work and family roles.

People who work too hard are likely to suffer negative physical as well as psychological consequences. The Japanese, for example, have been regarded as a society in which hard work is regarded as a virtue and people work intensely for many hours a week. The Japanese have a term, *karoshi*, meaning "death from overwork," that illustrates the negative health consequences of working too hard.[15] The major causes of death associated with *karoshi* are stress and stress-related heart attacks. The first reported case of *karoshi* (in 1969) was the death due to a stroke of a twenty-nine-year-old married male worker in the

[15]See, for example, en.wikipedia.org/wiki/Karoshi.

shipping department of a large newspaper company. The media began reporting this phenomenon in the latter part of the 1980s, when a number of high-ranking business executives in their prime working ages suddenly died of brain and heart ailments. Once the phenomenon received a label and its symptoms were publicized, people became more aware of it and statistics began to be published in 1987. It was estimated in 1990 that over 10,000 people were dying each year from *karoshi*.

A major consequence of overworking—whether produced by working too many hours or by working too intensely—is stress (e.g., Sparks, Cooper, Fried, and Shirom 1997).[16] Workers who feel rushed and experience great time pressure to get things done are more likely to feel stressed out. Overwork constitutes a major stressor (that is, a chronic strain and a daily hassle), along with major negative life events, such as a divorce or death of a loved one. Workers who experience a feeling of being rushed or not having enough time to get work done (called "high subjective time pressure," an indicator of high work intensity) are also more likely to report that they are depressed. Roxburgh (2004), for example, found that men and especially women who feel themselves under time pressure are more likely to be depressed.

Moreover, there is an overwhelming body of research that links stress to a wide variety of physical ailments, including heart attacks and strokes, as well as diabetes and a weakened immune system. In addition, overwork may lead to greater

---

[16]Stress, of course, is related to other mismatches too, such as unemployment (Chapter 7) and declining rates of pay (Chapter 8).

consumption of junk foods, further harming one's health. Workers who report that they have high levels of stress are also more likely to have high health care costs. A recent study, for example, estimated that highly stressed workers incurred health care costs 46 percent (or $600 per person) higher than other employees (Schwartz 2004).

Corporate reorganization has also been linked to health problems. Studies from Scandinavia, for example, have shown that there is a strong link between corporate downsizing and physical illness such as the risk of heart attacks (Schwartz 2004).

The negative health consequences of overwork are also likely to generate costs for employers and society. It has been estimated that workplace stress costs the US $300 billion each year in health care costs and missed work and that stress-related illnesses cost England 13 million working days each year (Schwartz 2004). In addition, workers who are stressed are more apt to make mistakes at work, which can have severe consequences depending on the nature of the job (Galinsky, Kim, and Bond 2001). Most people would rather not fly on an airplane if the pilot has not had enough sleep, for example, or be operated on by a surgeon who is overwhelmed by the number of patients she has to serve.

There are several factors that mitigate the impact of overwork on stress and other health outcomes. Assumptions about a zero-sum approach to time are based on the scarcity hypothesis of human energy, which emphasizes that playing multiple roles may result in role overload. The empirical literature supports this view only partially. Barnett and Baruch (1985), for example, found that it was the quality of experience, not necessarily the number of roles that people play, that affected outcomes such as role conflict, role overload, and anxiety. An alternative view to the scarcity hypothesis is the expansion approach, which argues that human activity produces as well as consumes energy; thus playing multiple roles may energize people rather than drain them (Marks 1977).

Another factor that may mitigate the negative consequences of working long hours or working intensely is the amount of control people have over their schedules as well as the content of their work. Workers who can control when they work have more flexibility and thus tend to experience fewer of the negative effects associated with working long hours or nonstandard schedules. Flexibility gives workers control over their work time, and control in itself is beneficial. The literature on the effects of job and personal control on health and well-being indicates that lack of control over scheduling matters a great deal for family and health outcomes (Fenwick and Tausig 2001).

About 27 percent of the US work force recently reported that they could change their daily starting and ending times of work, an increase from 12 percent in 1985 (Golden 2001). This increase in flexibility represents a step in the right direction, but the provision of flexibility in the timing of work is not keeping pace with the demand for control that has accompanied increases in hours worked and work intensity discussed in this chapter. The proportion of people who are overworked still exceeds those who are able to control their work schedules.

Moreover, there is a great deal of disparity in schedule flexibility based on workers' demographic, work, and job characteristics. Women, non-whites, and those with less education tend to have less control over their work schedules. On the other hand, control over schedules is greater for workers who work many hours (fifty hours or more a week), are highly educated, are married, and work part-time (Golden 2001).

The desirability of flexibility underscores the distinction between looking at mismatches from the point of view of workers as opposed to employers. Flexibility has different meanings and consequences for workers and employers. Thus, while workers desire to have flexibility in their own schedules, the notion of flexible jobs is often defined from the employers' perspectives. Workers are expected to come in at odd hours on short notice, with little regard for their outside obligations. This situation provides flexibility for employers, not workers.

REDUCING OVERWORK

Overwork results from both the choices made by workers (although these choices are often constrained by economic realities) and the pressures imposed by employers. Policies designed to alleviate overwork should thus focus both on giving workers more control over the duration and timing of work hours as well as on buffering them from the pressures of their jobs. At the same time, these policies need to be sensitive to the needs of employers for greater flexibility.

It is particularly important to give parents—especially working women and dual-earner couples—greater flexibility and control over their working time. Such control would also help to alleviate the work-family mismatches we discuss in Chapter 9. Flexibility would enable mothers and fathers to balance their economic needs with their roles as parents. Public policy should focus on creating more flexible schedules for the 73 percent of workers who do not have flexibility (Golden

2001). Organizations and employers in the United States have been slow to adapt to dual-earner families and need to help workers better balance their work and family lives.

Giving workers more control over their schedules and what they do at work would also help to reduce feelings of being rushed at work or feeling time pressure because of the intense pace of work. To some extent, the division of labor within organizations constrains the amount of control people can have over their work activities and schedules; the work of teams, for example, is often compromised if workers do not show up for work at certain times or work hard enough when things need to get done. These pressures are likely to increase, since there is more work being done in teams now. Nevertheless, there are more possibilities for providing flexibility to frontline workers than is often recognized.

Policies designed to alleviate overwork in the United States might draw upon lessons provided by debates about work time in other countries, especially in Europe. Compared to workers in the United States, European workers work fewer hours per week and per year; the proportion of Europeans working fewer than 35 hours increased dramatically between 1995 and 2000, and the proportion working more than 45 hours has fallen during this period (Boisard et al. 2003). Working couples also work fewer hours in European countries than they do in the United States. In addition to working fewer hours, workers in other countries have better benefits such as day care and family leave to ease the conflict between work and family. These benefits reduce the burden of overwork and ease the stress on family life (see Chapter 9).

There are important cultural differences as well as economic and political conditions that affect the nature of working time arrangements (Fagan 2001). In the Netherlands, France, and Germany, for example, there is strong commitment to reducing work time and flexible scheduling. In the Nordic countries, there are extended opportunities for parental leave and opportunities to work part-time in a wide range of occupations.

Time arrangements are being restructured across Europe along with the spread of arrangements for dual-earner couples. These changes are reshaping gender roles and providing more opportunities for men and women to develop new ways of combining their employment and domestic lives. By contrast, reduction of work time has failed to gain political support in Britain and the United States. A prerequisite for greater gender equality at home and in the workplace is a more even balance in the amount of hours that men and women are employed.

There are limits to what we can learn from these lessons from abroad, however. American companies are not the only ones trying to address problems of work intensity and overwork and their negative consequences for stress and physical health. European companies, such as those in Germany and France, are also experiencing economic problems and competitive pressures and see the possibility of raising the number of hours worked as a way to deal with these pressures (Landler 2004). One way European companies have responded to these competitive pressures is by reducing their generous vacation policies.

There has also been an intensification of work in Europe. For example, the proportion of workers who say that they have to work at very high speed and meet tight deadlines increased from 1991 to 1996 (Green and McIntosh 2001).

Overwork, then, might be seen as a necessary effect of increased pressures produced by internationalization, technological innovation, and other sources of competition among organizations. But overwork is not the only possible response to these pressures. Empowering workers by giving them greater control over their jobs and working time is another way to alleviate mismatches related to overwork as well as enhance an organization's competitiveness by reducing labor turnover and increasing productivity.

Chapter Seven
TEMPORAL MISMATCHES:
UNDERWORKING

EMILY IS AN ASIAN AMERICAN WOMAN who is employed for twenty hours a week as an accounting technician for a construction company near her home in the northeast part of the United States. She is forty-five years old and finished two years of college. She is married and has two children, a boy and a girl. She took this job fifteen years ago because it was close to her home and it enabled her to take care of her children and do housework and other chores. Now her children are attending private universities on the West Coast. She would like to work more hours in order to earn more money, which the family needs with the children in college. Her salary is $11.00 an hour, much less than full-time accountants in her area earn. She would also like to receive benefits such as health insurance, which her company provides only to full-time workers. However, Emily cannot find a full-time job in her area, and she does not want to move outside the region in order to look for a full-time job, because she has a large circle of friends in her church and is active in her community. While she is not happy with her job situation, she realizes things could be worse. In particular, she considers herself lucky compared to her sister Lynn, who also lives in her neighborhood and has been unable to find a job at all, despite trying for the past year.

Some workers are not able to work as much as they would

like, in contrast to the workers discussed in the previous chapter. We use the term *underworking* to denote a mismatch in which people are not able to work as many hours as they need or would like.

The most common form of underworking is represented by people who work part-time (in the United States, part-time is usually defined as working less than thirty-five hours a week) but would rather work full-time. Government statisticians define this group as involuntary part-time workers. These workers are employed part-time for economic reasons such as an inability to find full-time work because of slack business conditions or seasonality of the work; for example, construction workers in certain parts of the country are often unable to work full-time in the winter. These part-timers are distinguished from those who work part-time for non-economic reasons such as going to school, taking care of children and other family obligations, or other personal reasons. The latter group is referred to as voluntary part-time workers, and since they presumably work less than thirty-five hours a week because they have chosen to do so, we will not consider them mismatched to their jobs.

An extreme form of underworking is not having a job at all. The term "unemployment" refers to the situation when a person wants to work but is unable to find a job. Unemployment reflects the failure to establish a job-person match at all, rather than a mismatch. However, since government statisticians define unemployment as a condition in which a person is actively seeking a job but is unable to find one, unemployed persons might also be considered mismatched, since they do not have a job that enables them to work as much as they want. Workers who do not have jobs and who have given up looking for one are called "discouraged" workers rather than unemployed; these workers could also be regarded as mismatched because they might still want to work if they felt they had a realistic chance of obtaining a job. Being unemployed has important consequences for individuals and their families, as well as for employers and society in general; in this chapter we will consider unemployment a second form of underworking.

There are other ways to think about underworking. For example, the opposite of work intensity is working in a job that is dull and boring, and does not allow workers to perform up to their potential. Such people may work their desired number of hours, but in jobs they do not find challenging; an example might be the person who quits her job as a well-paid accountant because she is bored with it and decides to become a golf instructor.

Moreover, workers could be considered underworking if they engage in active or passive resistance (Hodson 2001) or if they fail to perform up to their potential at work because they are soldiering or shirking. These problems have often preoccupied managers, who have sought to design jobs so as to prevent this kind of underworking from interfering with an organization's productivity and performance. These additional types of underworking are not our concern in this chapter.

EXPLAINING UNDERWORKING

The basic reason why people are underworked or underemployed is that they have little power in the labor market and little control over their employment situations. People have low market power for two reasons that we have previously discussed. First, some underemployed persons lack the skills and other qualifications to find full-time jobs or any job at all. These people tend to be underqualified for the jobs that are available (Chapter 4). Second, other underemployed persons are not underqualified, but are still unable to compete for full-time jobs that fit their qualifications because they are geographically constrained for various reasons (Chapter 5).

But underworking, like all the mismatches we discuss in this book, is not explained solely by the characteristics of individuals. Rather, mismatches result from the interplay of individuals' attributes with the characteristics of jobs and workplaces. Thus, employers' desire for greater flexibility and reduced costs are major factors in the growth of part-time jobs, especially those that workers take involuntarily for economic reasons. Moreover, decreases in the demand for particular goods and services are likely to cause unemployment in the industries that produce them.

Underworking: Empirical Evidence
The three survey questions we used to assess overworking in the last chapter can also be adapted to determine the percentage of workers who would like to work more hours than they currently work. The percentages of workers considered underworked according to these three measures are presented in Table 7.1.

In the late 1990s, about 19 percent of men and women in the United States (slightly more men than women) said that the number of hours they wanted to work in a week was greater than the number of hours they actually worked. These percentages are only one-third as large as the percentages of workers who said the opposite—that their ideal number of hours was less than the number of hours they actually worked (see Table 6.1).

Table 7.1

PERCENTAGES OF PERCEIVED UNDERWORKING

IN THE UNITED STATES

	Men	Women
Actual hours worked<Ideal hours[a]	19.3	18.5
Want to spend more time on paid work[b]		
Full-time wants more hours	18	10
Part-time wants more hours	2	4
Part-time wants full-time	5	5
Want to work more hours and earn more money[c]		
1989	37.2	27.5
1998	37.5	28.3

[a]Source: National Study of the Changing Workforce, 1997. Reported in Jacobs and Gerson (2004), Table 3.1.
[b]Source: General Social Survey, 1998. Reported in Reynolds (2003), Table 2.
[c]Source: General Social Surveys, 1989, 1998, author's calculations.

When the question is changed slightly to ask whether workers wished to spend more or less time in paid work without specifying the number of ideal or actual hours, we find that a higher percentage of male workers (25 percent) and the same percentage of women (19 percent) said that they would prefer to work more hours. The majority of workers classified as underworked by this last measure were full-time workers who wanted to work even more hours. The proportion of employed men and women who work full-time but prefer to work part-time (9 percent and 21 percent, respectively—see Table 6.1) is higher than the proportion of workers who work part-time but say they prefer to work full-time (5 percent for both men and women—see Table 7.1).

Finally, when workers were asked whether they would like to work more hours and earn more money, the percentages of workers classified as underworked on this basis are much greater; about 37 percent of men and 28 percent of women in both 1989 and 1998 said they would like to work more hours if this meant that they would be able to earn more money. These percentages are considerably larger than the proportion of workers who said they want to work fewer hours and earn less money.

The results for this last measure of underworking underscore the financial pressures that are often the major motivation for people to want to work more hours. As in the previous chapter, this question is relevant mainly to workers whose compensation is tied explicitly to the number of hours they work; it is less important to those who earn the same amount of money regardless of how many hours they work. For some of these salaried workers, however, a desire to work more hours may be tied to their perceptions that working longer and harder would advance their careers, as illustrated by the example of Kelly the lawyer in the previous chapter.

INVOLUNTARY PART-TIME EMPLOYMENT

As we noted above, government statisticians assume that workers who work part-time for economic reasons, such as bad business conditions which prevent them from obtaining full-time jobs, are involuntary part-time workers, and those who work part-time for noneconomic or personal reasons such as taking care of a family are voluntary part-time workers.[17]

It is reasonable to assume that workers who work part-time because of poor business conditions or seasonal demand for their occupations are doing so involuntarily. These part-time workers have little control over their ability to find full-time work if their difficulty is due to poor economic conditions. Their hours of work may also be reduced by bad weather or shortages of raw materials; all these factors are beyond the worker's control. Thus, we assume that they would take a full-time job if it was offered and it makes sense to consider them mismatched to their jobs.

It may be less defensible to consider those who work part-time for noneconomic reasons as voluntary part-time workers. It may well be that many choose to work part-time because it provides them the flexibility to take care of children or other family members, or to engage in church, recreational, volunteer, or other activities. On the other hand, it also very likely that people's choices are constrained, and while workers may be said to choose their jobs, the range of choices available to them may be

---

[17]Between 1995 and 1999, the most common reason given by workers for working part-time involuntarily was slack work or poor business conditions (about 19 percent of men and 9 percent of women). Another 10 percent of men and 8 percent of women said that they could find only part-time work. The most common noneconomic reason given by women for working part-time in the 1990s is to satisfy family or other personal obligations (34 percent of women, compared to only about 3 percent of men). The most often cited noneconomic reason given by men for working part-time is to be able to go to school or to receive training (39 percent of men and about 22 percent of women) (see Hudson, Kalleberg, and Rosenfeld 2005).

greatly restricted. Their choices may still be involuntary in the sense that they are doing something they do not really want.

Indeed, what persons choose may depend largely on what they perceive as their other options. For example, some women classified as working part-time voluntarily might well prefer full-time work if they could obtain adequate and affordable child care (Cassirer 2003). Moreover, an unknown number of voluntary part-time workers are employed for fewer hours not because they do not want to work full-time, but because disability or inadequate transportation prevents them from doing so (Kalleberg 1995). While they may claim that they are voluntarily working part-time for personal or noneconomic reasons, they might have claimed involuntary part-time status if they were able to find suitable transportation or child care. Classifying such people as working part-time voluntarily underestimates the number of part-time workers who are mismatched.

Characteristics of Involuntary Part-Time Employment

In the late 1990s, the part-time workforce in the United States comprised nearly one-fifth of all American workers—more than 26 million. Women are much more likely than men to work part-time; only about 11 percent of men worked part-time, compared to 27 percent of women. This gender difference in part-time employment continues a consistent pattern in the United States for at least half a century.

In the late 1950s, only about 12 percent of the US labor force worked part-time. This figure increased slowly to around 14 percent in the late 1960s. Then, as large numbers of women began to enter the labor force and the economy began to shift from manufacturing to services, part-time employment increased sharply. Between 1968 and 1983, the part-time employment rate rose from 14 percent to 18.4 percent. Since the early 1980s, the proportion of part-time workers has remained fairly stable at about 18 percent of the labor force, although the figure has fluctuated up or down by 1 to 2 percent in response to movements of the business cycle.[18] The stability in the part-time employment rate over the past quarter century suggests that claims of a dramatic explosion of part-time jobs in recent years are exaggerated (M. Phillips 1997; *Economist* 1997).

The sharp rise in part-time employment between 1968 and 1983 was largely the result of large numbers of workers taking part-time jobs for economic reasons (involuntary part-time employment). Since the late 1960s, the proportion of involuntary part-time workers has increased at a rate of 15 percent each year (Stratton 1996), accounting for over 90 percent of the growth in part-time employment during this period (Tilly 1996, 15).

Of part-time workers during the mid-1990s, about 27 percent of men and about 15 percent of women were classified by the Department of Labor as working part-time involuntarily for economic reasons. Therefore, about 3 percent of employed men and about 4 percent of employed women work part-time involuntarily.[19]

---

[18]For more information on the number of part-time workers in the United States, see Nardone 1995 and the data on part-time work provided at www.bls.gov/webapps/legacy/cpsatab5.htm.

[19]10.8 percent of men work part-time, 26.8 percent of them for economic reasons, while 26.6 percent of women work part-time, 14.6 percent of them for economic reasons.

Individual Correlates of Involuntary Part-Time Work

People who work part-time involuntarily are more likely to have low qualifications. For example, workers who have a high school diploma (or less) are more likely to work part-time involuntarily than to be employed full-time. In addition, male and female workers who are not citizens of the United States (and thus less likely to have acquired the skills—especially soft skills—and qualifications that lead to success in the labor market) are more likely to work part-time involuntarily than are US citizens.

Moreover, nonwhites, especially blacks and Hispanics who can be classified in any racial group, are more likely to work part-time involuntarily than to have a full-time job. Whites are more apt to be employed full-time. These racial differences parallel those that we have seen elsewhere throughout this book and underscore the greater likelihood that nonwhites have jobs that do not match their needs and preferences.

Structural Determinants of Involuntary Part-Time Work

Some have argued that changes in the rate of part-time employment have been generated mainly by the demand side of the labor market and the needs of employers, rather than by supply side considerations such as the choices made by workers (Callaghan and Hartmann 1991). This position is consistent with the finding that almost all the cyclical changes in the part-time employment rate since the early 1970s can be attributed to the growth of involuntary part-time employment.

Moreover, part-time employment tends to be countercyclical, increasing when the unemployment rate is high and declining when it is low. A greater proportion of workers are likely to turn to part-time jobs in times of recession because full time work is less likely to be available. Workers who would otherwise be employed full-time are forced to work part-time because of poor business conditions.

In recessionary times, companies may reduce the number of hours people work in order to cut costs without layoffs. For example, the investment firm of Charles Schwab took a variety of steps in 2001 to avoid cutting staff—it designated some Fridays as voluntary days off without pay for employees without clients and encouraged workers to take unused vacation time and unpaid leaves. In this way employers may be able to reduce the number of hours that employees work without turning full-time jobs into part-time jobs. Similarly, manufacturers can cut overtime hours as a way to reduce payroll without resorting to layoffs (A. Bernstein 2001).

Companies may also seek to cut costs of benefits such as medical insurance and retirement by hiring more part-timers. It has been well documented that part-timers receive fewer fringe benefits than full-time workers in the United States, as well as earn lower wages per hour (Kalleberg, Reskin, and Hudson 2000). Employers in the United States are legally allowed to pay workers less per hour if they work part-time rather than full-time; indeed, paying workers differently based on the number of hours they work per week is one of the few legal bases on which employers can still discriminate. This potential cost saving constitutes an important motivation for employers to use part-timers, especially when business conditions are poor.

Part-time employment can also be seen as a way to create a just-in-time workforce that provides employers with greater flexibility to vary hours worked according to seasonal changes, as in retail sales, which has busy seasons such as Christmas, or in construction, where demand varies depending on the weather. When business conditions improve, however, workers will take full-time jobs if they can get them, and it may become harder for companies to sustain a strategy of hiring part-timers.

Many of the cost issues related to hiring part-time workers were illustrated dramatically by the strategy used by United Parcel Service (UPS). This company relied heavily on part-time workers, maintaining that the nature of the delivery business requires part-time work done at non-standard hours, such as sorting packages overnight. Utilizing part-time workers enabled UPS to pay a lower hourly wage than it paid to its full-time workers and avoid paying the part-timers fringe benefits. This strategy was challenged in a costly fifteen-day strike by the Teamsters Union in August, 1997, that highlighted the part-time issue and generated public support for giving these workers, many of whom had worked at UPS for a long time, a chance at full-time jobs. As a result, UPS agreed to create 10,000 full-time jobs over the next five years, expanding its full-time positions by 34 percent while part-time positions grew just 18 percent. Nevertheless, there are still many part-time workers at UPS who want full-time work but have not yet been able to obtain it (Grow 2002).

Workers who are not unionized (unlike UPS employees, who belong to the Teamsters) are more likely to be vulnerable to employers' efforts to cut labor costs by reducing hours worked or creating part-time jobs. Consistent with this reasoning, full-time workers are much more likely to belong to a union than are involuntary part-time workers.

Male workers in central cities are also more likely to work part-time involuntarily than to work full-time (see Hudson, Kalleberg, and Rosenfeld 2005); women's work is less likely to be affected by spatial mismatches (Chapter 5).

UNEMPLOYMENT

Some kinds of unemployment are regarded as more problematic than others. Frictional unemployment, for example, is temporary and occurs when people move from one job to another. This type of unemployment is a normal feature of an industrial society, as job vacancies are created through retirements, dismissals, and quitting and workers compete for these vacancies. This kind of unemployment is not really a mismatch but rather an indication that labor markets are operating efficiently and effectively.

More problematic is the type of unemployment discussed in Chapter 4—structural unemployment—which is likely to involve long-term joblessness. Here, there may be job vacancies as well as people seeking employment, but these jobs and people do not match for one reason or another. Explanations for the failure to achieve a match include job seekers being underqualified, limited by geographic constraints, or lacking information about job vacancies.

Workers not able to find jobs at all are likely to have many of the same disadvantages—lack of power in the labor market and low control over their employment situations—as those who work part-time involuntarily. For example, unemployed persons are likely to be underqualified for the jobs in their location and apt to face constraints on their mobility that prevent them from moving to areas where there are jobs that are compatible with their qualifications and needs. They may also be victims of discriminatory hiring practices that keep them from jobs that would otherwise constitute a good match.

Studying Unemployment

The official US unemployment rate is calculated as the percentage of persons in the civilian labor force (that is, at least 16 years of age and not in the military or a hospital) who (1) do not have paid jobs, (2) have actively sought work within the past four weeks through means such as answering a want ad or registering with an employment agency, and (3) are available for work if it is offered.

Table 7.2 shows unemployment rates in the United States from 1947 to 2004 broken down for men and women and for various race and ethnic groups. The overall 2004 unemployment rate is lower than the average rates for the years from 1973 to 1989, comparable to those for the period 1989–2000, and higher than the averages from 1947 to 1973.[20] Men had lower unemployment rates than women in the United States from 1947 to 1989, although in recent years women have had slightly lower unemployment rates.

Racial differences in unemployment rates have always been

[20]Up-to-date information on unemployment rates can be found on the home page for the Current Population Surveys conducted by the Bureau of Labor Statistics: www.bls.gov/cps/home.htm. Unemployment rates may differ over the course of a year, since some jobs are part-year or seasonal. Thus, annual averages are better indicators of the rate of unemployment.

Table 7.2

UNEMPLOYMENT RATES IN THE UNITED STATES, 1947–2004[a]

Annual averages	Total	Men	Women	White	African American	Hispanic
1947–1967	4.7	4.5	5.3	—	—	—
1967–1973	4.6	4.0	5.7	5.8	—	7.5
1973–1979	6.5	5.8	7.5	6.8	12.5	9.5
1979–1989	7.1	7.0	7.3	5.5	14.7	10.3
1989–2000	5.6	5.6	5.5	4.2	10.8	8.6
2001	4.8	4.8	4.7	4.2	8.7	6.6
2003	6.0	6.3	5.7	5.2	10.8	7.7
2004	5.5	5.6	5.4	4.8	10.4	7.0

[a]Source: Mishel, Bernstein, and Allegretto 2005, Table 3.1. Figures for 2004 were obtained from Bureau of Labor Statistics' Current Population Surveys.

more pronounced than gender differences. Whites, for example, have unemployment rates much lower than those for African Americans and Hispanics (who can be classified in any racial group); in the years 1989 to 2000, the average unemployment rate for whites was about 4 percent, compared to nearly 11 percent for African Americans and nearly 9 percent for Hispanics.

The unemployment rate also differs sharply among educational categories (not shown in Table 7.2); in 2003, for example, the rate for college graduates was about 3 percent, compared to almost 9 percent for those with less than a high school diploma. People with a high school diploma and some college had unemployment rates between 5 and 6 percent (Mishel, Bernstein, and Allegretto 2005, 232).

Unemployment rates in the United States are in the middle of the range of unemployment rates for other OECD countries.

The overall US unemployment rate of 5.8 percent in 2002, for example, was greater than the unemployment rates in the same year for Japan (5.4 percent), the United Kingdom (5.1 percent), Norway (3.9 percent), and Sweden (4.9 percent), but was less than the unemployment rates for Germany (8.6 percent), France (8.8 percent), Italy (9.0 percent), and Spain (11.3 percent) (Mishel, Bernstein, and Allegretto 2005, 419).

A criticism of the official government unemployment rate is that it underestimates the problem of joblessness because it doesn't count people who have given up looking for a job; one requirement for being considered unemployed by government statisticians is that the person reports having looked for work within the past four weeks. This criterion disqualifies people without jobs who would like to be employed but are not actively seeking a job, perhaps because they feel their chances of getting a job are so low (Castillo 1998). This is often the case with spatially mismatched workers, for example, who see no hope of finding suitable employment in their area. These discouraged workers consist of about 40 percent more people than those officially counted as unemployed in the OECD countries (Livingstone 1998, 66).

A broader measure of unemployment might be an *underemployment* rate. This category would include those who are officially counted as unemployed and those who are working part-time involuntarily. It would also include those who are marginally attached to the labor force such as discouraged workers as well as those who have looked for a job within the past twelve months as opposed to four weeks. Adding the involuntary part-time workers (4.3 million people) and marginally attached (5.1 million people) to those officially counted as unemployed in the United States in April 2005 (7.7 million people or 5.2 percent), for example, would yield an under-employment rate of 11.1 percent—a total of 17.1 million people.[21]

CONSEQUENCES OF UNDERWORKING

An important consequence of underworking is that people may not have adequate income from their jobs. Of course this is especially true for unemployment, since unemployment insurance benefits are inadequate to replace lost income and run out after a fixed period of time. Moreover, approximately only one-third of all unemployed people receive unemployment insurance benefits today, and less than half of the unemployed are even eligible for such benefits (Osterman 1999, 125).

But those who work part-time for economic reasons may also find their earnings are inadequate to meet their needs and those of their families. Moreover, part-time and unemployed workers do not receive fringe benefits such as health insurance or pension benefits, which are generally provided only to full-time workers, if at all. This contrasts sharply with the situation in many European countries, where health insurance is a right of citizenship, not a reward of employment.

Involuntary Part-Time Work

Workers who work part-time involuntarily are more likely to have substandard jobs—low-skilled, low-paying, low-security jobs that do not provide health insurance or retirement bene-

[21]Current information on official and hidden employment is provided by the National Jobs for All Coalition at their website (www.njfac.org/jobnews.html).

fits. These part-time jobs have been described by some (Tilly 1996) as constituting "half a job." These poor-quality part-time jobs are created by employers in order to obtain flexibility and to cut labor costs, as contrasted to those part-time jobs that employers create in an effort to retain valued employees by giving them more flexibility to take care of their family and other personal needs (Hudson, Kalleberg, and Rosenfeld 2005).

The negative economic consequences of working part-time involuntarily are more problematic for some people than others. A relatively high percentage of young workers (eighteen to twenty-nine years old) are working in part-time jobs for economic reasons. The proportion of young men involuntarily employed part-time is especially high (47.4 percent). We expect that many of these young people are likely to leave these kinds of jobs after they enter their thirties and move into full-time jobs. For these young workers, involuntary part-time employment is a temporary career stage on the way to better jobs in the future and may provide them with the flexibility to attend school and engage in other activities.

By contrast, there are a substantial number of single parents working part-time involuntarily without the help of a working spouse (Hudson, Kalleberg, and Rosenfeld 2005). For them, working in half a job means half an income and few, if any, benefits. These families are likely to suffer a range of negative consequences, economic and otherwise.

Unemployment

Unemployment also has a number of important negative economic and noneconomic consequences for individuals and their families, as well as the society in general. Unemployment results in a reduction of economic buying power. It reduces one's integration into the social world and thereby enhances feelings of alienation (or separation) from society. It often makes it difficult to replace the order and structure in one's life that are provided by going to work each day. Unemployment also creates a sense of insecurity and pessimism about the future and reduces people's ability to plan ahead for themselves and their families. The unemployed are also likely to lower their expectations regarding the kinds of jobs and earnings that they think they will be able to get in the future (so-called "job skidding"). In addition, the unemployed are apt to experience reductions in their confidence, self-esteem, and sense of control over their lives.

All these negative consequences are exacerbated if unemployment lasts for a long time. Long-term unemployment, generally defined by statisticians as seeking but going without paid work for twenty-seven weeks or more, is the most severe form of joblessness, and workers who are long-term unemployed face considerable financial and personal hardships often associated with health care difficulties and a loss of unemployment benefits.

The percentage of unemployed persons classified as long-term unemployed is growing and is the highest it has been so long after a recession ended than at any time since World War II (Uchitelle 2005).[22] Some groups in the population were

[22]The highest share of long-term unemployment on record in the United States was 23.9 percent in 1983 (the unemployment rate at this time was 9.9 percent), followed by 22.1 percent in 2003 (with an unemployment rate of 6.1 percent) (Mishel, Bernstein, and Allegretto 2005, 239). The relatively high share of long-term unemployment during these periods reflects the difficulties unemployed

more likely to experience long-term unemployment than others in recent years. For example, men are more likely to be unemployed for more than twenty-seven weeks than women, and whites are more apt to be long-term unemployed than African Americans or Hispanics. Long-term unemployed persons also tend to have relatively low education; over half of this group had a high school education or less in the 2000s. However, people with a bachelor's degree or more experienced a nearly 300 percent increase in long-term unemployment between 2000 and 2003, illustrating the weakness of the recovery from the 2001 recession in the information sector and in professional and business services (Mishel, Bernstein, and Allegretto 2005, 242–43). Indeed, the incidence of long-term unemployment among the groups most likely to suffer from long stretches of joblessness in the past, such as less educated blue-collar workers, appears to have fallen in recent years (Uchitelle 2005).

Reasons for the recent high levels of long-term unemployment include the reluctance of employers to hire workers on a permanent basis because of their uncertainty about the future of the economy, as well as the difficulties that baby boomers, men, and whites may have had in finding jobs (especially relatively well-paying jobs) that utilize their skills and experience and acquiring new skills after losing their jobs.

Unemployment also has profound impacts on society. The government provides income assistance to those out of work through unemployment insurance, at least for some people for some period of time. Society must also pay for the negative

---

workers had in obtaining jobs during these years, both of which followed recessionary periods.

consequences of unemployment experienced by individuals and their families that may result from increased stress and its psychological and physical correlates—depression, insecurity, family conflict, violence, and alcoholism, among others. Society also does without the goods and services that would have been provided by those who are not working.

Reducing Underwork

As we have argued, underworking results largely from workers' lack of power in the labor market and control over their employment situations. This vulnerability is often rooted in their inadequate skills and qualifications as well as constraints on their mobility because of family obligations, geographical mismatches, or lack of information about job opportunities. This vulnerability forces some people to work part-time rather than full-time or to go without work altogether.

Reducing this vulnerability is a necessary step toward alleviating mismatches associated with underworking. The strategies we discussed in Chapter 4 for raising workers' qualifications and in Chapter 5 for reducing spatial mismatch are likely also to help address the kinds of underemployment and underworking discussed in this chapter. Thus, workers are less likely to be underemployed if they have the skills and qualifications to do the jobs that are vacant, if they are able to obtain better information about the job opportunities that are available, and if they are able to move freely to locations where the jobs for which they are qualified are found.

Policy interventions directed at the labor supply side and at changing characteristics of workers are not likely to be sufficient to alleviate mismatches due to underemployment, however. As we have also argued in this chapter, the growth in part-time jobs which workers would rather not have, because they pay low wages, do not provide benefits, are insecure, and so on, is largely a result of employers' efforts to achieve greater flexibility in labor staffing and to cut labor costs by hiring part-time workers rather than full-timers.

Employers have been able to cut labor costs by creating part-time jobs and eliminating jobs entirely through downsizing and corporate restructuring because workers have not been able to organize and challenge these actions. Therefore, achieving greater control over labor market processes by reviving unions and other collective forms of worker power would help to enact legislation, perhaps modeled after European examples, that prevents earnings discrimination against part-timers. This would be an important step toward alleviating mismatches associated with underworking. Moreover, providing health insurance to all citizens regardless of their employment status would remove it from the costs of labor and reduce the employer's incentive to create part-time jobs.

Chapter Eight
EARNINGS MISMATCHES

RAMÓN IS A THIRTY-TWO-YEAR-OLD Hispanic man who has worked for the past three years as a nursing aide at a small regional hospital in the Southwest. He has a high school diploma and has taken a few classes at the local community college. His job as a nursing aide is hard work, since the hospital is busy and understaffed, and he now has primary responsibility for twenty patients. He works full-time (defined by the hospital as 40 hours a week) at $7.00 an hour and has not been able to take any time off for personal reasons in the past five years. His yearly earnings, less than $15,000 before taxes, are not nearly enough to support himself, his wife, and their two small children. To make matters worse, his wife has a disability which prevents her from working outside the home and she is barely able to care for their children when Ramón is at the hospital. Ramón's job does not provide health insurance, a big problem for him and his family. Ramón has been looking for a second job to supplement his earnings from the hospital, and he thinks he has found a part-time job as a night security guard. This job pays only minimum wage ($5.15 an hour in 2005, which has not increased since 1997) but he feels he needs to take it for his family in order to help make ends meet.

Edward is a fifty-two-year-old white male who spent most of life working his way up through the ranks at one of the biggest banks in the Southeast. He is a college graduate and is married with two college-age children. Ten years ago, he was promoted to assistant manager of a branch bank in a middle-size city and earned $80,000 per year. However, the bank was purchased by a larger bank based in the Northeast, and he was laid off. He tried for two years to find another job in banking, but was unable to find a job that paid as well as his previous one. As a result, a year ago he took a job for an accounting company that prepares people's taxes; he is able to put his banking experience to use by answering questions about financial matters. His salary on the new job is less than half what he earned on his previous job. Because of this, Edward and his wife, Ashley, were forced to sell their house in order to be able to pay their two children's college tuition bills, and they moved to a smaller house in a less prestigious neighborhood. Ashley has taken a job in a grocery store to help maintain their standard of living. Neither Edward nor Ashley has been able to obtain health insurance from their employers; they have been forced to purchase expensive individual policies.

Like Ramón, some people in the United States work for pay but do not earn enough money to meet their needs and those of their families. Some of these people work full-time, and some have more than one job. We refer to these workers as the "working poor," people whose jobs do not provide a livable wage even though they work full-time. These workers are mismatched in the sense that their jobs do not enable them to meet their basic needs.

But not all workers who have earnings mismatches are considered poor. Workers such as Edward are regarded as belonging to the middle class, yet they also have jobs that do not provide enough money to take care of their family's basic needs, such as providing for their children's education and living in their own home. The number of middle-class people who have experienced earnings mismatches has increased in recent years, as earnings have stagnated and layoffs of white-collar workers have become more common because of downsizing and corporate restructing. In addition to experiencing earnings mismatches, neither Ramón nor Edward has job-provided health insurance, so it is difficult or impossible for them to afford good medical care for themselves and their families. We will consider these two kinds of earnings mismatches in this chapter.

THE WORKING POOR

President Lyndon Johnson declared war on poverty in the United States on January 8, 1964. Initially, there was some progress; the official poverty rate decreased from 19.5 percent in 1963 to 11.1 percent in 1971. Unfortunately, this early progress was eroded, and the poverty rate rose again in the 1970s and 1980s before falling in the 1990s. In 2004 it increased to 12.7 percent, a figure slightly higher than thirty years ago. The poor are still very much with us.

The welfare reform movement in the United States in the mid-1990s sought to solve the problem of poverty through work. People were required to find jobs as a condition of receiving some welfare benefits. The problem of the working poor still remains, however, underscoring that work by itself is not the solution to poverty. Perhaps surprisingly, most poor people live in families in which someone is working (Quigley 2003, 20).

Who are the Working Poor?

Measures of poverty are ambiguous and somewhat arbitrary. It is artificial to pick an amount and say that anyone whose earnings fall below that amount is poor. The process of setting the threshold is often a political one; politicians do not like creating inclusive definitions of poverty that classify more people as poor while they are in office.

The poverty thresholds calculated by government statisticians are used for statistics, such as the estimated number of Americans in poverty each year.[23] These thresholds were originally created in 1963 by a government statistician, Mollie Orshansky. They were initially determined by the amount of income needed by low-income families to provide basic food in 1955.

These thresholds have been adjusted over time for different size families to keep pace with inflation, but they are less useful as measures of the poverty that currently exists because they have not been revised to keep up with changes in family budgets. Food made up about a third of the family budget in 1955, but this proportion has decreased since then, and the index does not reflect items that make up a larger part of families' budgets now, such as child care (J. Bernstein 2003) or items that have increased substantially, such as the cost of housing or health care. They also do not consider several other aspects of

---

[23]An additional measure of poverty is represented by the poverty guidelines, a simplification of the poverty thresholds used for administrative purposes such as determining financial eligibility for certain federal programs. For example, for the forty-eight contiguous states and Washington DC, the 2005 Health and Human Services poverty guideline for a family of four is $19,350 per year. About double that is considered "low income."

poverty, including variations in the cost of living from state to state, lack of assets, and nonmaterial aspects, such as poverty of opportunity.[24]

Regardless of the specific definition of poverty, it is generally agreed that the federal poverty thresholds and guidelines are far below the amounts required for a decent living. A recent study, for example, found that it took more than double the federal poverty threshold to provide for a family's basic needs in many places in the United States (Boushey et al. 2001).

In this chapter, we define the working poor as those who receive an hourly wage less than the amount a full-time, year-round worker must earn to sustain a family of four at the government's poverty threshold. In 2003, this hourly wage was $9.04 (Mishel, Bernstein, and Allegretto 2005). This figure is a very low standard for defining the working poor.[25] Using this amount as a reference point, it is clear that it is virtually impossible for a worker to survive in the United States—much less to support a family—while earning the federal minimum wage, which has been $5.15 since 1997, or the $6- to

[24]The poverty threshold also neglects to consider government subsidies such as the Earned Income Tax Credit (EITC), which may be worth as much as $4,000. The EITC, begun in 1975, is the largest federal cash transfer program for lower-income families. The goal of this program is to encourage those who choose to work by providing workers with a refundable credit against federal income taxes. Twenty-two million families currently receive a total of $34 billion from the EITC, helping to raise many families' incomes above the poverty level. Other subsidies include food stamps worth several thousand dollars and Medicaid, worth about another $4,000. Thus, the main government programs to fight poverty—especially the two most costly programs, EITC and Medicaid—are not even counted in the official poverty statistics.

[25]The official poverty line is too low; a more realistic figure is 125 percent higher, which would put the cutoff for poverty at $11.29 an hour.

Table 8.1

CHARACTERISTICS OF LOW-WAGE WORKERS IN THE UNITED STATES COMPARED TO TOTAL LABOR FORCE, 2003[a]

Share of Workforce	24.3%	100.0%
Number	28,280,343	116,288,910
Average hourly wage	7.09	17.15
Female	58.2%	48.2%
Race/ethnicity		
White	58.4%	69.6%
African American	14.0	11.2
Hispanic	21.9	13.4
Asian	3.7	4.2
Other	2.0	1.7
Education		
Less than high school	23.5%	10.6%
High school	36.8	30.6
Associate degree	6.4	9.3
Some college	24.5	20.4
College or more	8.9	29.1
Union member	6.4%	14.6%
Occupations		
Managers/professionals	11.8%	34.1%
Admin/office support	14.6	15.5
Blue-collar	21.6	23.3
Services	34.5	15.8
Sales	15.6	10.6
Other	1.9	0.7
Industries		
Construction	4.2%	6.4%
Manufacturing	9.0	13.6
Durable	4.6	8.5
Nondurable	4.4	5.1

Trade	20.7	14.6
Wholesale	2.1	3.2
Retail	18.6	11.4
Transportation and utilities	3.0	5.4
Financial and information services	5.9	9.9
Services	52.7	43.5
Government	2.2	5.2
Other	2.2	1.3

aSource: Table 5.12 in Mishel, Bernstein, and Allegretto (2005), 341.

$7-an-hour jobs vividly profiled by Barbara Ehrenreich (2001).

Table 8.1 provides an overview of some basic characteristics of low-wage workers in the United States in 2003 (first column) compared to characteristics of the labor force as a whole in that year (second column).

Nearly a quarter (24.3 percent) of the US labor force was classified as low-wage workers by this definition in 2003, accounting for slightly over 28 million workers who work full-time but earn poverty-level wages (see also Shulman 2003; Quigley 2003). This percentage has decreased during the past thirty years; it was nearly 30 percent in 1973 and slightly more than 30 percent in 1989, falling to 25 percent in 2000 (Mishel, Bernstein, and Allegretto 2005, Table 2.9). In the 2000s, poverty increased as the economy recovered from the recession of 2001; this was the first time in history that the poverty rate increased three years in a row at the beginning of an economic recovery.

Over half of the low-wage workers were women (58 percent), even though women constituted less than half the labor force. The working poor are also disproportionately nonwhite; whites constitute about 58 percent of low-wage workers but nearly 70 percent of the labor force as a whole. By contrast, African Americans and Hispanics are overrepresented in the low-wage category relative to their presence in the labor force; over a fifth of low-wage workers are Hispanic. It is also likely that a considerable number of Hispanics are immigrants who generally have a higher poverty rate than nonimmigrants, a gap that is growing (Krueger 2004). Asians, on the other hand, are less likely to be represented in the low-wage group compared to their presence in the labor force.

Low-wage workers are more likely than others to have relatively little education; nearly a quarter did not graduate from high school compared to about 11 percent of the labor force, and six in ten low-wage workers had a high school diploma or less. On the other hand, nearly a quarter (24.5 percent) of low-wage workers had some college education compared to about 20 percent of the labor force as a whole, and 9 percent of low-wage workers were college graduates compared to nearly thirty percent of all workers. These figures do not support the view that the working poor have no higher education or do not have college degrees, since about a third have at least some college education.

Half of all poor families are headed by single women (not shown in Table 8.1—see Shipler 2004). This group was impacted most directly by the welfare reforms enacted in the mid-1990s, which required people to find paid employment in order to qualify for some welfare benefits. By contrast, two-parent families are less likely to be in poverty, largely because such families are more likely to have two wage earners.

Some of the attributes of the working poor (low education and nonwhite) are similar to the characteristics associated with being underqualified or unemployed (see Chapters 4 and 7). Indeed, these three types of mismatch are strongly related to each other and overlap considerably.

Moreover, the working poor are more likely to be concentrated in certain kinds of jobs. For example, they are much more likely to be in service occupations; over a third (34.5 percent) worked in a service occupation, more than twice the percentage in the labor force as a whole. This is unfortunate, since some service occupations play a very important role in the economy and in the lives of many families. For example, there are more than 20,000 home health-care aides in New York City (a high cost of living area), and most are paid only $6–$7 an hour—some earn even less. Nearly all are women, and most receive no health care, no sick pay, and no vacations (Herbert 2002). Low-wage workers are also overrepresented in sales occupations, which include jobs in the big box stores such as Wal-Mart and Target. By contrast, low-wage workers are underrepresented in managerial and professional occupations.

These occupational differences are also reflected in the kinds of industries that employ low-wage workers. The working poor are most apt to be found in the service sector (over half of low-wage workers work in service industries) and in retail. Low-wage workers are less likely to work in manufacturing industries (especially manufacturing of durable goods such as automobiles and steel), financial and information services, and government.

Sales and services occupations, the majority of low-wage jobs, are concentrated in the industries of retail trade, health, social administrative support, personal services, entertainment and recreation, and business services (Thomson 1999). As noted above, the kinds of service jobs in which the working poor are employed are central to the American economy and support those in the population who are often much better paid. These service occupations include low-wage jobs such as: nursing home and health care workers; retail clerks in department stores, grocery stores, and convenience stores; housekeepers and janitors; call center workers; teaching assistants in schools; and child care workers. For examples of low-wage industries in the United States, see the case studies in Appelbaum, Bernhardt, and Murnane 2003.

In addition, the vast majority of low-wage workers (93.6 percent) do not belong to a union; only 6.4 percent of low-wage workers belong to a union, compared to 14.6 percent of the overall labor force.

A review of low-wage employment in Europe (Lucifora, McKnight, and Salverda 2005) concluded that people in the low-wage group in European countries are similar to those in the United States: young people; manual workers; and those working in industries such as retailing, hotels and catering, agriculture, and personal services.

EXPLAINING WORKING POVERTY

The causes of working poverty are complex and belie attempts to blame either the culture or the economy, the attributes of individuals or the structure of job opportunities. David Shipler (2004, 285) summarizes this complexity:

> working poverty is a constellation of forces that magnify one another: not just low wages but low education, not just dead-end jobs but limited abilities, not just insufficient savings but

also unwise spending, not just poor housing but also poor parenting, not just the lack of health insurance but also the lack of healthy households.

In general, the working poor share certain characteristics that exclude them from high-paying jobs, such as inadequate skills, and family or other obligations that limit job search. The extent of the working poor is also greater because of the abundance of low-wage jobs. The relative importance of these two general factors—inadequate skills or work motivations and the proliferation of low-wage jobs—has been the subject of considerable debate and is the framework for creating policy options to alleviate the situation of the working poor.

The view that the working poor are poor because they do not have the skills and education to qualify for higher-paying jobs was the basis for many of the policy interventions of the 1960s that sought to provide training and educational opportunities for workers. Education was widely regarded as the ticket out of poverty. The social scientific rationale behind these antipoverty programs was the human capital theory, which holds that investing in people by giving them more education and training would increase their skills and productivity (see also Chapter 3), making them more employable in higher-paying jobs. This strategy was partly successful, as indicated by the reduction in poverty rates during the 1960s noted above.

Ascribing the source of low-wage work to the inadequate skills and qualifications of workers is still a commonly held viewpoint, as reflected in the claims that there are skills shortages discussed in Chapter 4. Thus, it is often argued that racial minorities lack the technical and soft skills, such as appropriate motivation, to qualify for higher-paying jobs. Others maintain that since women are not willing to invest in the training and education needed to qualify for high-wage, higher-skilled jobs, they have consigned themselves to working in lower-skilled, low-wage jobs.

However, attributing the persistence of the working poor to low qualifications and skills is only partially correct. Otherwise, why would workers who are highly educated and skilled still work in low-wage jobs? As we saw in Table 8.1, for example, about a third of low-wage workers have some college training, and about nine percent of them have college degrees. Moreover, the reductions in the poverty rates achieved during the 1960s were reversed in the 1970s and 1980s, despite the continued emphasis on training and the growth in educational attainment described in earlier chapters.

In addition, people do not necessarily climb out of working poverty by acquiring more skills; their efforts depend also on the state of the economy and supply and demand in labor markets. The very tight labor markets in the United States of the late 1990s, for example, led employers to offer relatively high wages to low-skilled workers, resulting in a decline in poverty levels as low-income families experienced economic improvement. As the economy slowed in the 2000s, however, the demand for less-skilled workers declined, along with their wage gains.

The effects of the economic slowdown in the early 2000s were also exacerbated by the acceleration of globalization; outsourcing of production and labor depressed wages, as did the growth in the supply of low-skilled labor due to immigration.

Lessened demand for low-skilled workers contributed to the stagnation of real wages for most workers in the United States during the past few decades.

Therefore, a more complete understanding of the working poor requires us also to account for the existence and persistence of low-wage jobs.

The Problem of Low-Wage Jobs

In any industrial capitalist economy, there will always be jobs that are paid less than others; some people will be poorer than others. It does not follow from this observation, however, that there must be a large group of jobs that pay wages at or below the poverty level. To say that the problem of poverty will be solved by training the poor and giving these workers more skills neglects to consider whether there are opportunities for them to find jobs that pay above the poverty level.

There has been an increase in low-wage jobs in the United States in recent years as employment in low-paying, labor-intensive industries has expanded rapidly. The two lowest-paid industry categories, retail and service, increased their share of production and nonsupervisory employment from 30 percent to 48 percent from 1965 to 1998 (Shulman 2003, 105). In addition, some writers project that the low end of the job market, such as jobs requiring only short-term on-the-job training, will continue to grow (Hecker 2001).

Many of these low-wage jobs are portrayed as low-skilled and identified as requiring little training (Silvestri 1997). However, low-wage jobs that do not require much training or education should not necessarily be equated with unskilled or low-skilled jobs. Even the lowest-paying jobs in the economy require some skills, although these may not always be cognitive ones; they could also require the other kinds of skills—e.g., motor or interpersonal skills, or soft skills—discussed in Chapter 4.

Labeling jobs as low-skill is partly a distancing device (Shulman 2003, 9) that puts the blame on workers rather than employers who are not willing to pay people adequately for doing these kinds of jobs. Many of these low-skill jobs such as nurses' aides or teachers' aides are traditionally regarded as women's work, requiring emotional skills that are usually not seen as valuable in the labor market. For example, home health-care aides need compassion and psychological and emotional strength; call-center workers must be able to handle information and be patient with callers who are rude and not always aware of what they need. These are real skills just as much as the cognitive skills that are more apt to be rewarded in the labor market and that are usually defined in terms of educational attainment and technical skills.

Low-wage jobs are not necessarily low-skilled, as shown in a study by Howell and Wolff (1991). They found that between 1960 and 1985, high-wage low-skilled jobs, such as automobile assemblers, declined in goods industries, while low-wage jobs requiring moderate skill levels, such as some clerical occupations, nurses' aides, and cashiers, increased in service industries. This suggests that factors other than skill, such as unionization in goods industries, are at least somewhat responsible for the levels of earnings associated with occupations.

If low-wage jobs are not necessarily low-skilled jobs, then why do employers pay them so little? Robert Kuttner (2004, 60) explains the low-wage job problem as mainly the consequence of a new social contract strikingly dif-' ferent from that of the post-World War II boom. . . . the ground rules from the mid-1940s to the mid-1970s included stronger regulation of industries and of labor markets, broader acceptance of trade unions, and more insulation of the domestic economy from speculative international capital flows and low-wage competition. Consequently, ordinary wage and salaried workers had more bargaining power to command more of the total economic product.

Kuttner attributes the persistence and expansion of low-wage jobs to the reduced power of workers to negotiate the terms of their employment. Wage differentials reflect not only skill differences and market mechanisms, but also the relative power of employers and workers and other institutional forces. Low-wage workers are highly vulnerable to labor market processes and have little power to change their employment situations. Their low power is due to the political, economic, and social changes that have occurred in the United States over the past quarter-century, including the deregulation of highly unionized industries, growth in global trade, decline in unionization and in the social contract between business and labor, changes in immigration laws, expansion of temporary work agencies, and so on.

Some employers say they have little choice but to pay low wages. In the case of home health aides in New York City discussed above, most of whom earn $6–7 an hour and in most cases receive no benefits—no health care, no paid vacation, no sick days, no pensions—their union (1199/S.E.I.U.) called a strike against Premier Home Health Care Services, which employs about 3,500 home health aides. The president of Premier, which is reimbursed at the rate of $11 an hour but pays the aides $6.50 an hour, felt that it was horrible the way these workers are treated, but he felt he cannot pay more because the market wouldn't let him (Herbert 2002, A21). In order to be competitive in the marketplace, he felt his pricing needed to reflect what similar companies charged.

However, there is considerable evidence to suggest that employers do have choices about how they respond to economic changes such as increased competitiveness, and may choose to take either the high or low road (Gordon 1996). In the political climate of the United States, employers have not been pressured by unions to take the high road to economic competitiveness, which would involve the creation of high-wage, high-skilled jobs in which workers make more decisions about how to do their work. Rather, employers have often been allowed to take the low road, reducing costs by driving down wages and making their workers work harder. This decision on the part of employers has been supported by a pro-market political consensus that has not been challenged effectively by either political party.

The persistence of low-wage work is also often attributed to broad economic forces such as globalization and trade. It is unlikely that low-wage jobs are due primarily to globalization, since most such jobs are in the service and retail sectors (Herzenberg, Alic, and Wial 1998; Shulman 2003). However, it is probably true that the shrinkage of the higher-paying jobs in the manufacturing sector has resulted in part from globalization. Low-wage jobs such as service jobs (home health care, child care, teaching assistants, and retail clerks) cannot be done overseas. Other factors are likely to be responsible for the low wages associated with less skilled jobs, such as technological changes unrelated to trade; unexpected political developments, such as instability in various parts of the world; and firms' compensation policies (Freeman 1995).

Moreover, the presence of a union can make a big difference for the prospects of low-skilled workers such as call center workers who lack college degrees. Batt, Hunter, and Wilk (2003), for example, found that a unionized call center they studied invested more than twice as much in training and pay and benefits than a similar call center that was not unionized, and the union encouraged promotions. Evidence from Europe (see Lucifora, McKnight, and Salverda 2005) further suggests that unions and collective bargaining reduce the incidence of low-paid jobs.

A key question is whether low-wage jobs are dead-end jobs that trap workers for the rest of their careers, as suggested by the concept in the 1960s of the "secondary labor market," or whether most people are able to escape from them as they acquire more skills (Gordon 1972). Shulman (2003) rejects the idea that working in low-wage work is merely a career stage or a temporary step leading to better jobs, especially for young workers, and argues that low-wage job mobility is minimal, and the idea that people can move up job ladders out of poverty is a myth. In support of this view, Gottschalk and Danziger (1998), using data from the Panel Study of Income Dynamics, found that nearly half of people with earnings in the bottom 20 percent in 1968 were still in that group twenty-three years later. Osterman (1999) found a similar result using the same data; almost half of the men in the bottom earnings quartile in 1979 remained in that quartile in 1995.

There are also fewer better jobs to move into, since the growth in the American economy in recent years has been primarily in low-paying, labor-intensive industries as well as the top end of the occupational structure; there has been relatively little growth in the middle (Wright and Dwyer 2003). There are now fewer job ladders in low-wage jobs than there were in the past (Bernhardt et al. 2001).

A study of whether workers who begin their careers in minimum-wage jobs eventually progress to higher-paying jobs, using the 1979 National Longitudinal Study of Youth, found that after leaving school, most workers move on to higher-paying jobs. At the same time, a significant fraction of workers—more than 8 percent—also spend at least half of their first ten years after leaving school working in jobs paying less than the minimum wage plus $1.00; these workers are mainly women, minorities, and the less educated (Carrington and Fallick 2001). This study looked only at the early career, the first ten years, but the fact that wages generally grow more quickly in the early stages of one's career suggests that some workers will have minimum-wage careers for a long time.

There is also evidence to suggest that low-wage jobs are more likely to be dead-end jobs in the United States than they are in many other industrial countries. For example, one study found that low-wage workers in the United States were likely to remain in the low-wage labor market five years longer than low-wage workers in France, Italy, the United Kingdom, Germany, Denmark, Finland, or Sweden. In another study, poor households in the United States were found to be less likely to leave poverty from one year to the next than were poor households in Canada, Germany, the Netherlands, Sweden, and the United Kingdom (Mishel, Bernstein, and Schmitt 2001).

THE DECLINING MIDDLE CLASS

Earnings mismatches may characterize workers who earn more than the working poor. People who earn more than the poverty wage may be better off than the working poor, but they may still be unable to satisfy their families' needs through paid work. Sociologists often call this group the middle class, because they are midway in the class structure between the rich and the poor.

The middle class historically played an important role in the United States. It has been touted as the economic and political backbone of the country (K. Phillips 1993) and an important carrier of the idea of social mobility, a central component of the culture of economic opportunity in the United States. As long as those in the working poor feel that they can improve their living standards and eventually become part of the middle class, they are likely to remain motivated to work and to support the existing social and economic system, helping to preserve social stability.

The traditional middle-class jobs were the blue-collar, unionized, manufacturing jobs in industries such as automobiles or steel during much of the post-World War II period. These jobs provided workers with good pay, steady work, health insurance for themselves and their families, and pension benefits. Workers who worked hard and were committed to their employers were rewarded with relatively secure jobs.

These well-paid, unionized manufacturing jobs were not necessarily high-skilled jobs but were well-paid because of the bargaining power of the unions.

Moreover, these middle-class jobs were linked together on job ladders; working on one job promised advancement to other jobs that provided more responsibility and higher pay. These job ladders were used by industrial manufacturing firms to facilitate on-the-job training and to forestall collective action on the part of workers, since workers were motivated to climb the ladder of success rather than take the risk of joining with coworkers in opposing management (Edwards 1979).

Unfortunately for these workers, these middle-class jobs are fast disappearing and have been for some time because of developments in the world economy that surfaced in the 1970s. American companies began to feel the brunt of foreign competition, as markets for a variety of manufactured products such as automobiles and steel became global and international. The surge in competition from companies such as Toyota and Honda put increasing pressure on American manufacturers to cut costs and to reorganize their workplaces to remain competitive. Coupled with the growth of globalization was a restructuring of financial markets that linked stock prices and managers' salaries to short-term profits and forced managers to become increasingly concerned with the bottom line.

The result of these pressures was the restructuring of corporate America in the 1980s and 1990s, as companies sought to cut labor costs in order to enhance profits. The workplace on which the middle class relied during the postwar period has changed drastically since the middle of the 1980s. Massive downsizings occurred in this period, as companies sought to shed expensive workers and to become "lean and mean" enterprises.

The jobs that were affected and the regions in which layoffs were concentrated differed in the 1980s from the 1990s. In the years from 1981 to 1983, there were extensive layoffs in blue-collar manufacturing jobs in the Midwest and the South; due to downsizing, several million highly paid, unionized blue-collar production jobs disappeared in these areas in the early and mid-1980s, and many of the remaining jobs paid less.

In the years from 1991 to 1993, there were massive layoffs of office workers in the Northeast and on the West Coast; in the 1990s, millions of middle managers were laid off and other white-collar jobs were eliminated. The impact of this downsizing came as a shock, especially to middle-class, highly educated managers and professionals who had assumed that their jobs and careers would be protected by the employers in whom they had placed their trust and commitment. The trend toward downsizing continues to the present day; General Motors in late 2005 announced its plan to cut its blue-collar workforce in the United States to 86,000 by the end of 2008; at its peak, GM employed more than 600,000 (Hakim 2005).

The elimination of layers of middle management and other white-collar jobs was made possible by new information technology that enabled companies to computerize many of the tasks previously done by clerical workers. Corporate restructuring and the elimination of middle-class jobs was also fueled by the growing use of temporary workers on an as-needed basis and by the extensive use of subcontracting and outsourcing to produce goods and provide services once provided by permanent employees. The decline of union power (see Chapter 2) permitted managers to cut costs relatively freely. The decline of unions also reinforced an environment in which unions could not gain a foothold for bargaining with employers.

In addition to corporate restructuring, the growth of service sector industries also helped to eliminate middle-class jobs. In service industries such as insurance, retail, and finance, customers are divided; wealthier clients are served by different workers than low-status customers, making it difficult for people to move from entry-level jobs to higher-level ones, as opposed to the job ladders that characterized manufacturing firms in the past.

In one sense, corporate restructuring was successful, since it led to greater profits, at least in the short term, raising the economic position of the richest 5 percent of Americans. There is little evidence, however, that downsized companies were ever more productive. Moreover, these changes in the workplace increased the number of low-wage jobs. Indeed, " . . . the number of new low-wage jobs created since the late 1970s exceeds the number of additional high-wage positions" (Harrison and Bluestone 1988, xi).

These changes in the workplace and the replacement of high-wage manufacturing jobs by lower-wage service jobs caused an economic crisis for the middle class. Earnings for the majority of the labor force have been stagnant since the early 1970s, while the economic situation of the bottom 20 percent has declined. Average real wages stopped growing in 1973, and the gap between the well-paid and poorly-paid increased after that (Harrison and Bluestone 1988). Income inequality in the United States during the 1980s rivaled that of the Great Depression. Despite the prosperity enjoyed by those at the top, the percentage of people with middle-class purchasing power or incomes was 5 to 10 percentage points lower than 10 to 20 years earlier (K. Phillips 1993, 31). The median US family income in 1990 ($35,000) no longer guaranteed the middle-class status and lifestyle that a median income had brought twenty or thirty years earlier.

This decline in the size of the middle class reflected political changes in addition to economic and technological changes. One political change was President Reagan's tax policy that favored the unearned income of the wealthy over the earned income of jobholders. These changes were widely regarded as betraying the middle class by favoring the rich; they contributed to economic polarization or growing inequality between the rich on the one hand and the middle class and the poor on the other (K. Phillips 1993).

The growing plight of the middle class is reflected in political support for tax cuts, government restructuring, and debt financing that have left the middle class out of the political equation at the national level. As individual states have joined the chorus favoring unearned income over earnings from jobs, these governments too have restructured their tax systems to penalize the middle class (K. Phillips 1993).

The middle class during the 1980s and 1990s thus suffered from a combination of economic, social, and political setbacks—higher tax burdens, a decline in the quality and availability of public services, more expensive private services such as health care and higher education, and erosion of employee benefits such as health insurance and pensions.

One way that middle-class workers and households responded to their declining earnings was by working more hours, contributing to several of the mismatches we have discussed, such as overwork and work-family conflict as family leisure time declined. Middle-class families also maintained their level of consumption by taking on more debt, made easy by the expansion of available consumer credit. In addition, household savings declined since earnings were barely adequate to purchase goods and services required to satisfy the needs of their families. As a result, average household debt has increased substantially since the 1980s (Leicht and Fitzgerald 2006).

CONSEQUENCES OF EARNINGS MISMATCHES

The consequences of earnings mismatches are similar in many respects for the working poor and those we might consider to be middle class. Nevertheless, there are some notable differences between them, and so we consider these two groups separately.

Low-Wage Workers

The consequences of being a member of the working poor are especially pronounced and pervasive in a country such as the United States. Here, a person's economic status is largely determined by one's job, and there is not much of a safety net to take care of those unable to pay for health insurance or other fringe benefits.

The consequences of working in low-paying jobs, as is the case with many of the mismatches in this book, depend to some extent on one's family circumstances and age. Not all low-wage workers are in low-income families, for example, and some low-wage earners may have spouses or other family members who earn more and thus help the family escape poverty. Moreover, young workers living at home may not be mismatched to their low-wage jobs, since they do not depend on their earnings to satisfy their basic needs or those of their family.

Nevertheless, working in low-wage jobs entails serious consequences. First, there are health consequences of working in low-wage jobs; being a member of the working poor is a stressor, and these workers are more likely to experience depression and alcohol abuse (Friedland and Price 2002). These health difficulties are made worse because the poor are less likely to have health insurance; half the poor working full-time were uninsured in 2001, compared with 16 percent of all full-time workers (Pear 2002). Earnings mismatches are associated with benefits mismatches. Low-wage workers are also highly monitored (Ehrenreich 2001) and closely watched, further increasing stress levels. In addition, low-wage jobs have high injury rates (Shulman 2003).

Second, the working poor generally have inadequate housing. Housing costs have outpaced wages in the United States, and in no state can a low-income worker reasonably afford a modest one- or two-bedroom apartment. The National Low Income Housing Coalition (www.nlihc.org) estimated that in order to meet the expense of a modest two-bedroom rental, a full-time worker must earn a national median of $15.21 an hour, far above the $9.04 used in this chapter to characterize the working poor, not to mention the current federal minimum wage of $5.15 or the national median wage of about $12 (Clemetson 2003).

Third, family life is likely to suffer as a result of working in low-wage jobs. These jobs tend to be inflexible and generally do not provide time off to tend to a sick child or elderly parent or to attend a child's school activities. They also provide few vacation days. For all these reasons, low-wage jobs are especially hard on children of low-wage workers (Shulman 2003, 82–89).

Fourth, the conditions of low-wage work result in high turnover, low work quality, and low productivity, all of which have negative effects on the delivery of services to consumers and society. Workers constrained to work in low-wage service jobs are apt to be dissatisfied with their jobs and not likely to go the extra mile to provide their customers with high-quality service. The quality of services we obtain depends to a considerable extent on whether workers are satisfied with their working conditions and feel that they are treated equitably. Dissatisfied service or sales workers can be problematic if your family member needs care in a nursing home or hospital or if you need to buy goods quickly and don't know where in the store to find them.

Finally, people who work in low-wage jobs are less likely to vote and be engaged citizens than those with higher wages. The result is that the poor have little input into laws that have an impact on their lives, so that:

> most of the laws about working and nonworking poor people are formulated by nonpoor people, debated by nonpoor people, and mostly enacted due to lobbying that is not conducted by poor people (Quigley 2003, 27).

Middle Class
Many of the consequences of working in low-wage jobs also affect middle-class workers who have earnings mismatches. They

too experience stress from being unable to earn enough money to take care of their families' needs. Middle-class workers are also apt to suffer work-family mismatches, since they must work longer hours to meet their families' needs.

The economic distress increasingly faced by middle-class families is reflected in the high rate of bankruptcies in families with children; if current trends continue, one of every seven families with children will file for bankruptcy by 2010 (Warren and Tyagi 2003). This economic distress is due to the rising cost of essentials such as housing and education, not discretionary purchases like clothing. Middle-class workers, like the working poor, are also less likely to have health insurance and other benefits previously associated with a middle-class job and lifestyle.

The *New York Times* poll conducted in connection with the report *Downsizing of America* (see Chapter 6) underscores that middle-class workers experience some of the other mismatches we have discussed; 10 percent said they had been forced to work reduced hours, 42 percent frequently had to work more hours than usual, and 28 percent had to take an extra job.

This poll also documents the social and psychological suffering that comes to both those who are laid off and those who worry about being laid off. Over half the respondents felt that they were not as well off financially today as they expected to be at this point in their lives. The report illustrated that changes in the workplace led Americans to be more pessimistic about their future and to wonder if they would ever see the opportunities for bettering themselves that were available to previous generations.

POLICIES TO ALLEVIATE EARNINGS MISMATCHES

Again, we consider separately the two groups of earnings mismatched workers—the working poor and middle class—since the policies targeted at these groups are somewhat different.

Working Poor

For a long time experts thought the solution to poverty was to get people to work. This was the impetus, for example, behind the welfare reform efforts of the mid-1990s that sought to move people out of welfare and into the labor force. Aided by the booming economy of the late 1990s, this strategy resulted in a slight decrease in the number of working poor, although the poverty rate increased again during the recession in the early 2000s. The problem of the working poor is still a concern that needs to be addressed.

The reasons why some people are poor despite working full-time are complex, as we have discussed. Alleviating poverty requires more than simply providing people with money and jobs; it also necessitates changes in behavior such as marriage patterns and the ability and motivation to hold a job. Policy interventions need to be multidimensional and complex, and the various facets of poverty must be tackled at the same time in a holistic way (Shipler 2004).

How one goes about reducing the problem of the working poor recalls the old adage about which came first, the chicken or the egg. Sociologists since Marx have assumed that economic forces shape culture and behavior. This approach is consistent with William J. Wilson's argument that the ghetto underclass has limited aspirations rooted in their restricted economic opportunities, suggesting that demand-side policies to increase job opportunities, such as bringing jobs to poor areas, are needed to motivate people to acquire the skills necessary to escape from poverty and low-wage jobs.

The alternative view, held by many political conservatives, assumes instead that culture shapes economics, implying that changes in behavior, such as encouraging people to become more industrious, sober, and dependable, are the first step toward decreasing poverty (Brooks 2004). This perspective sees poverty as a result of people's character defects or inadequate skills, rather than inadequate economic opportunities.

It is clear that policies designed to alleviate the problem of the working poor need to reduce both the supply of workers who are underqualified for available jobs and the overabundance of jobs that pay low wages.

Labor supply programs expand the pool of qualified job seekers either by enhancing worker skills through job training programs and other investments in human capital or by inducing more people to look for work. Enhancing economic productivity by increasing the supply of skilled workers is essential in order to reduce working poverty. However, it is not sufficient, as has been illustrated by the experience of America's lowest-paid workers since the mid-1970s (Jencks 2004). We must also focus on the demand side of the economy.

Labor demand policies boost the number of jobs employers seek to fill by stimulating more economic activity, subsidizing private hiring, or creating public service jobs (Tilly 2002; see also Bartik 2001). In order to create jobs that reward people for their skills, it is essential that these jobs pay at least a living wage.

A key step toward this goal is to raise the federal minimum wage. Last increased in 1997, the federal minimum wage is currently $5.15 an hour, although a number of states have set their minimums higher; Alaska's is the highest at $7.15. The nation's median hourly wage in 2002 was about $12 an hour. Inflation has eaten away 14 percent of the value of the federal minimum wage since 1997, the last time it was raised. While relatively few workers earn the minimum wage or less (about 2 million workers in 2004, down from 4.8 million in 1997, according to the Bureau of Labor Statistics), there are a number of good arguments for raising it—75 percent of the workers affected by an increase in the minimum wage are adults, not teenagers, and workers at or near the minimum wage are those who have lost the most ground since the 1970s.

Not everyone agrees that raising the minimum wage is a good idea. Some economists have argued that raising the minimum wage will increase unemployment, since employers will be unwilling or unable to fill jobs at higher wages. Other economists do not agree; studies by Card and Krueger (1995), for example, found that after the last increases in 1996 and 1997, employment growth was stronger in low-wage states that were more affected by the rise in the federal minimum wage (Rives 2004).

Alleviating problems faced by the working poor needs to go beyond raising minimum wages and move toward a living wage. The campaign for a living wage began in the US in 1994 in response to growing economic inequalities, increases in poverty, declines in benefits, and the growing gap between the minimum wage and the real cost of living. Similar campaigns are underway in other industrial nations. Living-wage laws are enacted at the local level and are designed to enable a full-time worker to support a family above the poverty line without working two jobs. There are about ninety-five living-wage laws in the 3,106 counties in the United States. Quigley (2003, 3), an advocate of living-wage laws, suggests that we can end poverty in America by "amending our Constitution to guarantee every person the right to a job at a living wage."

Solutions based on the labor market—creating more jobs or turning low-skilled Americans into high-skilled ones—are not likely to eliminate working poverty completely. Some Americans, about 6 to 8 percent, are disabled or otherwise unable to work at non-poverty wages (Krueger 2004). Their existence underscores the importance of interventions outside the labor market to lift people out of poverty, to make sure living standards are not tied to low-wage jobs, and to provide a safety net to help people cope with the negative consequences of poverty. These interventions include health care and assistance with food and housing.

Some of these policies, such as the very successful Earned Income Tax Credit (EITC), might be linked to the notion of work. In addition, policies that seek to enhance asset development, such as providing savings accounts at birth for every person in America, are also worth exploring as ways to lift people out of poverty.

Mismatched Middle-Class Workers
As we discussed earlier, corporate restructuring and globalization has resulted in a decline in middle-class jobs and a growing gap between low-skilled, entry-level jobs and highly skilled, high-wage jobs. Low-wage jobs are likely to be dead-

226 THE MISMATCHED WORKER

end jobs; while it is important to get people into entry-level jobs, it is equally necessary to create job ladders to help workers in the middle class obtain jobs that would help them overcome their earnings mismatches, and to help low-wage workers to move upwards to better jobs.

In order to create job ladders, employers need to invest in both jobs and skills; one job should build upon the skills learned in others. Employers have the power to create job ladders and are more apt to do so if there are incentives for them to invest in training. Career ladders are facilitated by partnerships composed of employers, unions, community colleges and organizations, and government agencies (Fitzgerald 2004). Job ladders are also more likely if the firm is stable and big enough to afford investments in workers' skills, which can be recouped over time.

Finally, providing workers with the flexibility and support to care for their families properly through mechanisms such as paid family and medical leaves or day care would not only alleviate the problems of the working poor and the mismatched middle class, but it would also help reduce mismatches between work and family, a topic to which we now turn.

Chapter Nine
WORK-FAMILY MISMATCHES

KAYLA HAS WORKED as a registered nurse at a big hospital in the East for the past ten years. She is a thirty-five-year-old African American woman who graduated from a large public university. Kayla's husband, Luis, is a forty-one-year-old Hispanic male who graduated from the same university and then obtained an MBA from a prestigious private university in the Northeast. He is an account executive with the biggest advertising company in the state and has worked at this company for the past fifteen years. They both earn good salaries; Kayla brings in about $40,000 a year and could earn more if she were willing to put in more hours of overtime, and Luis earns about $90,000 a year. Both Kayla and Luis receive health insurance from their employers.

Kayla and Luis have four children between the ages of five and fifteen. They constantly juggle the demands of their busy work lives with the needs of their growing family. They try to take care of their children's and each other's needs and desires while still working the long hours required by their jobs. Kayla has some control over her schedule and is often able to take off from work to spend some time with her children, especially when they are out of school. Luis, however, is on call 24/7 and is frequently asked to travel out of the state to meet with clients. Luis is very ambitious and would like to become the

CEO of his company; Kayla is happy at her current job. Unfortunately, both Kayla and Luis experience a great deal of stress at work and they are worried that they are not giving their children the attention that they need during their formative years. Their marriage is also starting to show strain; they have not taken a vacation together for years and they find they are no longer able to spend much time together having fun and doing the things they used to enjoy.

Role-boundary mismatches is a term for situations in which people are not able to fulfill the behaviors and responsibilities associated with two or more of the roles they are expected to play (see Ashforth, Kreiner, and Fugate 2000 and Clark 2000). A prominent example of role-boundary mismatch, the one we will focus on in this chapter, occurs for many people when the activities and obligations associated with their work roles do not fit well with their family roles.[26]

Work and family are arguably the two most important roles adults have in an industrial society. Associated with each are sets of role behaviors and responsibilities that all adults are expected to perform. Potential mismatches are created when the demands of one of these roles make it difficult to satisfy the expectations associated with the other.[27]

We equate work-family mismatches with the various types of work-family conflict discussed in Chapter 1. Some people have obligations to care for elderly parents and other loved ones that they may not be able to honor due to their work responsi-

---

[26]A good source of information on work-family issues, including work-family conflicts, is wfnetwork.bc.edu.

[27]See Edwards and Rothbard (2000) for a discussion of the mechanisms that link work and family roles.

bilities, or they do not have enough time to spend with their spouses because of work-related obligations. Conflict may occur in the other direction as well—family responsibilities may limit one's ability to accomplish adequately what is needed at work. The type of work-family mismatch that has received the most attention, perhaps, is the conflict between the expectations of parental roles and work roles. This mismatch occurs when fathers and (especially) mothers cannot find jobs that enable them to balance their economic needs with their roles as parents.

Work-family mismatches can be looked at from the point of view of the individual and the family as well as that of the employer and society. Our emphasis in this chapter, as throughout the book, is on the worker and his or her family. As with all the mismatches we consider, however, we recognize that these work-family conflicts are likely also to affect employers and society in general.

EXPLAINING WORK-FAMILY MISMATCH

The basic reason for work-family mismatches is that workers have a great deal to do on their jobs as well as for their families and don't have the flexibility to fulfill their obligations for one role adequately without interference from the other. This conflict makes it difficult for the person to satisfy their responsibilities to both work and family.

Work-family mismatches are related to several of the other mismatches discussed in this book, especially overwork (Chapter 6). Indeed, a major reason why people experience work-family conflict is that they work more hours than they would like and feel they do not have enough time to spend with their families. The causality may also be reversed; the experience of work-family conflict may lead some people to desire to work fewer hours. Work-family mismatches are also closely linked to the problem of low-wage jobs and the working poor, as well as earnings mismatches among the middle class (Chapter 8). A prominent reason for the growth in dual-earner households is that a single breadwinner's earnings have become inadequate to support a family, forcing the other spouse to take a paid job. This happens especially in the middle class, since many poor families are single-parent households headed by women.

Work-family mismatch also underscores the fact that issues related to working time and overwork affect households and families, not just (or even primarily) single workers. In fact, the working time of employed couples has increased more dramatically in the United States than that of individual workers from 1970 to 2000; for example, among all couples, the average number of hours of paid work per week done by both husband and wife increased from 52.5 hours per week in 1970 to 63.1 hours per week in 2000 (Jacobs and Gerson 2004, 43). For this reason, work-family mismatches have become much more common in recent decades in the United States.

The emergence of work-family mismatches as a concern and social scientific interest in the United States stems from a combination of recent rapid changes in the paid employment of women, especially mothers, along with slower changes in the institutions that support paid market work and unpaid care work. The replacement of the traditional single breadwinner family by the dual-career family means that both spouses must increasingly share family obligations. At the same time, workers often have less time to take care of these family responsibilities because of the increases in work intensity described in Chapter 6 and the fact that organizations have not adapted sufficiently to accommodate the needs of dual-earner families. As a result of these changes, both high- and low-skilled workers may now have greater difficulties than ever before in balancing their work and family lives.

Mismatches between the demands of family life (especially for care of children and elders) and work have become more common, since there is no longer someone at home to provide the care that the wife and mother used to do. The extent to which this mismatch is problematic is related to sex roles and who is primarily responsible for various roles in the family. A brief overview of the changes in recent decades in the participation of women in the labor force and in the family composition of the labor force will help provide a better understanding of the reasons for work-family mismatches.[28]

Changes in Families and Labor Force Composition
In the United States after World War II, the typical American family consisted of a male breadwinner who worked outside the home and a female homemaker who took care of the house and the children. This kind of family has been referred to as the "Ozzie and Harriet" or "Leave it to Beaver" family, after the popular television situation comedies of the 1950s that featured these kinds of families.

This arrangement worked well for many people. The American work ethic emphasized that men obtain dignity from hard

[28]The following discussion draws heavily upon Appelbaum, Bailey, Berg, and Kalleberg (2002).

work and being the family breadwinner, no matter what their jobs were. Women, on the other hand, were encouraged by the prevailing ideology of "The Cult of True Womanhood" and the "Feminine Mystique" (Friedan 1963) to work in the home to support the family, leaving paid outside work to their husbands. Women were responsible for the labor in the home, while men worked outside the home.

This situation changed drastically with the dramatic growth in the participation of women in paid employment (Chapter 2). The increase in the labor force participation rates (LFPR) of married women has been especially great, increasing from 41 percent in 1970 to 62 percent in 2003 (US Census Bureau 2005). By contrast, the LFPR of single women grew from 57 percent in 1970 to 67 percent in 2002. Women's employment in the United States increased most rapidly among married women with children; their LFPR increased from about 40 percent in 1970 to about 70 percent in 2002. By 2004, 60 percent of married women (whose spouses were present) with children under the age of six were in the workforce, as were three-quarters of those with school-age children (six to seventeen) (United States Department of Labor 2005b, Table 6).

The growth in women's LFPR was fueled by the stagnant or declining wages of men, in addition to the reasons discussed in Chapter 2, such as economic pressures to supplement their husbands' earnings, declining fertility rates, increases in divorce rates, and desires to take advantage of educational investments. The standard employment arrangement that had provided men with rising wages over their working lives began to unravel during the 1970s. The oil price shocks and resulting stagflation led to a long period of falling real wages for men who did not have a college degree; men's wages fell from the mid-1970s through the mid-1990s and threatened the purchasing power and living standards of most families. Married couples staved off a decline in the family's standard of living by increasing the hours of paid work engaged in by both husbands and wives.

This growth in married women's LFPRs, especially among married women with children, coupled with the continued high percentage of men in the labor force, led to an increase in dual-earner couples, or families in which both parents work. For example, in 1940, in about two-thirds of all families with children, the husband was the wage earner while the wife stayed at home, like the traditional Ozzie and Harriet family; both husband and wife worked for pay in only about 10 percent of the families with children. By the end of the twentieth century, families with employed husbands and stay-at-home wives accounted for only 19 percent of all families, and both husband and wife worked for pay in 44 percent of families with children (Padavic and Reskin 2002, 151; see also United States Department of Labor 2005b, Table 23).

Among married women, the increase has been even more dramatic. Moreover, a growing number of families were headed by a single adult, because of the rise in divorce rates, a trend that contributed further to the demise of the Ozzie and Harriet family.

As a result of the emergence of the dual-income family, the average number of hours worked by married-couple households has grown explosively. Between 1979 and 2002, wives in prime age (between 25 and 54), married-couple families with children added between two months (for low- and high-income families) and three months (for middle-income families) to couples' time spent at work (Mishel, Bernstein, and Allegretto 2005, 102–03). Since husbands usually worked full-time in 1979, there was little room for them to expand their hours; hence, the increase in wives' hours accounted for the vast majority of growth in hours worked by the family. The large increase in hours worked by dual-earner families has intensified the pressures on them to fulfill their family obligations as well as their work obligations. Ralph Gomory and Kathleen Christensen (1999) of the Alfred P. Sloan Foundation described the situation this way: "In today's two-career family, there are three jobs, two paid and one not paid, but still only two people to do them."

Despite the increase in hours worked by family members, their obligations in the home did not decrease during this period; children still needed to be raised and cared for, and the aging of the population meant that working families were more likely to have older as well as younger dependents. The availability of labor-saving devices such as microwaves, dishwashers, and so on helped somewhat by making housework more efficient. But these time-savers did not eliminate domestic tasks such as running errands or feeding and entertaining children, that were formerly done by a full-time homemaker and now had to be shared by the two paid workers in the household.

Unfortunately, while the family's role in the labor force changed considerably, the workplace has not evolved to accommodate the changing nature of families, making the problems of work-family mismatch even worse. Corporate restructurings, downsizing, and the other kinds of cost-saving strategies discussed in previous chapters put greater, not less, pressure on workers to work more hours and to work more intensely in order to meet competitive pressures from domestic and foreign companies. Most organizations still operate as if workers still had a family member at home to take care of their family obligations; managers continue to treat women as well as male workers as if they still had a wife at home to take care of household and family-related activities (Williams 2000).

The entry of married women into the labor force in the United States was viewed by social policymakers not as a contribution to the nation's standard of living, but as a private response to the financial problems facing individual families. As a consequence, the US government and private employers have not felt a pressing obligation to address the work-family mismatches produced by the emergence of the dual-earner family. When conflicts arise, employers expect workers to compromise on the care side of the equation—time spent on housework and in the care of children and elderly parents.

This attitude contrasts to the response to the entry of men into the industrial labor force earlier, which was accompanied by the development of social insurance to meet the family's needs for financial support if the wage earner was unable to work. No similar response by the government to the entry of women into employment has been forthcoming, and arranging care for children while both parents work is regarded by working families, as well as by business and government, as a private family responsibility. The only federal government initiative was the passage in 1993 of the Family and Medical Leave Act requiring large companies to offer twelve weeks of unpaid family or medical leave to workers. Many workers cannot afford to take unpaid time off from work, however, and many others are not covered by the provisions of the law.

It is instructive to compare the US with Sweden, another Western industrial country with many working women. The rise of married women's participation in the labor force in both countries was fueled by advances in technology and industrialization as well as by steadily rising educational levels of women over the twentieth century.

In Sweden, however, the rapid entry of women into paid employment happened earlier and was the result of two developments. First people recognized that the small size of the population meant that the standard of living in the country required women as well as men to contribute to economic output. Society accepted women's employment and recognized the need to secure the well-being of children while promoting employment of both parents. Second, the development of the Swedish social welfare state greatly expanded employment opportunities for women in the caring professions and situated these activities in the public sector. As a result, care work is relatively well paid in Sweden, and the state provides a highly developed, publicly funded system to provide education services, health care, care for the elderly, and care of young children.

The Swedish example is not unique. Many other industrial countries help families achieve work-family balance by means of public policies that give people more vacation and personal time and provide them with greater control over when to use this time. In some cases, these public policies have been prompted by the actions of unions, as in Germany. In other countries, such as Japan and Italy, they are part of a governmental policy designed to increase labor force and population growth so as to address current and projected labor shortages.

HOW COMMON IS WORK-FAMILY MISMATCH?

There are different ways to experience work-family mismatches, and social scientists have measured them in a variety of ways. Perhaps the most common approach is to ask workers how much conflict or interference they feel there is between their work and family lives. Such questions provide an overall assessment of the extent to which workers have difficulty balancing their work and family lives.

Table 9.1 presents estimates of the percentages of men and women in the United States in 2002 who reported that they experienced various kinds of mismatches between their work and family lives, expressed as conflict between these two roles. These estimates are based on data from two recent national surveys of the labor force—the 2002 General Social Survey (GSS) and the 2002 National Study of the Changing Workforce (NSCW).

In Table 9.1 we report the percentages of workers who responded that they feel some degree of conflict between their work and family lives; there are separate figures for men and women and for parents and nonparents. In the NSCW study, "children" means the respondent is the parent or guardian of children of any age; in the GSS survey, it means the respondent has children eighteen or younger living in the home. We expect that workers with children will experience more conflict between their work and family lives, since we assume that their family responsibilities will be greater than for those workers without children.

Table 9.1

PERCENTAGES OF WORK-FAMILY CONFLICT
IN THE UNITED STATES, 2002

	Men		Women	
	No children	Children	No children	Children
Work-family conflict				
How much do your job and your family life interfere with each other? (A lot or Somewhat).[a]	32	48	34	42
How easy or difficult is it for you to manage the demands of your work and your personal or family life? (Very difficult, Difficult, or Sometimes easy and Sometimes difficult)[b]	48	58	50	62
Impact of family life on work				
How often does family life interfere with job? (Often or Sometimes)[a]	25	37	25	45
How often has your family or personal life kept you from doing as good a job at work as you could? (Very often, Often, or Sometimes)[b]	21	24	22	27
Impact of work on family life				
How often does job interfere with family life? (Often or Sometimes)[a]	36	57	33	45
How often has your job kept you from concentrating on important things in your family or personal life? (Very often, Often, or Sometimes)[b]	37	42	34	36

[a]Source: General Social Survey, 2002; author's calculations.
[b]Source: National Study of the Changing Workforce, 2002; author's calculations.

The responses suggest that a substantial number of Americans report having difficulty balancing their work and family lives, and that these difficulties are greater for workers with children. Overall, 44 percent of men and 40 percent of women say that their job and family life interfere with each other a lot or somewhat; results for the overall samples of men and women are not presented in Table 9.1. Workers with children are substantially more likely to say that work and family interfere with each other; nearly half the men (48 percent) and 42 percent of women with children say that there is a lot or some interference between their work and family lives, compared to only about a third of men and women without children.[29]

A second question asks "How easy or difficult is it for you to manage the demands of your work and your personal or family life?" About six in ten men and women with children find it difficult at least some of the time. The percentages are again considerably higher for men and women with children than those without children. About 10 percent of men and women with children say that it is difficult or very difficult for them to manage their work and family demands, compared to about 5 to 6 percent of men and women without children (these numbers are not presented in the table).

In addition to these general assessments of the extent to which people feel a lack of balance between their work and family lives, these surveys also included questions about the

[29]Overall, 13 percent of men and 11 percent of women say that their job and family life interfere with each other a lot. Among workers with children, 15 percent of men and 12 percent of women say that there is a lot of interference between their work and family lives, compared to 8 percent of men and women without children.

directionality of this work-family conflict—that is, whether workers' families had a negative impact on their work or whether work negatively affected their family life. Table 9.1 includes two questions that focus on these two directions.

It appears that the demands of work conflict with family roles, and that family responsibilities conflict with work obligations. Work, however, has a stronger negative impact on family life than vice versa, especially for men. Among people with children, for example, 57 percent of men and 45 percent of women say that their job interferes with their family life often or sometimes, but 37 percent of men and 45 percent of women say that their family life interferes with their job often or sometimes.

This result is consistent with the view that men regard their work role as more central to their identities than women, and so men are more apt than women—especially women with children—to place higher priority on their work as opposed to their family activities. This is the sort of asymmetrical permeability of boundaries that Pleck (1977) expected. Most studies, however, indicate that men and women experience similar levels of both work-to-life conflict and life-to-work conflict—see Greenhaus and Parasuraman 1999.

Both men and women without children are more likely to say that their work interferes with their family activities often or sometimes than they are to say that their family life interferes with their job (36 percent versus 25 percent for men, 33 percent versus 25 percent for women). That work interferes with family more than vice versa is a consistent finding in the literature on work-family conflict, attributed to the fact that the organization's demands are usually given primacy over family issues because of the essential economic contribution that work provides to the family (Greenhaus and Parasuraman 1999).

Further support for the notion that work negatively affects family life more than family impacts work, especially for men, is provided by the results of the other two questions in Table 9.1. About a quarter of men and women feel that their family or personal lives keep them from doing as good a job at work as they could very often, often, or sometimes (results not shown in the table). Men and women with children are more likely to respond this way, although at least two out of ten workers without children also feel that this is the case.

By contrast, larger percentages of workers—both parents and nonparents—feel that their job prevents them from concentrating on important things in their family or personal lives very often, often, or sometimes. Men are more likely than women to say that work detracts from their family life in this way, especially men with children (42 percent, compared to 37 percent for men without children). Women with children are about as likely as women without children (about 34 to 36 percent) to say that their job keeps them from concentrating on their family or personal lives. Again, this is consistent with the idea that women are generally more likely than men to attach greater primacy to their family and nonwork lives.

CONSEQUENCES OF WORK-FAMILY MISMATCH

When the demands of work conflict with those of the family, there will often be strain between these two roles as the individual tries to satisfy the responsibilities associated with both of them simultaneously (Goode 1960). Since most married couples in the United States—even those with young children—are dual earners, there are likely to be great stresses on household members as families are less able to meet the personal needs of working adults and to care for children, the sick, and the elderly.

Work-family mismatches are likely to have consequences for individuals' health and well-being, for their family lives, for the workplace, and for society in general (Voydanoff 2002). Workers must often choose between their roles as parents, spouses, and workers, and are increasingly pressured for both time and money. Members of dual-earner families feel higher levels of stress and lower levels of psychological well-being. The resulting stresses spill over into social institutions such as schools, social service agencies, religious institutions, the courts, and the police.

These institutions are not prepared to deal with the stresses generated by work-family mismatches, and so they are also apt to experience disruptions and increased costs. Employers also suffer because of high turnover, absenteeism, and loss of productive human capital.

The individual consequences of work-family strain are borne disproportionately by women, who still have the main responsibility for homemaking and child care but are increasingly expected to work outside the home (Andrews 2004). For them, working at home constitutes a second shift (Hochschild 1989) in addition to their paid job. Mothers with younger children at home are especially likely to shoulder a double burden.

Accordingly, most of the research on work-family conflict has focused on women. A number of studies document the time pressures and cultural barriers created when women enter labor markets where the separation of work and family is the norm and companies assume that unpaid caregivers are performing domestic tasks (Nelson and Bridges 1999). Women's earnings—especially the earnings of middle-class women—also suffer more than men's from time spent on domestic work (Shirley and Wallace 2004).

The situation may be changing somewhat as men, especially younger men, play a greater role in child care. While women are more likely to face the dual challenges of work and family, then, the rise of dual earner-couples has seen more men facing these challenges, and a growing number of studies now pay attention to the impact on men.

Men are affected by work-family mismatches both directly through increased stress and indirectly by the decreased time that their spouses can devote to them. One consequence of women working has been a negative impact on the health of their husbands.

Using longitudinal data, Stolzenberg (2001) shows that husbands of wives who work over forty hours a week are less healthy in various ways than husbands of wives who either do not work or work less than forty hours a week. He explains that when women work long hours, they are less able to devote the time needed to take care of their husbands' needs, such as reminding them to do things that will keep them healthy (such as getting enough sleep or exercise), or helping maintain the husband's emotional state by facilitating his interactions with supportive social contacts such as relatives, friends and acquaintances.

Some writers have argued that many women prefer to go to work rather than spend time with their family. Hochschild

(1997), for example, found that many women, especially those in highly demanding professional careers, chose to spend more time at the workplace; they were stimulated by the challenges of their work and their co-workers, and valued their employers' recognition of their efforts, which often exceeded the appreciation they received from their family members. The workplace is thus viewed by at least some women as a respite from family life.

Hochschild's description may be true of a relatively small group of women workers, especially those in large corporations and professional occupations, but the evidence suggests that most Americans, both men and women, do not wish to avoid family life through work, but rather are seeking a reasonable, if elusive, balance between work and family. Moreover, the results in Table 9.1 indicate that substantial proportions of workers say that they have difficulty balancing work and family life (see also Maume and Bellas 2001). Even workers who say they would rather spend time at the workplace than at home may have difficulty balancing work and family life; they may still feel the strain produced by guilt (see Brown and Booth 2002 and the response by Hochschild 2002).

The extent to which work-family mismatches have negative consequences depends in no small part on the amount of control people have over their working time. While most research on working time has focused on the number of hours that people work, a growing number of studies have suggested that it is not so much the sheer number of hours that is important for the quality of family and personal life, but rather whether one is able to control when one works and whether one is able to take time off as needed (Fenwick and Tausig 2001). With regard to timing, it is clear that working forty hours 9 to 5 Monday through Friday has a very different effect on one's participation in family activities than working forty hours on the night shift or flexible hours during the month.

The degree of control workers have over their time may affect the impact of work on family differently from the effect of family on work. This is illustrated by a study of self-employed persons, who have more control over the duration and timing of their work than most workers. For self-employed persons, work is less likely to interfere with their family lives because of their control over their work time. On the other hand, since many self-employed persons work at home, their life is more likely to interfere with their work (Reynolds and Renzulli 2005).

The effects of work-family mismatches also vary by race and ethnicity. As we have emphasized throughout this book, nonwhite workers are more likely to have jobs that pay lower wages, provide fewer fringe benefits, and provide less flexibility. At the same time, nonwhites also have larger families on average and thus are apt to have greater family responsibilities. For example, black women are often single mothers and so are especially vulnerable to work-family mismatches. The associated stresses help explain disparities between racial groups in overall health, coronary heart disease, and hypertension. In particular, black women generally fare the worst of any race and gender group on these indicators of health.

Moreover, the extent to which work and family conflict and the severity of mismatches and their consequences vary by phase in the life cycle. Mismatches are more severe at some ages and life stages than at others. For example, time pressures caused by both parents working are especially great when children are small, since the children cannot be left alone without some kind of supervision such as day care. When children are adolescents, they have lots of activities that require them to be driven to various places and constantly encouraged. Often adolescence occurs just when career-oriented parents are at critical junctures in their careers, when they need to devote large chunks of time to their work in order to earn promotions; thus work-family mismatches are likely to be especially pronounced during this period. When children go off to college, work-family mismatches ease off, and parents may be able to concentrate more on their working lives, and they may need to do this in order to pay for college. Later, children may "boomerang" and return to the household, although the amount of supervision and support they need will be less than before.

Work-family mismatches may also arise later in life for some families because of the need to take care of aging parents. This problem will grow worse as life expectancies increase and pension benefits become increasingly unreliable. Moreover, a growing number of workers are becoming part of the "sandwich generation" that needs to care simultaneously for young children and aging parents. In addition, some workers must care for chronically ill family members, underscoring the importance of good health benefits to alleviate work-family mismatches.

REDUCING WORK-FAMILY MISMATCH

The dual-earner family is not likely to disappear anytime soon. Economic pressures for two paychecks, combined with the noneconomic benefits that men and women derive from participating in paid employment, are likely to encourage both genders to continue working. It is also highly unlikely that dual-earner families will stop having children. Therefore, reducing mismatches between work and family will continue to pose a challenge for both public policy and businesses.

The conflicts between the demands of homemaking and those of paid employment, along with unrealistic expectations for women who have shouldered that double burden, have not yet been addressed adequately in the public discourse, largely because of the historical context within which women entered the labor force in the United States. The growth of dual-earner families was seen primarily as a private response to the financial problems facing individual families rather than as a way of addressing pressing social needs.

It is important to recognize that improving the fit between work and family is a social problem that has social causes. As with all the mismatches discussed in this book, work-family mismatches are not only personal troubles but also public issues that require social solutions that must be implemented at the societal level, not at the level of the individual family. Unfortunately, the absence of strong social policies to address work-family mismatches in the United States has led individuals to try coping with them on their own (Warner 2005) through various self-help and time-management strategies. Individuals have been forced to rely on their own decisions and to make compromises in order to cope with these mismatches. These strategies include compartmentalization (not bringing work home), delegation (hiring a nanny to take care of the children), elimination of role conflicts (working fewer hours or not at all), extension (I can't do housework because I have taken on new responsibilities at work), and so on (Goode 1960). Rather than leaving it up to individuals to solve these work-family mismatches as best they can, we need social policies that provide working families with opportunities and options for coping with work-family mismatches.

Unfortunately, the United States currently has no comprehensive social policies to deal with the interface of work and family roles that would include such things as paid family leave, mandatory benefits related to day care, or flexible working hours. While modern industrial economies inherently produce conflict between work and home, the United States is especially fraught with public policy conflicts over the interface of work and family. Despite the increase in the percentage of women in the US labor force, social supports for work have remain largely unchanged since the 1930s. In the United States, unemployment insurance and social security laws were written to protect families dependent on the wage of a male breadwinner. Not until 1993 did women have the legal right to take time off from work at the birth of a child. But federal law does not require that maternity leave be paid, limits such leave to twelve weeks, and does not apply to women who work in establishments that employ fewer than fifty workers. Moreover, there is no federal law in the United States that gives workers the right to paid vacation leave, sick leave, or parental leave, although some employers provide better programs than those mandated by federal law.

The situation is different in other industrialized countries. All western European countries, as well as Canada, offer some kind of maternity, paternity, and/or parental leave during at least the first year after a child is born or adopted. These countries also provide opportunities for high-quality part-time and flexible work. Moreover, governments of these countries generally provide early-childhood care and education programs (Meyers and Gornick 2003).

By contrast to these other industrialized countries, the US government is doing little to help families to balance their work and family lives, despite its expressed concern with the well-being of children. For example, despite the fact that most mothers work, the United States still lacks an adequate system of high-quality care for children. Care is provided, for the most part, by workers (mostly women), often untrained and underpaid, whose work is devalued and marginalized by the low wages and lack of career advancement opportunities typically associated with these jobs. Much the same can be said about care for the elderly. Earnings of the women who care for children and the elderly are extremely low, and turnover rates in these jobs are excessively high. As a result, the quality and continuity of care of the most vulnerable members of society suffer.

What the United States needs is a combination of "shared work and valued care" (Appelbaum et al. 2002). Shared work can be accomplished through shorter work weeks, flexible scheduling, job sharing, and providing access to good jobs for mothers. It also recognizes the need for men and women to share in caring for children and family members, and for the community and other public institutions to participate as well. "Valued care" means that workers need to have more flexibility and control over their work time so that they can meet their family responsibilities. It also underscores society's responsibility to provide high-quality care options to help workers take care of the young, the old, and the sick.

Implementing such family-friendly policies will require a combination of public and private policy interventions targeted at the reduction of work-family mismatches. To offer a generous package of paid family leave and child care, for example, the United States would have to spend between 1.0 and 1.5 percent of the gross domestic product ($115 to $175 billion per year), comparable to what France and Sweden spend (Meyers and Gornick 2003). These investments would reap considerable social benefits in terms of child development, educational performance, parental well-being, and social stability. These are valued goals that are widely shared in the United States, regardless of one's political views.

Companies also need to adopt family-friendly practices to help their employees resolve their conflicts between work and family, consistent with the emphasis in the United States on policy interventions at the workplace level. Some organizations are likely to do this out of a desire to be viewed as a good place to work. Examples of such companies are provided each October by *Working Mother* magazine.[30] Some of the practices adopted by these 100 Best companies, such as flexible scheduling and employee assistance programs, have been implemented by most companies in the United States, but other, more expensive options, such as various child care programs and paid paternity leave, are provided by very few.

Other companies might be motivated to adopt family-friendly practices by the values of their leaders, as was the case when Lewis Platt, then the CEO of Hewlett-Packard, found

---

[30]The list for 2005 can be found at: www.workingmother.com/100BEST _2005.html. Profiles of these companies are also provided on this website.

himself having to take care of children as a single parent. Most common organizational policies, such as day-care referral services, are relatively cheap for organizations to offer, though they don't help all that much, since some workers cannot afford these services. Organizations are likely to take the lead—for example, in providing more expensive forms of day care—only if they have to because of cost pressures imposed by labor shortages or other demands from workers.

S. C. Johnson & Son is a company that has instituted a variety of family-friendly policies.[31] Located in Racine, Wisconsin, this family-owned and managed company is one of the world's leading manufacturers of household cleaning products (Windex, Mr. Muscle, Shout) and insect control products (Raid and Off). S. C. Johnson also established a childcare learning center twenty years ago, one of the nation's first child care centers for the exclusive use of its employees and their families.

Another set of social policies is needed to reduce the length of the workweek, as a number of European countries have. A number of US companies have successfully timesized their workforces (see www.timesizing.com/1cases.htm). SAS Institute in Cary, North Carolina, for example, maintains a thirty-five-hour week instead of the standard forty hours; this is consistent with the CEO's belief that people are more productive if they work fewer hours.

Despite the need, the adoption of family-friendly practices in the United States is far from complete. Larger organizations and those with a higher proportion of women workers are more likely to adopt family-friendly policies (Davis and Kalleberg

[31]www.scjohnson.com/family.

2006). The paucity of family-friendly practices in US businesses is especially problematic in view of the lack of comprehensive social policies to alleviate work-family mismatches. In the mid-1990s, slightly more than a quarter of US businesses provided paid parental leaves to new parents, while less than a quarter provided some kind of assistance for dependent care (child care as well as elder care). Mandatory overtime is common, and there is no legal maximum number of hours of work in a day or a week.

The ability of the United States to alleviate work-family conflicts and their consequences is important not only for the well-being of individual families, but for the economic and social health of the society. As global competition accelerates, it will become increasingly important to develop flexible institutions that are able to sustain new forms of work organization, as well as strong family structures. Nations that are unable or unwilling to address problems such as work-family conflicts through coherent and effective public policies are likely to suffer economically as well as socially (Carnoy 2000).

Chapter Ten
REDUCING MISMATCHES:
A POLICY AGENDA

IN THIS BOOK we have discussed seven mismatches, situations in which people are unable to find jobs that allow them to fulfill their needs, preferences, or expectations. Each is likely to result in dissatisfaction with the job and a desire to change the work situation to improve the match or, if possible, to leave the job in the hope of finding one that fits better. Each mismatch is problematic for some people and their families as well as detrimental, at least indirectly, to their employers and society in general. All these parties would benefit if workers had jobs that enabled them to satisfy their preferences and needs.

Some mismatches are particularly likely to produce stress and other negative psychological and physical consequences that spill over into nonwork situations. Overworking, work-family conflict, and working in low-wage jobs are especially apt to lead to high stress. These mismatches are also liable to have adverse consequences for the well-being of the family and are likely to be particularly difficult for workers who are primarily responsible for supporting their families. These consequences cost the nation billions of dollars each year in social services such as hospitals and family support to help people cope with the disruptions caused by these kinds of mismatches.

Other kinds of mismatches, such as overqualification, underqualification, and underworking, often result in both private and social underutilization of human capital, since people (along with their employers and society) are denied the opportunity to employ fully their talents and abilities (Sullivan 1978, 11–12). The underutilization of our workforce is a serious issue that costs employers and the society billions of dollars in lost productivity.

Many of these mismatches have become more prevalent in the United States in the past several decades. Work-family conflict and overworking, for example, are more common now than ever before. There has also been a growth in recent years in mismatches related to underworking, earnings, and benefits. Overqualification and geographical mismatches are also on the rise. Consequently, the problems associated with mismatches have become more urgent now than at any time since World War II. They must be addressed immediately.

This urgency is magnified when one recognizes that these mismatches are outgrowths of trends that will continue to shape the nature of employment relations, labor markets, and work organization in the United States and other industrial nations. These trends include globalization, the explosive growth of information technology and the escalating importance of knowledge in the economy, the increasing geographic dispersion of people and workers, and the growing diversity of the labor force.

This concluding chapter provides an overview of the kinds of social policies and business strategies that are necessary to alleviate these seven mismatches. Many of these public and private policy suggestions have been mentioned in the previous chapters, as we discussed ways of reducing each of the mismatches. This chapter brings these suggestions together and presents a policy agenda that outlines the directions that social policies and business strategies need to pursue in order to reduce mismatches between work and workers in the United States.

ALTERNATIVE APPROACHES

There are several ways to try to reduce these mismatches. Some argue that labor markets will solve the problem if only they are allowed to operate freely. Others feel that markets by themselves are incapable of eliminating mismatches, but must be guided by social solutions, especially government intervention.

Let Markets Do It

Debates about policies designed to improve the fit between persons and jobs in capitalist industrial countries generally center on the role of the labor market, the major arena in which people are matched to jobs. Relying on labor markets to alleviate mismatches between people and jobs is often the subject of debate between conservatives, who generally favor letting market mechanisms operate competitively, thus preserving the status quo, and liberals, who want the government and institutions such as unions to intervene, make markets work more fairly, and reduce the vulnerability of certain groups to the effects of market processes (see Massey 2005). This political debate is part of broader disagreement about values and the desirability of government intervention in markets.

Conservative politicians and many economists argue that if labor markets operated competitively, they would be more efficient, and mismatches would not occur, or at least they would be temporary. For them, the problem is that labor markets are not allowed to operate freely because of constraints imposed by the government, employment and labor laws, unions, and other forces operating on the market.

This view is consistent with the promarket consensus in the United States, which holds that markets are the answer to our problems and that the government and other institutions should not get involved in the operation of free markets. This position maintains that the interests of the society as a whole will be maximized if labor markets are allowed to function without interference, labor is simply a factor of production to be controlled, and labor costs should be minimized as much as possible. Advocates of free labor markets assume that employers should be allowed to organize work so as to make as much profit as possible, regardless of the consequences for workers, communities, or other stakeholders.

This overriding commitment to free markets in the United States is linked to other ideological and institutional features of American society. For example, individualism is a central value in the United States, and some believe that individuals should be free to make their own bargains with each other and with employers without outside interference. This view disapproves of institutions that interfere with negotiations between an individual and an employer, such as unions or government.

Labor markets on their own are not likely to produce satisfactory outcomes such as the elimination of mismatches between persons and jobs. As Quigley (2003, 7–8) puts it:

> The market has no inherent interest in the common good . . . Expecting only the unguided market to steadily create good jobs at good wages is like expecting your car to watch your

kids. The common good is irrelevant to the market. Looking after the common good is the job of civil society and democratic government . . . On its own, the market will give us recessions and depressions as well as good times . . . most people who advocate for a free market actually mean a business climate that is free of any regulation on commerce for the common good . . . Blind trust in the market, or neutrality, or a hands-off attitude, is essentially acceptance of the status quo.

There is little reason to assume that labor market matching mechanisms, left unfettered, will reduce the kinds of mismatches between persons and jobs that we have discussed. Markets don't operate freely; they are created by social actors according to a set of rules. Expressions such as the "need for a free market" or "let the market decide" are simply rhetorical devices used to justify the status quo—such as the enormous inequality between the earnings of top managers and their workers in the United States—and to protect those whose interests are best served by the current set of rules (Massey 2005).

Our findings in previous chapters suggest strongly that labor markets have not been effective in producing good fits between persons and jobs. Moreover, the processes that govern the matching of people to jobs in labor markets are not only economic; they are embedded in other social institutions, even in highly market-oriented, capitalist societies such as the United States. These social institutions include labor laws, collective bargaining agreements, and families. This fact underscores the need for social policies that shape the operation of labor markets so as to alleviate mismatches and temper their consequences.

The Need for Governmental Intervention

Alleviating mismatches ultimately requires social policies rather than relying on workers to find individual solutions. Some individuals may be able to achieve better matches through their own strategies, such as pursuing further training and education, or finding child care to help them balance their work and family responsibilities. But the structural nature of these mismatches implies that individual solutions are not likely to be effective for the vast majority of people. Most individuals cannot hope to achieve better fits by their own actions, since they may not have the money to obtain more education or find suitable child care. Hence, the alleviation of these mismatches needs to be a focus of the government's social and economic policies.

The government's role is central in any effort to alleviate the mismatches we have discussed in this book. As Shipler (2004, 289) describes the role of government:

> The state exists not just to preserve freedom. It exists to protect the weak. It exists to strengthen the vulnerable, to empower the powerless, to promote justice. It exists to facilitate "the pursuit of happiness."

Government intervention is required because the roots of the mismatches are public issues that result from institutional and social structures, rather than private troubles that are the fault of individual workers. Moreover, the workers who are most likely to be mismatched—especially those who are underqualified, spatially mismatched, underemployed, and low-wage workers—are often powerless to change their situations.

The government should help to alleviate mismatches, especially those associated with the working poor, not only for reasons of social justice, but also for social efficiency. Society has to pick up the tab for poverty in general and working poverty specifically, when it has to deal with the varied consequences of poverty discussed earlier. For example, the government has to provide assistance so that disadvantaged children can learn at a pace equal to their peers. Those who never catch up because of inadequate education and inability to find jobs that pay living wages are more likely to become criminals, and their crime costs the government even more money. Moreover, the negative consequences of health problems that result from working in jobs that do not offer health insurance are likely to cost much more than it would have cost to provide preventive health measures.

The Role of Business

Government cannot eliminate mismatches by itself; social and economic policies must have the support of business. History has taught us that the government cannot mandate that business act in a certain way in a capitalist economy. All the government can do is to provide incentives for business to adopt certain policies and then hope that these are effective.

Businesses need to decide that it is in their interests, individually and collectively, to reduce mismatches. For example, businesses need to realize that an underqualified workforce or workers who are not able to work as many hours as they would like constitute a drag on productivity and profits, and they would be better served if workers were able to work up to their full potential. Moreover, businesses must decide that having workers who are able to balance their work and family lives and obtain sufficient earnings to satisfy their basic needs is not only just, but is good business.

There are thus two essential components of a policy agenda to alleviate mismatches—*governmental social and economic policies* that give businesses incentives to provide high-quality jobs, better prepare people for work, and make a safety net available to workers; and *business strategies* that seek to enhance competitiveness through workplace practices that enable workers to participate in decisions and become integral parts of their workplace communities.

EVOLVING WORK AND WORKERS

Policies designed to reduce mismatches and alleviate their consequences must be sensitive to the economic, political, and social transformations that will occur in the coming decades and have profound effects on the composition and attributes of the labor force and the structure of the workplace. We will first outline some of the changes likely to take place in the labor force and in job structures. These trends suggest strongly that the kinds of mismatches we have discussed will persist.

Changing Labor Force

Projected trends in labor force composition (Table 2.1) suggest that nearly half of the labor force will still consist of women, and a large proportion of them will be married with children. Since workers with families will continue to dominate the workforce, work-family mismatches will remain problematic, and issues related to working families will stay at the forefront of policy needs (Kochan 2004). Providing family-friendly practices such as child care, flexible work scheduling, and parental leave will thus remain pressing concerns.

The American labor force will also continue to be racially and ethnically diverse; the percentage of the labor force that is white will steadily decline. In particular, the percentage of the labor force that is Hispanic will grow and is projected to make up nearly a quarter of the labor force by 2050.

The growth in Hispanics is linked to immigration from Latin America, raising questions about the desired number of immigrants and the conditions under which they are admitted to the United States. Growth in immigration requires more training and education programs in order to alleviate mismatches such as underqualification and to enable these workers to find jobs that pay wages above poverty levels. Some of this training may be in English as a second language to enable foreign workers to compete effectively for jobs with native-speaking workers.

The increased diversity of the labor force will also require managers to develop skills that appreciate this diversity and enable them to motivate workers from different cultural backgrounds to work together. If cooperation and teamwork can be achieved, employers would have even less reason to discriminate against workers based on their race or ethnicity.

The proportion of the labor force made up of workers aged fifty-five and older is also apt to increase during the next few decades from about 13 percent in 2000 to about 19 percent in 2050 (Table 2.1). Baby boomers may not be able to retire as early as they would like because of declines in the value of their stock portfolios, cutbacks in pension benefits, and a possible rise in the Social Security retirement age. The greater proportion of older workers will increase the need for continued education and training in order to keep their skills current and keep them qualified for changing jobs. The growth in the older group of workers is likely to cause a decline of workers aged thirty-five to fifty-four, which may cause a shortage of skills in some occupations and industries.

The American workforce is thus projected to become increasingly gray in the next few decades, raising a number of questions that policy makers must address. For example, to what extent will older workers be displaced from their jobs and perhaps become underqualified because of industrial restructuring and reorganization of work? What strategies are available to match older workers' accumulated skills to new job situations, and how can they best be retrained to function effectively in these new jobs? What is the impact of geographical mobility on older people, since they may have to break long-standing community relationships and friendships to pursue jobs?

Whether these changes in the labor force result in mismatches depends also on what happens to jobs. For instance, workers with low skills will not be underqualified if they are able to find jobs that require few skills; working mothers with small children will be less likely to experience work-family conflict if they are able to arrange for child care.

Changing Job Structure

The opportunities likely to be available for people to fulfill their work-related needs and preferences are even less clear. The way work is organized, controlled, and rewarded depends greatly on what employers choose to do and how they decide to organize their workplaces; the evolution of jobs and workplaces will not necessarily follow a predictable trajectory. Rather, aspects of jobs that people value highly, such as economic and noneconomic rewards or job security, are the result of social and political processes that take place in labor markets and in individual workplaces.

Nevertheless, certain trends in the evolution of the occupational structure are fairly clear. Globalization and internationalization of work will accelerate, and companies will continue to face both domestic and foreign competition. Thus, employers must continue to be as competitive as possible, whether by cutting costs or restructuring work to enhance productivity.

Moreover, computers and other technological innovations will become even more integral to the organization of work and the workplace. There will be further growth in knowledge workers such as professional and technical occupations, especially those involved with computers, microelectronics, communications, and other aspects of the exchange of information. Technological change is likely to be even more rapid than in the past few decades, providing opportunities for employers to reorganize workplaces in ways that now we can only imagine.

Achieving greater flexibility, innovation, and teamwork will still be major goals. Skill requirements of some jobs will increase, creating the need for new skills and abilities on the part of individuals. Greater use of teams, for example, involves social and organizational skills as well as cognitive skills. The continued growth of the service sector underscores the importance of people skills and places less emphasis on the motor skills that were valued in manufacturing industries. The persistent need for these kinds of skills will require additional training and education if workers are to be capable of doing these jobs.

There will be continuing need for diverse and ongoing education and training for workers in order to adapt to the changing skill requirements of jobs. Who will provide this training is not clear. The growing insecurity of employment relations in the past few decades has made it less likely that workers will remain with one employer for their careers or even for an extended period of time. Employers are less likely to provide expensive training to their workers for fear that these employees will leave their organizations and take with them their expensive training. It is necessary to create incentives to encourage employers to invest in training and to avoid the temptation of a free ride on other employers' investments.

Other social and economic trends are likely to affect the evolution of the job structure in ways that are harder to predict. What will be the impact of technological changes, such as the growth of the Internet and e-commerce, on the nature of work and workers? The use of computers enables employers to downsize and eliminate layers of management as information is centralized. On the other hand, computers also provide opportunities to reduce geographical mismatches, since work can be done far from the main workplace. Moreover, computers enable flexible work hours, making it easier for workers to coordinate their work and family lives.

SEARCHING FOR BEST PRACTICES

Alleviating mismatches presents major challenges for social policy. Despite these challenges, the negative costs of these mismatches compel us to try to reduce them and to temper their consequences. Doing so must remain high on the agenda for social and economic policy in the United States in the twenty-first century.

It will be tricky to alleviate these mismatches, because many of them represent deep-rooted disjunctures between institutions in our society, as we discussed in Chapter 2. Initiatives on the part of diverse social and economic stakeholders, including business, Congress, the courts, the White House, Wall Street, educational institutions, and unions, to name a few, often diverge from one another and are propelled by forces that are extremely difficult to control. For example, the valuation of business performance by Wall Street in terms of the quarterly bottom line encourages managers to relocate plants to low-cost areas of the country or the world, even though the workers left behind are underemployed or unemployed. Pressures to cut costs also lead to the creation of low-wage jobs. Once these initiatives are set in motion, they take on a life of their own. Changing the way companies are governed—for example, from the shareholder model, in which companies base decisions primarily on whether they benefit stockholders, to a stakeholder model in which the company is responsive to workers as well as owners—will not be an easy task.

Reducing mismatches is also complicated because some of them are mutually exclusive. It is probably not possible to achieve good matches on all dimensions at the same time. For example, raising the skill requirements associated with jobs may help to reduce overqualification, but may also exacerbate underqualification. Similarly, creating a thirty-hour work week may reduce the incidence of overworking, but it could increase the likelihood that some people may not be able to work as much as they would like.

Any effort to use social and economic policy to attain certain ends involves the political process. For the past thirty years the United States has largely neglected these mismatches and their impacts on the middle class, dual-earner families, marginal workers, and the other groups we have discussed. Yet alleviating these mismatches and their consequences—and doing so now—is not only likely to be economically and socially efficient, it is also the right thing to do.

In order to develop a social policy agenda designed to address these concerns, it is helpful to draw upon existing models of best practices, both from other countries and within the United States.

Lessons from Abroad

The mismatches we have discussed are especially likely to occur in the United States, since employers in this country have an unusually free hand to determine how work is organized. In recent years, this freedom has increased because of the decline in union membership and the deregulation of markets that began in the 1980s. Moreover, the emphasis on individualism in the United States promotes the idea that workers should find jobs that fit their needs and preferences without government interference.

Differences in the institutions and cultures of other countries, especially those in western Europe, make it less likely that workers experience the mismatches that occur in the United States. These cross-national differences demonstrate the extent to which mismatches depend on the social context; they can be reduced or magnified by social policies. In previous chapters, we have provided some illustrations of how the various mismatches differ in other countries.

For example, workers in many European countries have much more flexible working hours than American workers, and so are less likely to experience overworking. The issue of work time has been a central focus of policy initiatives and collective bargaining in the European Union during the 1990s. This legislation has been advanced by unions and works councils in many of these countries, such as Germany, Sweden, and the Netherlands, ensuring that workers will have ample vacations and not work an excessive number of hours per week. In addition, the standard workweek in France has been reduced to thirty-five hours (Berg, Appelbaum, Bailey, and Kalleberg 2004). Part-time work is also more common in countries such as Sweden and the Netherlands than in the United States. The Netherlands, for example, avoided severe unemployment by creating part-time jobs as a result of an agreement between the employers' federation and the leading unions. Many people, particularly mothers with children, preferred part-time jobs.

Spatial mismatches are apt to be less common in countries with efficient public transportation that facilitates commuting to work and makes it possible for people to travel long distances from their homes. The Japanese train system is able to move large numbers of people quickly and efficiently and enables workers to live far from the Tokyo city center and still get to work in a relatively short time. This system represents a public commitment to move people from their homes to their workplaces.

The number of workers who are poor is relatively high in the United States because of the negligible influence of unions, which also helps account for the rise in income inequality in the United States since the 1980s. In countries where unions and worker associations are strong, such as Sweden and Norway, levels of poverty, especially working poverty, are relatively low, and incomes are more equally distributed.

European countries have also implemented a variety of practices to help reduce work-family conflict. The restrictions on excessive work time and greater opportunities for part-time and flexible work have surely helped. There are also much better provisions for child care in many European countries as well as early-childhood education programs, in addition to generous parental leave policies, all of which help to reduce work-family mismatches.

Most European countries also have much better safety nets to protect workers from the negative consequences of working in low-wage and otherwise inadequate jobs. Persons receive benefits as rights of citizenship in these countries rather than as benefits of employment given only to those who work a certain number of hours or who are employed by companies of a certain size, as in the United States. As a consequence of these safety nets, part-time or low-wage workers have medical insurance and retirement benefits, and so are less likely to suffer many of the negative consequences associated with inadequate work. People are also more apt to work part-time voluntarily, since their part-time jobs provide them with flexibility to deal with family matters or other activities. They are not forced to work full-time for health insurance and other benefits.

Lessons from US Companies

Employers choose how they will compete. They may continue to cut labor costs as much as possible through a low road strategy that pays low wages, provides few benefits, trims the workforce through downsizing and layoffs, offshores jobs to low-wage countries in Asia and Latin America, and encourages the immigration to the United States of low-skilled workers willing to work at low wages. Such low road strategies are likely to intensify mismatches such as overworking and underworking, geographical and earnings mismatches, and work-family conflict.

Alternatively, employers may choose high road strategies that seek and utilize high-skilled, highly committed workers. High-performance work practices encourage the discretionary effort of workers, who are given opportunities to participate in business decisions, the training to be able to take advantage of these opportunities, and the incentives to do so, such as a share of the profits generated through their efforts. These high road business strategies are likely to reduce overqualification as well as earnings mismatches.

An example of a high road strategy is provided by textile companies in North Carolina—such as DeFeet, which makes high-quality bicycle socks—that are trying to reverse the trend toward offshoring by finding niche markets where knowledge and flexibility are more important than large-scale, low-cost production. Other examples of high-performance companies include Jet Blue and Southwest Airlines in the airline industry; the family-friendly companies we discussed in the previous chapter; and the joint Toyota-General Motors automobile venture, the New United Motors Manufacturing (NUMMI) plant in Fremont, California. These companies have been successful because they have drawn upon the skills and commitment of their workforces to produce high-quality products and services.

A POLICY AGENDA

The lessons of the high road strategies practiced in other countries and by innovative employers in the United States suggest that government policies and business strategies must try to accomplish three main goals.

First, we need to create good, high-quality jobs. The proliferation of low-wage, often low-skilled jobs and the disappearance of middle-class jobs in recent years has contributed to the rise in earnings and benefits mismatches, along with underworking, overqualification, and geographical mismatches. Social policies and business strategies are needed to reverse these trends toward bad jobs; we must create better jobs that require higher levels of skill, provide a living wage, and allow workers to have more flexibility over their worktime.

Second, we must give workers the education and training they need to obtain and perform these high-quality jobs. Some people lack the skills and behavioral traits to qualify for high-skill jobs, which contributes to mismatches such as underqualification, underworking, and geographical and earnings mismatches. Social policies and business strategies ought to promote investments in human capital through training and education and enhance people's social capital, such as their network connections to other people and communities. Both human and social capital is needed to help workers learn about job vacancies and acquire the skills needed to function well in the knowledge and service economy of the future.

Third, it is necessary to build a safety net to protect people from the negative consequences of mismatches. It is inevitable that some mismatches will occur in a dynamic industrial society such as the United States, and some people will always be more vulnerable than others to earnings and geographical mismatches, work-family conflicts, and temporal and skill mismatches. Therefore, social policies must focus also on protecting workers from the negative consequences associated with these mismatches. The government has a responsibility to provide all its citizens with basic protections such as health insurance and retirement benefits and not leave the distribution of such benefits up to the benevolence and economic success of individual employers.

All three of these elements of the policy agenda have become more problematic over the past three decades or so because of the economic pressures on employers and the social and political changes we discussed in previous chapters. Thus, achieving these three goals is a matter of great urgency and must be at the forefront of the nation's agenda. We turn now to some government and private sector initiatives needed to achieve these three fundamental policy goals.

Creating Good Jobs

People define a good job in different ways. Some people define a good job as one that pays well and provides fringe benefits such as health insurance. Others define it as one that is interesting and challenging or that provides opportunities for advancing to higher-level jobs. Still others view a good job as one that is secure. Finally, some people may feel that their job is good if they have friendly coworkers or supervisors, an easy commute, or the opportunity to help other people. A job that has one of these characteristics may not necessarily have all the others; for example, a job that pays well may not necessarily be secure, or one that is challenging may not necessarily lead to opportunities for advancement.

Despite these individual differences, most people believe that the minimum standard for a good job is that it pays at least a living wage. In addition, the job should also provide workers with opportunities to utilize their skills to avoid being overqualified and some flexibility in the hours worked or the schedule so they can balance other aspects of their lives with their work.

Government Social and Economic Policies

Governmental social and economic policies can enhance the quality of jobs in several ways. Perhaps the most direct way is by reestablishing standards in labor markets. Government can increase the federal minimum wage, for example, which, as we noted in Chapter 8, has remained at $5.15 since 1997. While relatively few people earn the federal minimum wage, a mandated increase in this yardstick would put pressure on employers to raise wages to at least half the average wage (around $7.75 today), so as to be more in line with living wage levels that differ by geographical area. The government could also oblige businesses supported by public funds to pay a living wage to their workers.

The government can also require employers to pay part-time workers the same hourly wages and benefits as full-time workers. One of the last ways in which employers in the

United States are legally allowed to discriminate among workers is on the basis of hours worked; part-time workers thus earn less per hour than full-time workers. Moreover, under the Employment Retirement Security Act, employers can exempt from pension plans workers who are employed fewer than 1,000 hours a year (Kalleberg, Reskin, and Hudson 2000). Legislation to extend such rights to part-time workers would remove the incentives that employers now have to create part-time jobs. An expansion of rights for part-time workers could also be coupled with legislation that moves the country toward working fewer hours by reducing the full-time workweek to thirty or thirty-five hours, mandating a minimum amount of vacation time for all workers, and providing time for personal leave and sick leave.

The government can also stimulate the growth of new jobs through labor demand policies such as creating public sector jobs, as was done at the end of the Great Depression; stimulating economic activity by reducing corporate taxes; and subsidizing private hiring by means of strategies such as tax breaks.

The use of tax breaks as incentives for employers to create high-quality jobs may be a particularly promising approach to alleviate mismatches. Such financial incentives could encourage employers to adopt creative flextime work schedules to accommodate workers' family needs and invest in innovative, high-skilled technologies and occupational structures. Government support of high-wage business through its investments in research and development would enhance economic development as well as send a strong signal about the importance of a high-wage economy.

Labor demand programs should also be targeted at the hard-to-employ workers and at high unemployment areas and involve subsidies to employers to encourage them to create jobs especially for these groups.

Business Strategies

All companies in a particular industry may face similar market pressures, but it is clear that managers have some discretion about employment and wage policies. As we have noted, a number of companies in the United States have adopted high road strategies and compete based on jobs that pay well, demand high skills, and involve the participation of workers. Unfortunately, the use of such strategies is far from universal; recent estimates suggest that only about one-third of American workplaces have implemented such strategies (Osterman 2001).

Government incentives such as tax breaks can encourage employers to adopt high road strategies. However, employers also need to be persuaded that these are good business strategies that are likely to result in higher productivity and profits. The proof that high road competitive strategies actually increase productivity and profits is mounting across a broad range of manufacturing industries, including apparel, steel, and medical electronics (see Appelbaum, Bailey, Berg, and Kalleberg 2000). Such strategies are associated with high wages and require considerable investments in training, but they still pay off because they result in higher-quality products, faster response times, and reductions in labor turnover (Appelbaum, Bernhardt, and Murnane 2003). In addition to increasing organizational performance, such strategies also benefit workers by providing high-quality jobs.

Employers are also more likely to adopt high road strategies if they are pressured to do so by workers. It is not surprising, for example, that Southwest Airlines and NUMMI, two examples of high-performance work organizations discussed earlier, are highly unionized. Employers have been able to get away with low road strategies largely because of the lack of opposition from the labor movement. Thus increasing the power of workers is a vital component in efforts to encourage companies to take the high road to increasing competitiveness.

Preparing Workers: Investing in Human and Social Capital
Workers also need to be prepared to perform the higher-quality jobs that will be created as a result of these demand-side policies. As we have discussed, there are skill shortages in a number of areas of the economy, and workers are often underqualified for the jobs that are available. There are also inequalities in education and training that lead to underworking and underqualification as well as earnings and geographic mismatches.

Therefore, labor supply policies are needed to make sure that workers are adequately prepared for high-quality jobs. Such programs would seek to expand the pool of qualified jobseekers, either by augmenting worker skills or by inducing more people to look for work. These policies need to focus on developing people's human capital—their skills and abilities— as well as their social capital—network connections and membership in various kinds of social groups.

Government Social and Economic Policies

Government policies can enhance the skills of job seekers in several ways. Most directly, social policies need to remedy deficiencies in the public education system and ensure that all Americans have the opportunity to obtain a high-quality education, from kindergarten through college. Educational inequalities tied to differences in the ability of local school systems to fund schools must be eliminated; such inequalities are a major cause of the continued segregation of housing and therefore the problem of spatial mismatch, and are closely linked to problems of underworking and underqualification.

Educational policies must be supplemented by job training strategies to provide workers with the skills they actually need to perform jobs. These include both technical skills such as cognitive and motor skills and soft skills such as motivation and proper work attitudes (see Chapter 3). The government has an important role to play here, since it can absorb some of the costs associated with such training.

How can the government best fund training programs, and what are the most effective methods of skill acquisition? One likely institutional venue for training programs is the community college, which offers great potential for preparing workers in an area for the jobs that are created there. Governments could play a major role by creating networks to connect universities, industries, and companies, as is illustrated by the North Carolina textile industry.

Government policies should also be targeted at training people who are especially powerless in the labor market, such as low-skilled immigrants. They could also mainstream workers with disabilities and mental deficiencies into the labor force in jobs where they can find rewarding work and make valuable contributions to society.

Business Strategies

Employers in the United States have generally not invested much in training their workers, as we discussed earlier. In the absence of institutions that guard against free rider problems, employers will be reluctant to invest in training workers who may then move on to other companies.

Agreements among groups of employers in an industry to share the risks of providing job training could help avoid concerns about free riding. Employers can use new labor market institutions to help them, such as when companies band together to train workers (in industries as diverse as hospitals, hotels, and hosiery) and set industry skill standards (see the case studies in Appelbaum, Bernhardt, and Murnane 2003). Comprehensive retraining programs that require contributions from employers help to ensure that employers have a financial stake in retraining and will make certain that they get their money's worth by providing high-end jobs.

Employers are sometimes assisted by local governments and community colleges. For example, the Hosiery Technology Center (HTC) at Catawba Valley Community College, in partnership with individual firms, industry suppliers, and the regional industry trade association, has helped the hosiery industry to survive in North Carolina. The HTC provides training specific to this industry and is geared toward the largely immigrant labor force in the area who do not have much for-

mal education. The HTC has also retrained machine techni-
cians to repair and maintain the new, computerized knitting
machines (Willis, Connelly, and DeGraff 2003).

The presence of unions makes a big difference in whether
businesses will adopt training programs. A number of the companies discussed in Chapter 4 that adopted training programs
were persuaded to do so by pressure from unions, who often
acted as a partner with management in implementing these
programs. In addition, the study of call centers discussed in
Chapter 8 found that a unionized call center invested more
than twice as much in training and pay and benefits than a similar call center that was not unionized (Batt, Hunter, and
Wilk 2003).

The Wisconsin Regional Training Partnership illustrates
how unions, business, and the colleges can act together to promote training. This program is a consortium of forty employers
in the metalworking, electronics, plastics, and related manufacturing industries—along with unions and technical colleges—
in the Milwaukee metropolitan area. The partnership facilities
communication among these groups and develops skill standards to help workers transfer skills across employers. The
members of the partnership are also undertaking an apprenticeship program and a training program for inner-city residents to
provide access to entry-level jobs (Osterman 1999, 143).

Building a Safety Net
The third component of the policy agenda is the creation of a
better safety net to protect people from the negative consequences of working in low-wage jobs and other forms of inadequate work, particularly the consequences associated with

overwork and underwork, underqualification and earnings, and geographic and work-family mismatches.

Workers should have access to this safety net regardless of whether or not they work a minimum number of hours for an employer willing and able to pay for benefits. This plan differs from the employer-centered model that currently provides benefits in the United States. The origin of this system dates to the 1930s, when Franklin Roosevelt and his advisors devised social security and unemployment insurance plans funded and distributed through employers. The rise of unions during the next several decades extended and reinforced this employer-centered system, and, as new benefits such as health insurance and private pensions were added to attract workers, these too were distributed through employers (Kochan 2004, 76). Since wage and price controls during World War II prevented employers from raising wages, instead they offered fringe benefits such as health insurance to attract workers.

This employer centered model worked, at least for some workers, as long as the economy was growing and jobs were relatively stable. However, it became much less viable as economic pressures on employers to cut costs mounted and workers could no longer count on having a secure job. As a result of corporate restructuring such as downsizing, this system was no longer viable. In its place, we need a system in which basic social protections are not dependent on working for a particular employer. These protections must be portable and transferable from one employer to another.

Perhaps the most basic element of the safety net is the provision of universal health insurance. Employment-based health insurance is now the only real source of health coverage for

Americans not yet eligible for Medicare and not poor enough to qualify for Medicaid. Comprehensive national health insurance would include a program of parental leave to help children get off to a good start in the first two years of life and insurance for catastrophic illness.

A program of comprehensive health care would not only protect workers from mismatches such as low-wage jobs; it would also help to eliminate some of these mismatches. One reason for the existence of low-wage jobs is that employers have been forced to divert a large portion of their productivity gains to fund their rising health-care costs. A vivid example is the automobile industry; General Motors is on the verge of bankruptcy largely because of its long tradition of providing high-quality health care to its employees. As a result of these commitments, the costs of health care now exceed the costs of raw materials such as steel to produce each car. We need to remove health-care costs from the employers' labor costs and make them an expense borne by the government. A nationalized health-care system would not only remove a major source of stress and uncertainty for both employers and their employees; it is also likely to provide higher-quality health care at lower cost than at present.

Government policies also need to assist workers to balance their work and family lives. Working-time legislation modeled after some European countries would provide working parents with some of the flexibility that they need to take care of their families. The government can also provide tax incentives to companies to implement comprehensive day care programs for children, preferably at the work site. Like many of the elements on the policy agenda, these programs must be supported by employers to ensure that they have a stake in them and that nobody gains a competitive advantage by not participating.

Existing government programs should also be expanded to protect workers better from the negative consequences associated with mismatches. For example, extending unemployment insurance would give workers greater security in times of economic adversity. As we noted in Chapter 7, only one-third of all unemployed people receive unemployment insurance benefits today.

Moreover, we need to strengthen the earned income tax credit (EITC), which, as we discussed in Chapter 8, is a useful antipoverty measure that ties benefits to work and provides wage subsidies for low-income workers. In addition, we need to help workers save more money to supplement their social security benefits upon retirement. A 2001 study found that only half of the households with retirement accounts that were approaching retirement had savings of $55,000 and one-fourth had less than $13,000 (Kochan 2004, 81). Providing greater opportunities for workers to open and maintain savings and investment accounts would help workers build assets, a key factor in reducing poverty. Such retirement funds also need to be portable.

Implementing the Policy Agenda

Successfully implementing this policy agenda requires us to overcome a number of obstacles, some of which result from various social, economic, and political actors pursuing their interests. Examples include businesses seeking flexibility by cutting costs and the government protecting those who are best able to use markets to advance their interests. Moreover, the currently huge and growing federal budget deficit limits the discretionary resources available to alleviate mismatches and build the safety net. It is not very likely that the federal government will endorse the notion that big government will solve the problems we have identified anytime soon.

Consequently, government intervention at the federal level needs to be supported by initiatives at community, local, and state levels. Various states are experimenting with a range of programs to reduce mismatches, reminiscent of the early twentieth century, when a number of states such as Wisconsin and New York experimented with unemployment insurance and other protections that eventually ended up in the federal New Deal legislation (Kochan 2004). For example, California has recently adopted the first paid family leave program in the United States, a hopeful harbinger of things to come in other states. Moreover, the kinds of partnerships involving communities, business, labor, and education discussed above illustrate the grassroots efforts and cooperative ventures to provide training and create high-quality jobs that might be implemented at the national level.

Enhancing Workers' Labor Market Power
It took the corrective actions of unions to help pass the legislation that improved the oppressive employment conditions of the Depression era. In similar fashion, neither government policies designed to alleviate mismatches nor high road business strategies will be adopted unless workers have sufficient power to press for their interests. During the past several decades, employers have had free rein to implement human resource policies and workplace practices designed to cut labor

costs and maximize shareholder value without taking into consideration the views of workers, who were not a countervailing force because of their inability to organize.

Workers need power in the labor market to ensure that they share in gains in productivity and profits. This has not been the case in recent years. During the boom years of the 1990s, for example, the record profits enjoyed by American companies were not shared with their workers, despite John F. Kennedy's famous claim that "a rising tide lifts all boats." Thus, while it is important to encourage economic growth in order to create healthy and profitable businesses, it is equally important for workers to get a fair share of the gains.

Our discussions have underscored how the seven mismatches all result in one way or another from workers' lack of market power and low degree of control over their employment situations. Social, economic, and political changes in the United States have made large segments of the population especially vulnerable to market forces because of low skills and qualifications, constraints on their geographic mobility, and other characteristics that prevent them from obtaining jobs that satisfy their needs and preferences. Some workers—especially women, non-whites, young and older people, and people with little education—are especially likely to have low control over their employment situations and are more apt to be vulnerable to market forces. We must reduce the vulnerability of these workers to market forces and provide them with sufficient market power and control over their employment conditions so that they can find and keep jobs that fit with their needs and preferences.

Enhancing the power of workers requires collective organization and action and depends on the reaffirmation of the right of workers to organize and bargain collectively. Labor revitalization hinges on our ability to reverse the antiunion climate in America and to build a more hospitable environment for workers to join unions and benefit from them. The decline of unions in the past several decades has been fueled by antiunion behavior on the part of employers, who have discouraged workers from organizing as well as taken steps to avoid unionization such as moving workplaces to areas of the United States and the world where unions are weak. Legislation such as the Employee Free Choice Act[32] would facilitate labor organizing, as would stronger enforcement of existing rights to organize by watchdog agencies such as the National Labor Relations Board.

Growth in labor unions in the past has occurred in explosive bursts rather than in steady increments (Clawson 2003). Efforts to increase membership are needed, but if the AFL-CIO, the largest federation of unions in the United States, were to add twice as many new members per year as it now does, it will still take a very long time for membership to reach the levels of the early 1980s. Instead, in the current environment unions need to ally themselves with other social movements, such as the women's movement, racial movements, living wage campaigns, movements to provide support for working families, and movements concerned with global justice. These movements represent efforts of people who are most vulnerable in the labor market to better their situations and to enhance their market power. By collaborating with these movements, unions will gain strength and be in a better position to help these

---

[32]See www.unionvoice.org/campaign/sponsorefca/explanation.

groups—and all workers—to alleviate the mismatches we have discussed.

CONCLUSIONS

Mismatches between persons and jobs are diverse and reflect the many ways in which people and their jobs differ in a complex industrial society. These mismatches have important and far-ranging consequences for individuals, their families, the organizations for which they work, and ultimately for the society in which they live. The seven types of mismatches we have discussed are rooted in the structures and institutions of our society. Alleviating them requires social solutions, since individuals cannot be expected to reduce these mismatches through their own actions. This chapter has outlined some of the governmental social and economic policies and business strategies needed to alleviate these mismatches.

These public and private policies must anticipate the changes that are apt to occur in the structure of jobs and in the composition of the labor force, since transformations along each of these dimensions will affect the nature of mismatches and the likelihood that they will occur. These changes will create opportunities as well as challenges for workers. The direction of change will help to answer questions such as whether the job structure will be able to accommodate the needs of working families, the growth in diversity, and other characteristics of the changing workforce.

The issues we have discussed in this book are likely to take on added importance in the coming years. Skill requirements for jobs are increasing in some sectors of the economy, while in other sectors there has been a proliferation of low-skilled and low-wage jobs. Pressures to do more with less have increased the chances that people are overworked in some sectors of the economy, putting more stress on them and their families. In other sectors, the need to cut costs has led employers to create part-time jobs or to lay off workers and reduce wages, so that even full-time workers have now joined the ranks of the working poor.

These economic pressures are likely to continue to generate mismatches between work and workers in the twenty-first century. Improving the fit between people and jobs will thus remain an ongoing challenge for American society, as we seek to enhance both the quality of work experienced by individuals and the competitiveness of the American economy.

REFERENCES

Alesina, Alberto, Edward Glaeser, and Bruce Sacerdote. 2005. "Work and Leisure in the U.S. and Europe: Why so Different?" *NBER Macroeconomic Annual*, National Bureau of Economic Research.

Andrews, Edmund L. 2004. "Survey Confirms It: Women Outjuggle Men." *New York Times*, September 15.

Appelbaum, Eileen, Thomas Bailey, Peter Berg, and Arne L. Kalleberg. 2000. *Manufacturing Advantage: Why High-Performance Work Systems Pay Off*. Ithaca, NY: Cornell University Press.

———. 2002. *Shared Work, Valued Care: New Norms for Organizing Market Work and Unpaid Care Work*. Washington DC: Economic Policy Institute.

———, Annette Bernhardt, and Richard Murnane, eds. 2003. *Low-Wage America: How Employers are Reshaping Opportunity in the Workplace*. New York: Russell Sage Foundation.

Ashforth, Blake E., Glen E. Kreiner, and Mel Fugate. 2000. "All in a Day's Work: Boundaries and Micro Role Transitions." *Academy of Management Review* 25 (3): 472–91.

Autor, David H., Frank Levy, and Richard J. Murnane. 2003. "The Skill Content of Recent Technological Change: An Empirical Exploration." *Quarterly Journal of Economics* 118: 1279–1334.

Barley, Stephen R. 1996. *The Brave New World of Work*. London: Needhams Design and Print.

Barnett, Rosalind Chait, and Grace K. Baruch. 1985. "Women's Involvement in Multiple Roles and Psychological Distress." *Journal of Personality and Social Psychology* 49(1): 135–45.

Bartik, Timothy J. 2001. *Jobs for the Poor: Can Labor Demand Policies Help?* New York: Russell Sage Foundation.

Batenburg, Ronald, and Marco de Witte. 2001. "Underemployment in the Netherlands: How the Dutch 'Poldermodel' Failed to Close the Education-Jobs Gap." *Work, Employment and Society* 15(1): 73–94.

Batt, Rosemary, Larry W. Hunter, and Stephanie Wilk. 2003. "How and When Does Management Matter? Job Quality and Career Opportunities for Call Center Workers." In

Eileen Appelbaum, Annette Bernhardt, and Richard J. Murnane, eds., 2003, 270–313.

Bell, Daniel. 1976. *The Coming of Post-Industrial Society: A Venture in Social Forecasting.* New York: Basic Books.

Bell, Linda A., and Richard B. Freeman. 1995. "Why Do Americans and Germans Work Different Hours?" In F. Butler, W. Franz, R. Schettkat, and D. Soskice, eds., *Institutional Frameworks and Labor Market Performance*, Chapter 5. London: Routledge.

Berg, Ivar. 1970. *Education and Jobs: The Great Training Robbery.* New York: Praeger.

———. 2003. *Education and Jobs: The Great Training Robbery*, with a new introduction by the author. Clinton Corners, NY: Percheron Press.

———, and Janice Shack-Marquez. 1985. "Current Conceptions of Structural Unemployment: Some Logical and Empirical Difficulties." *Research in the Sociology of Work*, 3: 99–117.

Berg, Peter, Eileen Appelbaum, Thomas Bailey, and Arne L. Kalleberg. 2004. "Contesting Time: International Comparisons of Employee Control of Working Time." *Industrial and Labor Relations Review* 57 (3): 331–49.

Berger, Joseph. 2004. "4-hour Trek Across New York for 4 Hours of Work, and $28." *New York Times*, May 6, A1, A29.

Bernhardt, Annette, Martina Morris, Mark S. Handcock, and Marc A. Scott. 2001. *Divergent Paths: Economic Mobility in the New American Labor Market.* New York: Russell Sage Foundation.

Bernstein, Aaron. 2001. "The Human Factor." *Business Week*, August 21: 118, 120–22.

———. 2002. "Too Many Workers? Not For Long." *Business Week*, May 20: 124, 127–30.

Bernstein, Jared. 2003. "Who's Poor? Don't Ask the Census Bureau." *New York Times*, September 26.

Bernstein, Nina. 2005. "Decline Is Seen in Immigration." *New York Times*, September 28, A1, C19.

Bills, David B. 1992. "The Mutability of Educational Credentials as Hiring Criteria." *Work and Occupations* 19: 79–95.

Bluestone, Barry, and Bennett Harrison. 1982. *The Deindustrialization of America: Plant Closings, Community Abandonment, and the Dismantling of Basic Industry.* New York: Basic Books.

———, and Stephen Rose 1997. "Overworked and Underemployed." *The American Prospect* 31: 58–69.

Boisard, Pierre, Damien Cartron, Michel Gollac, and Antoine Valeyre. 2003. *Time and Work: Duration of Work.* Dublin: European Foundation for the Improvement of Living and Working Conditions.

Bond, James T., Ellen Galinksy, and Jennifer E. Swanberg. 1998. *The 1997 National Study of the Changing Workforce.* New York: Families and Work Institute.

Borghans, L., and A. de Grip, eds. 2000. *The Overeducated Worker?* Cheltenham, UK: Edward Elgar.

Boushey, Heather, Chauna Brocht, Bethney Gundersen, and Jared Bernstein. 2001. *Hardships in America: The Real Story of Working Families.* Washington DC: Economic Policy Institute.

Bowles, Samuel, and Herbert Gintis. 1976. *Schooling in Capitalist America.* New York: Basic Books.

Braverman, Harry. 1974. *Labor and Monopoly Capital.* New York: Monthly Review Press.

Brooks, David. 2004. "More than Money." *New York Times*, March 2.

Brown, Susan L., and Alan Booth. 2002. "Stress at Home, Peace at Work: A Test of the Time Bind Hypothesis." *Social Science Quarterly* 83 (4): 905–20.

Brynin, Malcolm. 2002. "Overqualification in Employment." *Work, Employment and Society* 16(4): 637–54.

Burris, Val. 1983. "The Social and Political Consequences of Overeducation." *American Sociological Review* 48 (August): 454–67.

———. 2005. "Overeducation: Then and Now." *Work and Occupations* 32(3): 319–21.

Callaghan, Polly S., and Heidi Hartmann. 1991. *Contingent Work: A Chart Book on Part-Time and Temporary Employment.* Washington DC: Economic Policy Institute.

Card, David, and Alan B. Krueger. 1995. *Myth and Measurement: The New Economics of the Minimum Wage.* Princeton, NJ: Princeton University Press.

Carnoy, Martin. 2000. *Sustaining the New Economy: Work, Family, and Community in the Information Age.* New York: Russell Sage Foundation.

Carrington, William J., and Bruce C. Fallick. 2001. "Do Some Workers Have Minimum Wage Careers?" *Monthly Labor Review* (May): 17–27.

Cassirer, Naomi. 2003. "Work Arrangements Among Women in the United States." In *Nonstandard Work in Developed Economies: Causes and Consequences*, Susan Houseman and Machiko Osawa, eds., 307–49. Kalamazoo, MI: W. E. Upjohn Institute for Employment Research.

Castillo, Monica D. 1998. "Persons outside the Labor Force Who Want a Job." *Monthly Labor Review* 121(7): 34–42.

Charles, Maria, and David B. Grusky. 2004. *Occupational Ghettos: The Worldwide Segregation of Women and Men.* Stanford, CA: Stanford University Press.

Chatman, J. 1989. "Improving Interactional Organizational Research: A Model of Person-Organization Fit." *Academy of Management Review* 14: 333–49.

Clark, Sue Campbell. 2000. "Work/Family Border Theory: A New Theory of Work/Family Balance." *Human Relations* 53(6): 747–70.

Clarkberg, Marin, and Phyllis Moen. 2001. "Understanding the Time-Squeeze: Married Couples' Preferred and Actual Work-Hour Strategies." *American Behavioral Scientist* 44(7): 1115–36.

Clawson, Dan. 2003. *The Next Upsurge: Labor and the New Social Movements*. Ithaca, NY: ILR/Cornell University Press.

Cleeland, Nancy. 2002. "Workers Might Be Going Too Fast." *Raleigh News and Observer*, July 17, E1.

Clemetson, Lynette. 2003. "Poor Workers Find Modest Housing Unaffordable, Study Says." *New York Times*, September 9, A15.

Clogg, Clifford C. 1979. *Measuring Underemployment*. New York: Academic Press.

———, and James W. Shockey. 1984. "Mismatch between Occupation and Schooling: A Prevalence Measure, Recent Trends, and Demographic Analysis." *Demography* 21(2): 235–57.

———, Scott R. Eliason, and Kevin T. Leicht. 2001. *Analyzing the Labor Force: Concepts, Measures, and Trends*. New York: Kluwer Academic/Plenum Publishers.

Cohn, Elchanan, and Shanina P. Kahn. 1995. "The Wage Effects of Overschooling Revisited." *Labor Economics* 2: 67–76.

Collins, Randall. 1979. *The Credential Society: An Historical Sociology of Education and Stratification*. New York: Academic Press.

Committee on Techniques for the Enhancement of Human Performance. 1999. *The Changing Nature of Work: Implications for Occupational Analysis*. Washington DC: National Academy Press.

Davis, Amy E., and Arne L. Kalleberg. 2006. "Family-Friendly Organizations? Work/Family Programs in the 1990s." *Work and Occupations* 33(2): 191–223.

Durkheim, Emile. 1933. *The Division of Labor in Society*. New York: The Free Press.

Edwards, Jeffrey R., and Nancy P. Rothbard. 2000. "Mechanisms Linking Work and Family: Clarifying the Relationship between Work and Family Constructs." *Academy of Management Review* 25(1): 178–99.

Edwards, Richard. 1979. *Contested Terrain*. New York: Basic Books.

Ehrenreich, Barbara. 2001. *Nickel and Dimed: On (Not) Getting by in America*. New York: Henry Holt.

Elder, Glen H., Jr., and Richard C. Rockwell. 1979. "The Life-Course and Human Development: An Ecological Perspective." *International Journal of Behavioral Development* 2: 1–21.

Elder, Glen H., Jr., Linda K. George, and Michael J. Shanahan. 1996. "Psychosocial Stress over the Life Course." In Howard B. Kaplan, ed., *Psychosocial Stress: Perspectives on Structure, Theory, Life Course and Methods*, 247–92. Orlando, FL: Academic Press.

Ellwood, David. 1986. "Spatial Mismatch Hypothesis: Are There Teenage Jobs Missing in the Ghetto?" in Richard B. Freeman and Harry J. Holzer, eds., *The Black Youth Employment Crisis*, 147–90. Chicago: Chicago University Press.

Epstein, Cynthia Fuchs, and Arne L. Kalleberg, eds. 2004. *Fighting for Time: Shifting Boundaries of Work and Social Life*. New York: Russell Sage Foundation.

The EQW National Employer Survey: First Findings. 1994. Philadelphia: National Center for the Educational Quality of the Workforce.

Fagan, Colette. 2001. "The Temporal Reorganization of Employment and the Household Rhythm of Work Schedules: The Implications for Gender and Class Relations." *American Behavioral Scientist* 44(7): 1199–1212.

Farber, Henry S. 2005. "Union Membership in the United States: The Divergence between the Public and Private Sectors." Working Paper 503, Princeton University, Industrial Relations Section (September).

Farkas, George, and Paula England. 1985. "Integrating the Sociology and Economics of Employment, Compensation, and Unemployment." *Research in the Sociology of Work* 3: 119–46.

Fenwick, Rudy, and Mark Tausig. 2001. "Scheduling Stress: Family and Health Outcomes of Shift Work and Schedule Control. *American Behavioral Scientist* 44(7): 1179–98.

Fernandez, Roberto M. 1994. "Race, Space, and Job Accessibility: Evidence from a Plant Relocation." *Economic Geography* 70(4): 390–416.

———, and Celina Su. 2004. "Space in the Study of Labor Markets." *Annual Review of Sociology* 30: 545–69.

Fitzgerald, Joan. 2004. "Pathways to Good Jobs: Can Career Ladders Solve the Low-Wage Problem?" *American Prospect* 15(1): 57–59.

Flanigan, James. 2005. "Now, High-Tech Work is Going Abroad." *New York Times*, November 17, C6.

Ford, Paul Leichester, ed. 1897. *The Writings of Thomas Jefferson*, vol. 8. New York: G. P. Putnam's Sons.

Form, William. 1987. "On the Degradation of Skills." *Annual Review of Sociology* 13:29–47.

———, and Joan Huber. 1976. "Occupational Power." In Robert Dubin, ed., *Handbook of Work, Organization, and Society*, 751–806. Chicago: Rand McNally.

Freeman, Richard B. 1976. *The Overeducated American.* New York: Academic Press.

———. 1995. "Are Your Wages Set in Beijing?" *Journal of Economic Perspectives* 9(3): 15–32.

Friedan, Betty. 1963. *The Feminine Mystique.* New York: Bantam Doubleday Dell.

Friedland, Daniel S., and Richard H. Price. 2002. "Underemployment: Consequences for the Health and Well-Being of Workers." Unpublished paper, Institute for Social Research, University of Michigan, Ann Arbor, MI.

Friedman, Thomas L. 2005. *The World Is Flat: A Brief History of the Twenty-First Century.* New York: Farrar, Straus and Giroux.

Galbraith, James K. 1998. *Created Unequal: The Crisis in American Pay.* New York: The Free Press.

Galinksy, Ellen, Stacy Kim, and James Bond. 2001. *Feeling Overworked: When Work Becomes Too Much.* New York: Families and Work Institute.

George, David. 1997. "Working Longer Hours: Pressure from the Boss or Pressure from the Marketers?" *Review of Social Economy* 55: 33–65.

Golden, Lonnie. 2001. "Flexible Work Time: Correlates and Consequences of Work Scheduling." *American Behavioral Scientist* 44(7): 1157–78.

———. 2003. "Overemployed Workers in the U.S. Labor Market." Paper presented at the Industrial Relations Research Association (IRRA) ASSA Conference, San Diego, CA.

Gomory, Ralph, and Kathleen Christensen. 1999. "Three Jobs—Two People." *Washington Post*, June 2.

Goode, William J. 1960. "A Theory of Role Strain." *American Sociological Review* 25(4): 483–96.

Gordon, David M. 1972. *Theories of Poverty and Underemployment*. Lexington, MA: D. C. Heath and Company.

———. 1996. *Fat and Mean: The Corporate Squeeze of Working Americans and the Myth of Managerial "Downsizing."* New York: The Free Press.

Gottschalk, Peter, and Sheldon Danziger. 1998. "Family Income Mobility—How Much Is There, and Has It Changed?" In James A. Auerbach and Richard Belous, eds., *The Inequality Paradox: Growth of Income Disparity*, 92–111. Washington DC: National Policy Association.

Granovetter, Mark. 1981. "Toward a Sociological Theory of Income Differences." In Ivar Berg, ed., *Sociological Perspectives on Labor Markets*, 11–47. New York: Academic Press.

Green, Francis, and Steven McIntosh. 2001. "The Intensification of Work in Europe." *Labour Economics* 8: 291–308.

Greenhaus, Jeffrey H., and Nicholas J. Beutell. 1985. "Sources of Conflict between Work and Family Roles." *Academy of Management Review* 10(1): 76–88.

———, and Saroj Parasuraman. 1999. "Research on Work, Family, and Gender." In Gary N. Powell, ed., *Handbook of Gender and Work*, 391–412. Thousand Oaks, CA: Sage Publications.

Greenhouse, Steven. 2004. "Lawsuits and Change at Wal-Mart." *New York Times*, November 19, A20.

Grow, Brian. 2002. "UPS Doesn't Deliver for Part-timers." *Business Week* online, July 17.

Hakim, Danny. 2005. "For a G.M. Family, the American Dream Vanishes." *New York Times* online, November 19.

Halaby, Charles N. 1994. "Overeducation and Skill Mismatch." *Sociology of Education* 67 (January): 47–59.

Halbfinger, David. 2002. "Factory Jobs, Then Workers, Leaving Poorest Southern Areas." *New York Times*, May 10, A16.

Handel, Michael J. 2003. "Skills Mismatch in the Labor Market." *Annual Review of Sociology* 29: 135–65.

Harrison, Bennett, and Barry Bluestone. 1988. *The Great U-Turn: Corporate Restructuring and the Polarizing of America*. New York: Basic Books.

Hecker, Daniel E. 2001. "Employment Outlook: 2000–2010: Occupational Employment Projections to 2010." *Monthly Labor Review* (November): 57–84.

Herbert, Bob. 2002. "The Invisible Women." *New York Times*, September 13, A27.

Herzenberg, Stephen A., John A. Alic, and Howard Wial. 1998. *New Rules for a New Economy: Employment and Opportunity in Postindustrial America*. Ithaca, NY: Cornell University Press.

Hochschild, Arlie. 1997. *The Time Bind: When Work Becomes Home and Home Becomes Work*. New York: Metropolitan Books.

———. 2002. "Reply: A Dream Test of the Time Bind." *Social Science Quarterly* 83(4): 921–24.

———, with Anne Machung. 1989. *The Second Shift: Working Parents and the Revolution at Home*. New York: Viking.

Hodson, Randy. 2001. *Dignity at Work*. New York: Cambridge University Press.

Holland, John L. 1973. *Making Vocational Choices: A Theory of Careers*. Englewood Cliffs, NJ: Prentice Hall.

Holzer, Harry J. 1991. "The Spatial Mismatch Hypothesis: What Has the Evidence Shown?" *Urban Studies* 28(1): 105–22.

———. 1996. *What Employers Want: Job Prospects for Less Educated Workers*. New York: Russell Sage Foundation.

Howell, D. R., and E. N. Wolff. 1991. "Trends in the Growth and Distribution of Skills in the U.S. Workplace, 1960–1985." *Industrial and Labor Relations Review* 44: 486–502.

Hudson, Kenneth, Arne L. Kalleberg, and Rachel A. Rosenfeld. 2005. "How Good is Half a Job? Part-Time Employment and Job Quality in the United States." Unpublished paper, Department of Sociology, University of North Carolina at Chapel Hill.

Hummel, Marta. 2004. "Adapting and Persevering." *News and Record*, September 26.

Inlanfeldt, Keith R., and David L. Sjoquist. 1998. "The Spatial Mismatch Hypothesis: A Review of Recent Studies and Their Implications for Welfare Reform." *Housing Policy Debate* 9(4): 849–92.

Jacobs, Jerry A., and Kathleen Gerson. 2004. *The Time Divide: Work, Family, and Gender Inequality*. Cambridge, MA: Harvard University Press.

Jencks, Christopher. 2004. "The Low Wage Puzzle: Why Is America Generating So Many Bad Jobs—and How Can We Create More Good Jobs?" *American Prospect* 15(1): 35–37.

Johnston, William B., and Arnold H. Packer. 1987. *Workforce 2000: Work and Workers for the 21st Century*. Indianapolis, IN: Hudson Institute.

Kain, John F. 1968. "Housing Segregation, Negro Employment, and Metropolitan Desegregation." *Quarterly Journal of Economics* 82(2): 175–97.

Kalleberg, Arne L. 1977. "Work Values and Job Rewards: A Theory of Job Satisfaction." *American Sociological Review* 42(1): 124–43.

———. 1995. "Part-Time Work and Workers in the United States: Correlates and Policy Issues." *Washington and Lee Law Review* 52: 771–98.

———, and Aage B. Sørensen. 1973. "The Measurement of the Effects of Overtraining on Job Attitudes." *Sociological Methods and Research* 2(2): 215–38.

———, Michael Wallace, and Robert P. Althauser. 1981. "Economic Segmentation, Worker Power, and Income Inequality." *American Journal of Sociology* 87: 651–83.

———, and Ivar Berg. 1987. *Work and Industry: Structures, Markets and Processes.* New York: Plenum.

———, Barbara F. Reskin, and Ken Hudson. 2000. "Bad Jobs in America: Nonstandard Employment Relations and Job Quality in the United States." *American Sociological Review* 65: 256–78.

Kasarda, John D. 1990. "Urban Industrial Transition and the Underclass." *Annals of the American Academy of Political and Social Science* 501: 26–47.

———, and Jurgen Friedrichs. 1985. "Comparative Demographic-Employment Mismatches in U.S. and West German Cities." *Research in the Sociology of Work* 3: 1–30.

Katz, Lawrence F., and Kevin F. Murphy. 1992. "Changes in Relative Wages, 1963–1987: Supply and Demand Factors." *Quarterly Journal of Economics* 107: 35–78.

Knoke, David, and Arne L. Kalleberg. 1994. "Job Training in U.S. Organizations." *American Sociological Review* 59(4): 537–46.

Kochan, Thomas A. 2004. *Regaining Control of Our Destiny: A Working Families' Agenda for America.* Cambridge, MA: MIT Workplace Center.

Krueger, Alan B. 2004. "Economic Scene: After 40 Years, What Are Some Results and Lessons of America's War on Poverty?" *New York Times*, January 8, C2.

Kuttner, Robert. 2004. "High-Wage America: How We Can Reclaim a Middle-Class Society." *American Prospect* 15 (January): 60–62.

Lambrew, Jeanne. 2004. "Uninsured America." www.americanprogress.org (August 26).

Landler, Mark. 2004. "Europe Reluctantly Deciding It Has Less Time for Time Off." *New York Times*, July 7, A1, C2.

Lazaroff, Leon. 2005. "Effort Focuses on Work Habits." *Raleigh News and Observer*, May 22, 6E.

Leicht, Kevin T., and Scott Fitzgerald. 2006. *Post-Industrial Peasants: The Illusion of Middle-Class Prosperity.* New York: Worth Publishers.

Levy, Frank, and Richard J. Murnane. 2004. *The New Division of Labor.* Princeton, NJ: Princeton University Press.

Livingstone, David W. 1998. *The Education-Jobs Gap: Underemployment or Economic Democracy.* Boulder, CO: Westview Press.

Lucifora, Claudio, Abigail McKnight, and Wiemer Salverda. 2005. "Low-Wage Employment in Europe: A Review of the Evidence." *Socio-Economic Review* 3(2): 259–92.

Maher, Kris. 2005. "Skill Shortage Gives Training Programs New Life." *Wall Street Journal*, May 3, Economy Section.

Mandel, Michael J. 2005. "College: The Payoff Shrinks." *Business Week* (September 12), 48.

Marks, Stephen R. 1977. "Multiple Roles and Role Strain: Some Notes on Human Energy, Time and Commitment." *American Sociological Review* 42: 921–36.

Marsden, David. 1999. *A Theory of Employment System: Micro-Foundations of Societal Diversity.* Oxford: Oxford University Press.

Marx, Karl. 1961. *Capital,* Vol. 1–3. Moscow: Foreign Language Press. (Originally published in English, 1887).

Massey, Douglas S. 2005. *The Return of the "L" Word: A Liberal Vision for the New Century.* Princeton, NJ: Princeton University Press.

———, and Nancy A. Denton. 1993. *American Apartheid: Segregation and the Making of the Underclass.* Cambridge, MA: Harvard University Press.

Maume, David J., Jr., and Marcia L. Bellas. 2001. "The Overworked American or the Time Bind?" *American Behavioral Scientist* 44(7): 1137–56.

Merton, Robert K. 1968. *Social Theory and Social Structure.* New York: The Free Press.

Meyers, Marcia K., and Janet C. Gornick. 2003. *Families that Work: Policies for Reconciling Parenthood and Employment.* New York: Russell Sage Foundation.

Milkman, Ruth. 1987. *Gender at Work: The Dynamics of Job Segregation by Sex during World War II.* Urbana, IL: University of Illinois Press.

Mills, C. Wright. 1959. *The Sociological Imagination.* London: Oxford University Press.

Mishel, Lawrence, and Ruy A. Teixeira. 1991. *The Myth of the Coming Labor Shortage: Jobs, Skills, and Incomes of America's Workforce 2000.* Washington DC: Economic Policy Institute.

———, Jared Bernstein, and John Schmitt. 2001. *The State of Working America 2000/2001.* Washington DC: Economic Policy Institute.

———, Jared Bernstein, and Sylvia Allegretto. 2005. *The State of Working America 2004/2005.* Ithaca, NY: Cornell University Press.

Moen, Phyllis, and Patricia Roehling. 2005. *The Career Mystique. Cracks in the American Dream.* Lanham, MD: Rowman and Littlefield.

Moffitt, R. A. 2002. *From Welfare to Work: What the Evidence Shows.* Welfare Reform and Beyond. Policy Brief 13. Washington DC: Brookings Institution.

Moss, Philip, and Chris Tilly. 2001. *Stories Employers Tell: Race, Skill, and Hiring in America.* New York: Russell Sage Foundation.

Mouw, Ted. 2002. "Are Black Workers Missing the Connection? The Effect of Spatial Distance and Employee Referrals on Interfirm Racial Segregation." *Demography* 39(3): 507–29.

Nardone, Thomas. 1995. "Part-Time Employment: Reasons, Demographics, and Trends." *Journal of Labor Research* 16: 275–92.

Nelson, Robert L., and William P. Bridges. 1999. *Legalizing Gender Inequality: Courts, Markets and Unequal Pay for Women in America.* Cambridge: Cambridge University Press.

New York Times. 1996. *The Downsizing of America.* New York: Times Books.

"No Part-Time Job Explosion." 1997. *Economist,* August 16, p. 23.

O'Connor, Anahad. 2004. "Cracking under the Pressure? It's Just the Opposite, for Some." *New York Times,* July 7, A1, A22.

O'Reilly, C., J. Chatman, and D. Caldwell. 1991. "People and Organizational Culture: A Profile Comparison Approach to Assessing Person-Organization Fit." *Academy of Management Journal* 34: 487–516.

Osterman, Paul. 1999. *Securing Prosperity: How the American Labor Market Has Changed and What to Do about It.* Princeton, NJ: Princeton University Press.

———. 2001. "Work Reorganization in an Era of Restructuring: Trends in Diffusion and Effects on Employee Welfare." *Industrial and Labor Relations Review* 53(2): 179–96.

———, Thomas A. Kochan, Richard M. Locke, and Michael J. Piore. 2001. *Working in America: A Blueprint for the New Labor Market.* Cambridge, MA: MIT Press.

Padavic, Irene, and Barbara Reskin. 2002. *Women and Men at Work,* 2nd ed. Thousand Oaks, CA: Pine Forge Press.

Parkin, Frank. 1971. *Class, Inequality and Political Order: Social Stratification in Capitalist and Communist Societies.* New York: Praeger.

Pear, Robert. 2002. "After Decline, the Number of Uninsured Rose in 2001." *New York Times,* September 30, A21.

Peck, Jamie. 1996. *Work-Place: The Social Regulation of Labor Markets.* New York: Guilford Press.

Perlow, Leslie A. 1999. "The Time Famine: Toward a Sociology of Work Time." *Administrative Science Quarterly* 44: 57–81.

Peter, Laurence J., and Raymond Hull. 1969. *The Peter Principle: Why Things Always Go Wrong.* New York: Morrow.

Phillips, Kevin. 1993. *Boiling Point: Republicans, Democrats, and the Decline of Middle-Class Prosperity.* New York: Random House.

Phillips, Michael M. 1997. "Part-time Work Issue Is Greatly Overworked." *Wall Street Journal,* August 11.

Pleck, Joseph H. 1977. "The Work-Family Role System." *Social Problems* 24(4): 417–27.

Presser, Harriet B. 2003. *Working in a 24/7 Economy: Challenges for American Families.* New York: Russell Sage Foundation.

Quigley, William P. 2003. *Ending Poverty as We Know It: Guaranteeing a Right to a Job at a Living Wage.* Philadelphia: Temple University Press.

Reynolds, Jeremy. 2003. "You Can't Always Get the Hours You Want: Mismatches between Actual and Preferred Work Hours in the U.S." *Social Forces* 81(4): 1171–99.

———, and Linda A. Renzulli. 2005. "Economic Freedom or Self-imposed Strife: Work-Life Conflict, Gender, and Self-employment." *Research in the Sociology of Work* 15: 33–60.

Riley, Matilda W., Robert L. Kahn, and Anne Foner. 1994. *Age and Structural Lag: The Mismatch between People's Lives and Opportunities in Work, Family, and Leisure.* New York: John Wiley and Sons.

Rives, Karin. 2004. "Minimum-Wage Issue Stirs Up Maximum Debate." *Raleigh News and Observer,* June 16, 1D, 6D.

———. 2005. "CEO: Skills Gap a Problem." *Raleigh News and Observer*, October 31, 9B.

Rivlin, Gary. 2005. "Wooing Workers in New Orleans." *New York Times*, November 11, C1, C4.

Robinson, John, and Geoffrey Godbey. 1997. *Time for Life: The Surprising Way Americans Use Their Time*. University Park, PA: Pennsylvania State University.

Rosenbaum, James E. 2001. *Beyond College for All: Career Paths for the Forgotten Half*. New York: Russell Sage Foundation.

———, and Amy Binder. 1997. "Do Employers Really Need More Educated Youth?" *Sociology of Education* 70: 68–85.

Rothstein, Richard. 2002. "Teacher Shortages Vanish When the Price Is Right." *New York Times*, September 25, A16.

Roxburgh, Susan. 2004. "There Just Aren't Enough Hours in the Day." *Journal of Health and Social Behavior* 45(2): 115–31.

Rumberger, Russell W. 1981. *Overeducation in the U.S. Labor Market*. New York: Praeger.

Schor, Juliet. 1991. *The Overworked American: The Unexpected Decline of Leisure*. New York: Basic Books.

———. 1997. "Civic Engagement and Working Hours: Do Americans Really Have More Free Time than Ever Before?" Paper presented at the Conference on Civic Engagement in American Democracy, Portland, Maine.

Schwartz, John. 2004. "Always on the Job, Employees Pay with Health." *New York Times* online, September 5.

Shipler, David K. 2004. *The Working Poor: Invisible in America*. New York: Knopf.

Shirley, Carla, and Michael Wallace. 2004. "Domestic Work, Family Characteristics, and Earnings: Reexamining Gender and Class Differences." *The Sociological Quarterly* 45 663–90.

Shulman, Beth. 2003. *The Betrayal of Work: How Low-Wage Jobs Fail 30 Million Americans*. New York: The New Press.

Sicherman, Nachum. 1991. " 'Overschooling' in the Labor Market." *Journal of Labor Economics* 9: 101–22.

Silvestri, George T. 1997. "Employment Outlook: 1996–2006: Occupational Employment Projections to 2006." *Monthly Labor Review* (November): 58–83.

Smith, Herbert L. 1986. "Overeducation and Underemployment: An Agnostic Review." *Sociology of Education* 59 (April): 85–99.

Smith, Vicki. 2001. *Crossing the Great Divide: Worker Risk and Opportunity in the New Economy*. Ithaca, NY: Cornell University Press.

Sparks, K., C. Cooper, Y. Fried, and A. Shirom. 1997. "The Effects of Hours of Work on Health: A Meta-Analytic Review." *Journal of Occupational Health Psychology* 1999 (4): 307–17.

Spenner, Kenneth I. 1983. "Deciphering Prometheus: Temporary Change in the Skill Level of Work." *American Sociological Review* 48: 824–37.

Sørensen, Aage B., and Arne L. Kalleberg. 1981. "An Outline for a Theory of the Matching of Persons to Jobs." In Ivar Berg, ed., *Sociological Perspectives on Labor Markets*, 49–74. New York: Academic Press.

Stolzenberg, Ross M. 2001. "It's about Time and Gender: Spousal Employment and Health." *American Journal of Sociology* 107(1): 61–100.

Stratton, Leslie S. 1996. "Are 'Involuntary' Part-time Workers Indeed Involuntary?" *Industrial and Labor Relations Review* 49: 522–36.

Sullivan, Teresa A. 1978. *Marginal Workers, Marginal Jobs: The Underutilization of American Workers.* Austin, TX: University of Texas Press.

Thomson, Allison. 1999. "Employment Outlook: 1998–2008: Occupational Employment Projections to 2008." *Monthly Labor Review* (November): 33–50.

Thurow, Lester. 1975. *Generating Inequality: Mechanisms of Distribution in the U.S. Economy.* New York: Basic Books.

Tilly, Chris. 1996. *Half a Job: Bad and Good Part-Time Jobs in a Changing Labor Market.* Philadelphia: Temple University Press.

———. 2002. "Review of *Jobs for the Poor.*" *Contemporary Sociology* 31(6): 700–702.

Toosi, Mitra. 2002. "A Century of Change: The U.S. Labor Force, 1950–2000." *Monthly Labor Review* (May): 15–28.

Tufekci, Zeynep. 2004. "They Can Point and Click, but Still End up Painting Walls." *The Washington Post*, January 25, B4.

Tyler, J., Richard J. Murnane, and Frank Levy. 1995. "Are More College Graduates Really Taking 'High School' Jobs?" *Monthly Labor Review* 118: 18–27.

Uchitelle, Louis. 2005. "The New Profile of the Long-Term Unemployed." *New York Times*, May 24, C1–2.

United States Bureau of the Census. 2005. *Statistical Abstract of the United States 2004–2005.* (Table 573 for Chapter 2, Table 579 for Chapter 9).

United States Department of Labor. 1991. *Dictionary of Occupational Titles*, 4th ed., revised. Washington DC: US Government Printing Office.

United States Department of Labor, Bureau of Labor Statistics. 2005a. *Occupational Outlook Quarterly* 49(3): 36.

———. 2005b. *Women in the Labor Force: A Databook* (Report 985). Washington DC (May).

United States National Commission on Excellence in Education. 1983. *A Nation at Risk: The Imperative for Educational Reform.* Washington DC: US Government Printing Office.

Vaisey, Stephen B. 2006. "Education and Its Discontents: Overqualification in America, 1972–2002." *Social Forces* 85(2): In press.

Voydanoff, Patricia. 2002. "Linkages between the Work-Family Interface and Work, Family, and Individual Outcomes: An Integrative Model." *Journal of Family Issues* 23(1): 138–64.

Warner, Judith. 2005. *Perfect Madness: Motherhood in the Age of Anxiety*. New York: Penguin Group, Riverhead Books.

Warren, Elizabeth, and Amelia Warren Tyagi. 2003. *The Two-Income Trap: Why Middle-Class Mothers and Fathers are Going Broke*. New York: Basic Books.

Weber, Max. 1947. *The Theory of Social and Economic Organization*, trans. A. M. Henderson and Talcott Parsons. New York: Oxford University Press.

Weintraub, Arlene, with Jim Kerstetter. 2003. "Revenge of the Overworked Nerds." *Business Week*, December 8, 41.

Wilk, Steffanie L., Laura Burris Desmarais, and Paul R. Sackett. 1995. "Gravitation to Jobs Commensurate with Ability: Longitudinal and Cross-Sectional Tests." *Journal of Applied Psychology* 80(1): 79–85.

Williams, Joan. 2000. *Unbending Gender: Why Family and Work Conflict and What To Do About It*. New York: Oxford University Press.

Willis, Rachel, Rachel Connelly, and Deborah S. DeGraff. 2003. "The Future of Jobs in the Hosiery Industry." In Eileen Appelbaum, Annette Bernhardt, and Richard J. Murnane, eds., 2003, 407–45.

Wilson, William J. 1996. *When Work Disappears: The World of the New Urban Poor*. New York: Knopf.

Wirtz, Ronald A. 2002. "Shall We Dance? As Jobs Grow But the Labor Pool Doesn't, Job Matching Becomes Essential to Make Sure Everybody Gets the Right Partner." *Fedgazette*, Federal Reserve Bank of Minneapolis (July): minneapolisfed.org/pubs/fedgaz/02-07/dance.cfm.

Wright, Erik Olin, and Rachel E. Dwyer. 2003. "The Patterns of Job Expansions in the United States: A Comparison of the 1960s and 1990s." *Socio-Economic Review* 1(3): 289–325.

Wrzesniewski, Amy, and Jane E. Dutton. 2001. "Crafting a Job: Revisioning Employees as Active Crafters of Their Work." *Academy of Management Review* 26(2): 179–201.

INDEX